Herrn Dr. Burlingame mit besten
Empfehl:n.

REPORT

OF THE

SPECIAL COMMISSIONER OF THE REVENUE

FOR

THE YEAR 1868.

WASHINGTON:
GOVERNMENT PRINTING OFFICE.
1868.

REVENUE.

REPORT

OF THE

SPECIAL COMMISSIONER OF THE REVENUE

For the year 1868.

JANUARY 5, 1869.—Referred to the Committee of Ways and Means and ordered to be printed.

TREASURY DEPARTMENT, *January* 5, 1869.

SIR: I have the honor to present to you herewith the report of the Special Commissioner of the Revenue, and respectfully ask the attention of Congress to its recommendations.

I have the honor to be, very respectfully, &c.,

H. McCULLOCH, *Secretary.*

Hon. SCHUYLER COLFAX,
Speaker House of Representatives, Washington, D. C.

IN THE SENATE OF THE UNITED STATES,
January 12, 1869.

Resolved, That there be printed for the use of the Senate ten thousand copies of the Report of the Special Commissioner of the Revenue, with the appendices complete.

IN THE HOUSE OF REPRESENTATIVES,
January 19, 1869.

Resolved, That twenty thousand copies of the Report of the Special Commissioner of the Revenue, with the appendices complete, be printed for the use of the House, and one thousand bound copies of the same for the use of the Treasury Department.

REPORT

OF THE

SPECIAL COMMISSIONER OF THE REVENUE.

TREASURY DEPARTMENT,
OFFICE OF SPECIAL COMMISSIONER OF THE REVENUE,
Washington, D. C., January, 1869.

SIR: I propose in this my third annual report, which I have the honor herewith to present, to ask through you the attention of Congress to the results of a somewhat extended investigation, instituted with a view not of establishing or confirming any particular theory, but rather of determining, through the collection of positive data, what policy in legislation is likely to prove hereafter most advantageous to the revenue, and most certain to establish the credit and industry of the whole country upon a sound and substantial basis.

As all reasoning in respect to the future must necessarily be predicated upon the experience of the past or present, it is obvious that the first step or starting point of this inquiry is involved in the determination of the question as to what is

THE PRESENT CONDITION OF THE CAPITAL AND INDUSTRY OF THE COUNTRY.

The facts which constitute an answer to this question are to a considerable degree contradictory and paradoxical. On the one hand there is much that indicates that the country is rapidly recovering from the effects of the war, and resuming that wonderful career of progress and development which especially characterized its history during the period embraced in the thirteen years from 1847 to 1860. On the other hand there is another class of facts which as unmistakably indicate the existence of agencies which tend to arrest or obstruct national development, and which foster speculation, idleness, extravagance of living, discontent with moderate and slow gains, haste to be rich, and the spirit of trading as distinguished from the spirit of production.

It is proposed, in the first instance, to briefly state the evidence in support of the first proposition; and although this evidence has been presented in great part already by the Commissioner in his two previous reports, yet a recapitulation of the leading elements of national wealth, on which rest the elements of national credit, can never be considered as untimely so long as a distrust of the resources of the nation is for any purpose fostered and encouraged—particularly by persons holding official or other public positions. This evidence may be grouped as follows:

FIRST; IMMIGRATION.—From the 1st of July, 1865, to the 1st of December, 1868, about 1,000,000 natives of foreign countries have sought a permanent home in the United States. Investigations made some years ago (since when the character of the immigration has greatly improved) showed that these immigrants bring with them specie or its equivalent to the average amount of eighty dollars per head; while their average value to the country as producers cannot be estimated at less than half the average value of an ordinary laborer in the south prior to the war, viz: $1,000 each. Immigration, then, since the termination of the war, may be regarded as having added $80,000,000 directly, and $500,000,000 indirectly, to the wealth and resources of the country.

SECONDLY; A GENERAL INCREASE IN THE PRODUCTS OF DOMESTIC INDUSTRY.—The Commissioner is fully aware of the difficulties attendant upon the determination of estimates in this department; prices, with the present irredeemable, fluctuating currency being wholly valueless as a measure; while a statement of quantities, to be strictly accurate, must be considered not only with reference to quality, but also to the normal increase in production, which under all circumstances accompanies an increase of population. Nevertheless, the wealth of the country is its capacity for annual production; and an analysis of this production is the surest, and at present the only, available method of testing that wealth.

Speaking generally, however, in the first instance, the Commissioner asserts that all the available data tend to establish the following conclusions, viz: That within the last five years more cotton spindles have been put in operation, more iron furnaces erected, more iron smelted, more bars rolled, more steel made, more coal and copper mined, more lumber sawed and hewn, more houses and shops constructed, more manufactories of different kinds started, and more petroleum collected, refined, and exported, than during any equal period in the history of the country; and that this increase has been greater both as regards quality and quantity, and greater than the legitimate increase to be expected from the normal increase of wealth and population.

To support this general statement, the following specific evidence may be adduced:

1. *Cotton manufacture.*—The number of cotton spindles in the United States, according to the census of 1860, was 5,235,727. From 1860 to 1864 there was little or no increase of cotton machinery, but possibly a diminution—many mills, under the great demand for army clothing, having been converted into establishments for the manufacture of woollens. The number of spindles, however, at present in operation, is shown by the recent returns of the American Cotton Manufacturers and Planters' Association* to be about 7,000,000, a gain of 31.78 per cent. in from four to five years, and mainly since the termination of the war in 1865.

* The experience of this association strikingly illustrates the importance as well as immediate practical benefits of organized and properly conducted inquiries in respect to specialties of industry. Thus, one of the first steps taken by the association referred to, immediately after its organization in the spring of 1868, was to ascertain definitely, through its members, the number of cotton spindles in operation in the country; which number the most reliable and accepted estimates then available had placed at about 5,250,000. When the returns sent in were collated, it was found that the number of spindles actually in operation was largely in excess of prior estimates, and approximated or exceeded 7,000,000, a conclusion which at once led to another very important inference; for, making all due allowance for differences in the character of the manufactured product, (fine work requiring less cotton than coarse,) it followed that the minimum consumption of the raw material by the cotton mills of the United States could not have been much less, for the cotton year 1867-'68, than 900,000 bales. The commercial returns of the receipts of cotton, published weekly, indicated, however, a very much less rate of consumption in the United States; and even when corrected on the 1st of September, the end of the cotton year, the quantity stated as having been consumed was considerably less than what the returns made to the manufacturers' association would indicate.

This error has arisen from the change in the system of transportation. Before the war the receipts at the ports afforded a sufficiently accurate indication of the quantity of cotton delivered by the planters, as very little cotton was then sent north by inland routes; but it is now estimated that from 25 to 35 per cent. of the cotton consumed in the north is carried by

An estimate, based on less perfect data, given in the last annual report of the Commissioner, fixed this increase at only from 15 to 20 per cent.

2. *Woollen manufacture.*—Imperfect statistics, collected by the North-western Woollen Manufacturers' Association, show the increase in the woollen manufacture of seven States of the west, viz., Ohio, Michigan, Indiana, Illinois, Wisconsin, Iowa, and Minnesota, to have been since 1860 as follows:

	No. of establishments.	Capital invested.	Sets of machinery.
1860	259	$1, 616, 740	294
1868	557	5, 448, 000	995

3. *Pig iron production.*—In the department of iron industry the Commissioner would again call attention to the fact stated in his previous report, that the recent average annual increase in the production of pig iron is remarkably uniform and greatly in excess of the ratio of increase of population; the latter, at the present time, being assumed at about the ratio of increase from 1850 to 1860, viz., 3½ per cent., while the annual increase in the product of pig iron, during the last five years, has been as follows:

Annual product of pig iron from 1863 *to* 1868.

	Tons.	Annual increase.
1863	947, 604	
1864	1, 135, 497	19. 82 per cent.
1866	1, 351, 143	9. 50 per cent.
1867	1, 447, 771	7. 16 per cent.
1868, (estimated)	1, 550, 000	7. 06 per cent.

For the seven years from 1860 (when the production was 913,770 tons) to 1867, the average annual increase has been 8.35 per cent.

This increase is in excess of the present average annual increase of the pig iron product of Great Britain, which since 1863 has been as follows

	Tons.	Increase.
1863	4,510,040	
1864	4,767,951	5.71 per cent.
1865	4,819,254	1.08 per cent.
		Decrease.
1866	4,523,897	6.50 per cent.

In France the annual product of pig iron was in 1866 1,253,100 tons, and in 1867, 1,142,800 tons, showing a decline of 110,300 tons.

In Austria the official returns of the iron trade show a diminution of 42 per cent. in 1866 as compared with 1860; and of 60 per cent. as compared with 1862.

inland routes directly to the mills, being sent north *via* Memphis, Louisville, Cincinnati, &c., and thence by railroad to the points of consumption.

The weekly commercial statements indicated a crop of little more than 2,300,000 bales; but when the final corrections were made, partially making allowance for the previous error, the crop statement was brought up to about 2,500,000 bales. In other words, the third free-labor crop of the country was 65 per cent. or more of the average crop for five years preceding the war; or, if we take the estimate of consumption from the manufacturers' returns, it was nearer 70 per cent.

4. *Copper.*—The product of the copper mines of Lake Superior from 1860 to 1867, inclusive, is returned as follows:*

	Tons.
1860	6,000
1861	7,400
1862	9,062
1863	8,548
1864	8,472
1865	10,790
1866	10,375
1867	11,735

During the same period the copper product of Great Britain largely declined, viz: from 15,968 tons in 1860, to 11,153 tons in 1866, and 10,800 tons in 1867.

5. *Petroleum.*—In 1862 the export of petroleum was returned at 10,887,701 gallons. During the years 1864 and 1865, with the advantage of a high premium on gold, the export increased to an average of about 30,000,000 gallons. In 1867 the export was 67,052,020 gallons, and for 1868 the export is returned at 97,179,919 gallons.

6. *Coal.*—The recent increase in the production of anthracite coal, which may be taken as a measure of the product of all American coal, is reported as follows: 1862, 7,499,550 tons; 1866, 12,379,490 tons; 1867, 12,650,571 tons; 1868, to December 12, 13,500,000 tons. During the past year the supply of anthracite coal has been seriously affected by strikes and constant interruptions of labor; otherwise there is no reason to doubt that the aggregate product mined would have shown a much larger increase than has been indicated. But as the case stands the increase which has actually taken place proves that the conditions of ability to consume—which conditions are mainly industrial—have not been impaired, but have increased during the past year in about a three-fold ratio to the estimated increase of population.

7. *Lake tonnage.*—The following table prepared for the Chicago Board of Trade shows the recent increase of tonnage upon the northern lakes, (exclusive of canal boats,) for the years ending March 31, 1864, 1866, and 1867:

	Vessels.	Tonnage.	Increase.
1864	648	202,304	
1866	997	251,077	24 per cent.
1867 †	1,196	279,981	11 per cent.

8. *Consumption of sugar and coffee.*.—In Europe some measure of the prosperity of the people can, it is believed, be obtained by noticing the rise or fall in the consumption of certain articles which cannot be considered as belonging wholly to the catalogue of necessities, such as sugars, tea, coffee, &c. Making use of this standard, the following results are obtained:

The average monthly consumption of imported sugars for the 11 months

* Portage Lake Mining Gazette.

† Gratifying as this increase is, it should not be concealed that the amount of tonnage upon the lakes is even now less than in the early years of the war, viz: 1862 and 1863. On the other hand, the aggregate tonnage, number of vessels, and of seamen, which cleared from the port of Chicago for the year 1867, was greater than for any former period, as is shown by the following table:

	Vessels.	Tonnage.	Seamen.
1862	7,270	1,915,554	66,936
1863	8,457	2,161,221	76,332
1864	12,140	2,512,676	106,344

ending November 30, 1868, as indicated by the distribution from the five principal Atlantic ports, was 82,149,760 pounds, as compared with 70,088,480 pounds for the corresponding period of 1867, and 68,296,600 pounds for that of 1865; while the average monthly consumption of coffee for 1868, deduced from the same data, has been 8,294 tons, as compared with 7,560 tons in 1867, and 5,999 tons in 1866.

THIRDLY; THE CONTINUED INCREASE IN THE AGRICULTURAL PRODUCT OF THE UNITED STATES, WHETHER MEASURED BY QUANTITY OR VALUE.—The aggregate crops of the northern States for 1867 were believed to be greater than those of any previous year, while the crops for the past year are known to exceed in quantity and quality those of 1867.

As specific evidence, a few statistics are presented which have recently been published on what seems reliable authority.

In the State of Ohio the recent increase of sheep, hogs, and cereals, is reported as follows:

Number of sheep in 1865	6,305,796
Number of sheep in 1868	7,580,000

In the eight years last past the sheep of Ohio are reported as having more than doubled.

Number of hogs in 1865	1,400,000
Number of hogs in 1868	2,100,000

Cereal crops, including wheat, corn, and oats:

	Bushels.
1865	107,414,278
1866	118,061,911
1868	141,000,000

The commercial return of the number of hogs packed at the west since the season of 1864–5, is as follows:

1865–'66	1,705,955
1866–'67	2,490,791
1867–'68	2,781,084

This latter number was, however, exceeded during the first three years of the war.

The present ratio of the increase of the crop of Indian corn for the whole country is put by the best authorities at an average of three and one-half per cent. per annum. The crop of 1859 was returned by the census at 830,451,707 bushels, and adopting the above ratio of increase, the crop of 1868, acknowledged to be a full one, must be estimated at 1,100,000,000 bushels, and if sold at the assumed low average of 46 cents per bushel, would net over $500,000,000.

As respects the agricultural products of the southern States, the returns collected by the Association of cotton manufacturers and planters before referred to, show that the crop of 1867–8 was at least 2,500,000 bales, or about 65 per cent. of the average crop for the five years immediately preceding the war; while for the year 1868–9 the estimates are generally in favor of 2,700,000 bales. The results of the two crops upon the interests of the south will, however, be materially different. During the crop year 1867–8 the south did not raise food sufficient for its own subsistence, and a large part of the proceeds of the cotton of that year were used for the purchase of food, and also to repay advances for the previous purchase of stock and implements. This year, 1868–9, the south has raised food in excess of its necessities, and the proceeds of nearly the entire crop may be considered in the light of a surplus for future development.

The following are the estimated cotton crops of the south since the termination of the war: 1865–'66, 2,154,476 bales; 1866–'67, 1,954,988 bales; 1867–'68, 2,498,895 bales; 1868–'69, estimated 2,700,000 bales.

The culture of rice at the south, which at the termination of the war practically amounted to nothing, has also so far been restored that the product of the present year is estimated at 70,000 tierces; an amount probably sufficient for home consumption, and giving certain promise of a speedy renewal of the former extensive exports of this article.

The following is an estimate of the tobacco crops of the United States since 1850, prepared by a committee of the trade for the use of the Committee of Ways and Means, at the first session of the 40th Congress:

	Pounds.
1850	201,350,663
1863	267,353,082
1864	177,460,229
1865	183,316,953
1866	325,000,000
1867	250,000,000

Fourthly, railway extension and movement.—The total number of miles of railroads in the United States at the close of 1835 was 1,098; at the close of 1867, 39,244; giving an average increase of 1,156 for each year of the intervening period. The annual progress of railroad extension during and subsequent to the war is shown by the following table:

	Miles.
1860	1,846
1861	621
1862	864
1863	1,050
1864	738
1865	1,277
1866	1,832
1867	2,227
1868 (estimated)	2,500

It will thus be seen that since and including the year 1865, the year of the termination of the war, nearly 8,000 miles of railroad have been constructed in the United States, and that the present ratio of increase is more than double the average of railroad history prior to 1860, (viz: 1,156 miles.)

On the other hand the average annual increase of railroads in Great Britain from 1860 to 1865 was only 571 miles, and in France during the same period 509 miles.

An analysis of the railway system of the United States, which has been made for the first time during the past year,* presents us, however, with results which, were they not founded on incontrovertible data, would seem fabulous. Thus the ratio of the gross earnings to cost of the railroads of the whole country for the year 1867 was equal to about 21 per

* Rise, Progress, Cost, and Earnings of the Railroads of the United States.—H. V. Poor, New York, 1868.

cent.; for the northern States about 23 per cent. The railroads of the country, therefore, now receive their cost in a little more than four years, and this ratio of gross earnings to cost is steadily increasing with the increase of the railway system and traffic of the country.

Again, "the average number of tons of freight carried upon the railroads of the country is estimated at 2,000 tons per mile of road. The tonnage of the railroads of Massachusetts, in 1867, equalled 3,812 tons per mile; that of the railroads of New York, 3,100 tons; and that of Pennsylvania, 6,000 tons. The gross tonnage of the 39,284 miles of railroad in existence at the close of 1867, at the above estimate, was equivalent to 78,568,000, and if we deduct from this amount 15,000,000 tons for coal and other cheap material, and an equal amount for duplications of the same tonnage on different roads, there will be left 48,488,000 tons of merchandise moved annually upon all the railways of the United States. At an estimated value of $150 per ton for this tonnage, the total annual value of the merchandise traffic of all the roads at present equals $7,273,200,000."

The total amount of tonnage transported on all the roads of the country for the year 1851, is estimated by good authorities at not exceeding 10,000,000 tons. If from this we deduct 3,000,000 tons for coal and other cheap materials, and 1,000,000 tons for duplications, there will be left a merchandise tonnage of 6,000,000 tons in 1851, against 48,488,000 tons in 1867. The rate of increase in this period, therefore, has been equal to 800 per cent., and the actual increase 42,488,000 tons. At the estimated value of $150 per ton, the increase in the value of the railway merchandise of the country in 16 years has been $6,373,200,000, or at the rate of nearly $400,000,000 per annum. And it should also be noted that one-half of this total increase has taken place in the seven years that have elapsed since 1860.

The increased movement on the railways of the United States, which in the main represents increased product, also affords some indication of the progress of the development of the country. Thus, the earnings of the ten principal railway lines of the west exhibit for the first ten months of 1868 (with a decrease rather than an increase of freight rates) a gain of eight per cent. as compared with earnings of the corresponding months for the year 1867. Taking also the movements on the railways and canals of the State of New York, which are known to be accurate, and at the same time accessible, as a measure of comparison for the whole country, we find that the total annual tonnage increased from 7,138,917 tons, in 1858, to 16,032,006, in 1868, an increase of 124 per cent.; while the annual value of the tonnage thus moved increased from $486,816,505, in 1858, to $1,723,330,207, in 1867, a gain of 254 per cent.

An examination of the railroad statistics of the whole country for the above period further indicates that during the ten years above referred to, or from 1858 to 1868, the increase of tonnage moved on the railways of the United States has been at a rate *sixteen times greater than the ratio of the increase of population.*

Telegraphic extension.—The recent extension of the telegraphic system of the United States is reported to be approximately as follows:

1866, miles of wire	2,000
1867, miles of wire	3,000
1868, miles of wire	6,000

REDUCTION OF STATE DEBTS.

As affording some further indication of the material prosperity of the country, the Commissioner, as in his former report, would here call attention to the progress which has been made during the past year in the reduction of the indebtedness of the several States, incurred in great part by reason of the war. Thus, for example, the reduction of the debt of the State of New Hampshire for the year 1868 was 6.9 per cent., of Vermont, 16.2 per cent. as against 7.7 per cent. in 1867, of Rhode Island, 13.7 per cent., Connecticut, 3.4 per cent., Kentucky, 21 per cent., Ohio, 4.5 per cent., Michigan, 6.4 per cent., and Indiana, 23 per cent. During the years 1867 and 1868 the State of Illinois reduced her debt 30.5 per cent.; while New York, which has comparatively the largest State indebtedness, reduced her debt during the past year to the extent of about 12 per cent., as compared with a reduction of 7.6 per cent. for the year 1867. West Virginia, Kentucky, Iowa, Wisconsin, Nebraska and Minnesota have at the present time practically no indebtedness. For further information on the present condition of State indebtedness reference is made to the appendix of this report, marked C.

AGENCIES CONCERNED IN NATIONAL DEVELOPMENT.

One subject at this point of our inquiry is well worthy of attention. It is this: To what agencies are our seemingly fabulous national development to be attributed and to what extent especially is it to be referred to positive legislation?

In answer to this it is to be said that all investigation clearly shows that these agencies have been mainly two, viz: first, great natural resources in respect to abundant and fertile territory, great natural facilities for intercommunication, abundant and cheap raw material, and diversity without insalubrity of climate; and secondly, a form and spirit of government which heretofore has left man and capital, over an area almost continental, free and unrestrained to work out their own development. Since 1840, especially, other agencies have come in as powerful adjuncts, viz: a continued influx of population and capital from the old world; a continued invention and application of labor-saving machinery, and a most rapid extension of the railway system; which last, by giving a market to all the products of our national domain, has greatly stimulated the spirit of industry and enterprise. With these, also, should undoubtedly be included the purchase of California and the discovery of gold on the Pacific.

As respects the relation of legislation by the national government to the results under consideration, if we except the adoption of a liberal policy in the disposition of the public lands, it is difficult, at least for the period which elapsed between 1840 and 1860, to affirm much that is positive, unless, in conformity with the maxim, that that government is best which governs least, absence of legislation is to be regarded in the light of a positive good. If important results followed the acquisition of California, such results were certainly neither foreseen nor anticipated; while as regards commercial legislation, a review of all the facts cannot fail to suggest a doubt whether the evils which have resulted from instability have not far more than counterbalanced any advantage that may have proceeded from the experience of a fluctuating policy.

The Commissioner is well aware that this opinion will not be readily accepted by those who have been educated to believe that the industrial and commercial prosperity of the country was seriously affected by the legislation which took place during the years which elapsed from 1842 to 1846. But upon this point all investigation shows that the facts are entirely contrary to what may be regarded as the popular belief, which, indeed, in this particular, would appear to be based on little else than mere assertions, which, remaining for a long time unquestioned, have at last acquired the force of accepted historical truth. Thus, for example, it has been constantly asserted, both in Congress and out of Congress, that the production of pig iron was remarkably stimulated under the tariff of 1842—rising from 220,000 tons in 1842 to 800,000 tons in 1848—and that under the tariff of 1846 the same industry was remarkably depressed. Now, these assertions may be correct, but the most reliable statistics to which we have access, viz: those gathered by the American Iron Association, instruct us as follows:

Production of pig iron in 1830, 165,000 tons; in 1840, 347,000 tons. Increase in 10 years, 110 per cent.

Production in 1845, 486,000 tons; increase in 5 years, 40 per cent.
Production in 1850, 564,000 tons; increase in 10 years, 62 per cent.
Production in 1855, 754,000 tons; increase in 5 years, 33 per cent.
Production in 1860, 913,000 tons; increase in 10 years, 61 per cent.

It thus appears that the great annual increase in the production of pig iron took place prior to the year 1840, and for 30 years was remarkably uniform at the rate of 10 to 11 per cent. per annum; and that since then, no matter what has been the character of the legislation, whether the tariff was low or high, whether the condition of the country was one of war or peace, the increase of the production has been at the average of about 8 per cent. per annum, or more than double the ratio of the increase of population.

Again, as another curious illustration of an apparent misconception of the effects of past legislation upon the development of the country, take the following paragraph from the recent report of a Congressional committee:

No business man of mature age need be reminded of the revulsion which followed in consequence of the free trade system of 1846—the decline of production, of immigration, of wages, of public or private revenue, until the culmination of the system in the tariff of 1857, with the memorable crises of that period; the general ruin of manufacturers and merchants; the suspended payments of the banks; the reduction of the treasury to the verge of bankruptcy, and the unparalleled distress among the unemployed poor.

Now, with all due deference to the committee, the Commissioner would ask attention to the following statistics bearing on the question under consideration:

Increase in the production of pig iron: In 1840, 347,000 tons; in 1845, 486,000; in 1850, 564,755; 1855, 754,178; 1860, 913,770.

Increase in the production of Pennsylvania anthracite coal: 1842, 1,108,418 tons; 1846, 2,344,005; 1847, 2,882,309; 1849, 3,217,641; 1855, 6,486,097; 1860, 8,143,938.

Increase in the domestic consumption of cotton, north of the Potomac: 1840, 297,000 bales; 1845, 422,000; 1849–'50, 476,000; 1851–'52, 588,000; 1855, 633,000; 1858–'59, 760,000; 1859–'60, 792,000.

Increase in immigration: 1840, 84,000; 1845, 174,000; 1850, 310,000; 1854, 427,000.

Increase in public revenue: 1840, $19,000,000; 1845, $29,000,000; 1850, $52,000,000; 1855, $74,000,000.

Increase of national wealth: From 1840 to 1850, 80 per cent.; from 1850 to 1860, 126 per cent. In 1854 the six per cent. bonds of the United States, issued in 1848, commanded a premium of 21 per cent.

Commercial tonnage of the United States: In 1840, 2,180,000; 1850, 3,535,000; 1860, 5,353,000.

Exports and imports: In 1840, $239,000,000; 1845, $231,000,000; 1850, $330,000,000; 1855, $536,000,000; 1860, $762,000,000.

Increase in ship-building: 1842, 129,084 tons; 1845, 146,018; 1850, 272,219; 1855, 583,450.

Annual increase of railroad construction: 1842, 491 miles; 1845, 256 1847, 669; 1849, 1,369; 1853, 2,452; 1856, 3,643 miles.

In short, there does not seem to be any reliable evidence which can be adduced to show that the change which took place in the legislative commercial policy of the country in 1846 had any permanent or marked effect whatever; while, on the other hand, the study of all the facts pertaining to national development from 1840 to 1860, and from 1865 to the present time, unmistakably teaches this lesson; that the progress of the country through what we may term the strength of its elements of vitality is independent of legislation and even of the impoverishment and waste of a great war. Like one of our own mighty rivers, its movement is beyond control. Successive years, like successive affluents, only add to and increase its volume; while legislative enactments and conflicting commercial policies, like the construction of piers and the deposit of sunken wrecks, simply deflect the current or constitute temporary obstructions. In fact, if the nation has not yet been lifted to the full comprehension of its own work, it builds determinately, as it were, by instinct.

EFFECT OF THE WAR IN CHECKING NATIONAL DEVELOPMENT.

What would have been the condition of progress during the decade from 1860 to 1870 had not the war intervened is a question that cannot be definitely answered; but that many branches of production would have experienced a development limited only by the amount of available capital and skilled labor cannot be doubted. Investigation shows that in many departments of industry the cost of skilled labor and of raw material in Great Britain and the United States very closely approximated in 1860; while the advantage in the cost of food of domestic production, and of certain articles of import, such as sugars, teas, and coffee, was largely in favor of this country. In 1860 American coarse cottons were obtaining the command of most extra-European markets. In 1860, wooden ships, allowing for quality, could be built cheaper in the United States than in any other country, although it is a noticeable fact that, probably from an inability to supply the demand for iron vessels, the decline of the ship-building interest in the United States, so much commented on of late, really began several years before the breaking out of the war.*

In 1860 copper in the pig was exported from the United States in profitable competition with the mines of Cuba and of South America; and evidence has also been presented to the Commissioner showing that in some instances pig iron was manufactured with profit at rates far lower than the average of Europe, while the purchasing power of the wages paid for the same was considerably greater than at present.

But the war came, bringing with it certain inevitable results, and these results now constitute the *per contra* upon the national ledger before referred to. The feature about them which, in contrast with the facts above cited, seems contradictory and paradoxical, is that while our resources as a nation have, on the whole, continued unimpaired; while we continue to possess and enjoy the greatest area of fertile territory, the most unrivalled means of intercommunication, natural or artificial, and the freest and most popular form of government; while the aggre-

*The largest amount of tonnage constructed in any one year in our history was in 1855, viz: 583,450 tons. From this period construction began to decline, being, in 1856, 469,394; 1857, 378,805; 1858, 242,287; 1859, 156,602; and in 1860, 212,892.

gate annual products of the soil have continually increased and not diminished, and those of the anvil, the forge, the loom, and the spindle have also multiplied; there is, nevertheless, hardly a single domestic article or product, agricultural or manufactured, in behalf of which the claim, either directly or indirectly, has not been made within the last two years that the same could be produced to greater advantage or profit in some other country than the United States; increased protection even being demanded for oil paintings, rough building stone, Indian corn, fire-wood, bibles, and ice—the last to the extent of 15 per cent., gold; and this claim the Commissioner is obliged to admit is, to a very great extent, in exact accordance with the truth.

The United States finds itself, therefore, in the anomalous position of a great nation, favored in many respects as no other nation upon which the sun shines, unable to exchange its products on terms of equality with the products of any other country; the marked exception being always its product or supplies of the precious metals. Inquiry is now to be made into the causes to which these results must be attributed, and as to the measures which seem likely to prove remedial, avoiding in so doing, to the greatest extent possible, any repetition of the facts and arguments which have been presented by the Commissioner in his former reports, or by others who have discussed this subject; and aiming to present rather the results of a continued investigation and of an enlarged experience.

AGENCIES ADVERSE TO NATIONAL DEVELOPMENT.

The immediate cause of the anomalous condition of affairs in question must unquestionably be referred to the greatly increased cost of nearly all forms of labor and commodities as compared with the price for the same that prevailed in the decade immediately preceding the war; while these in turn must be regarded as the resultant mainly of three agencies growing out of the war, viz: *irredeemable paper currency; unequal and heavy taxation*, and *a limited supply of skilled labor*, the last manifesting itself at the present time in specialties rather than in general.

INFLUENCE OF AN IRREDEEMABLE PAPER CURRENCY.

As the specific influence of the first agency has been of late so often and so thoroughly discussed, the Commissioner will only ask attention, under this head, to a few points of presumed novelty or interest; and, first, to a specific statement of actual experience, illustrative of the manner in which an irredeemable paper currency, or what is the same thing, a national abnegation of specie payments, unavoidably tends to destroy all profitable commercial relations with foreign countries in which trade and industry is conducted on a specie basis. The statement is furnished to the Commissioner by a manufacturer of furniture in one of the middle States, who, previous to the war, had built up an extensive export business to the West Indies, Central and South America, of a variety of "cane-seated" and "cane-backed" furniture suited to warm latitudes.

Thus on the 1st of March, 1861, gold and currency being at par, $1,000 in gold possessed a purchasing power sufficient to obtain for the South American importer 111$\frac{1}{9}$ dozen of what are termed in the trade, "ordinary square-post cane-seat chairs." About the 1st of January, 1862, gold began to command a premium, and advanced during the next three years with great rapidity. This movement was not, however, participated in at first, to any considerable extent, by either labor or commodities, and in consequence the purchasing power of gold greatly increased; so much so that on the 1st of July, 1864, the $1,000 gold which in 1861 bought 111 1/9 dozen chairs, then bought 143 dozen. Under these circumstances, as was to be expected, trade increased, as the foreign purchaser found the American market by far the best for his interest; but from July, 1864, a movement commenced in an exactly opposite direction, gold receding and labor and commodities advancing in very unequal ratios. Thus in January, 1865, the $1,000 gold, which four years previous had a purchasing power of 111 1/9 dozen chairs, and on the 1st of July, 1864, of 143 dozen, then commanded but 126⅔ dozen; in February, 1866, a still smaller number, viz: 91½ dozen, and ultimately attained its minimum in January, 1867, when the purchasing power of the sum named was only 89⅔ dozen. From this point the purchasing power has gradually increased, and for the past year, 1868, has remained at the rate of about 102 dozen, or nine dozen less than could be bought with the same money in 1861.*

The result has been that the foreign purchaser now goes to France or Germany; while the products of American industry, in the form of furniture, being no longer available to exchange for sugars, spices, or dyewoods, gold has necessarily been substituted; and, to use the words of the manufacturer describing his condition, "unless there is a speedy return to specie payments, custom will soon so fix the channels and currents of trade that any attempt on my part to divert them will be attended with great difficulty;" and what has thus been shown to be the case in respect to the export trade of the United States in furniture, may be accepted as true of almost every other manufactured product, which, as a nation, we were accustomed, before the war, to exchange for foreign commodities.

RELATIVE AMOUNT OF CURRENCY IN USE AND REQUIRED IN THE UNITED STATES, GREAT BRITAIN, AND FRANCE.

Another investigation to which the Commissioner would ask attention under this head is one which has been undertaken with a view of deter-

* The fluctuations in prices above referred to are exhibited in detail in the following table:

Table showing the purchasing power of gold as applied to chairs, (ordinary square-post, cane seat,) from March 1, 1861, to July 1, 1868.

	Gold.	Price per dozen, currency.	Purchasing power per dozen of $1,000 gold.
March 1, 1861	Par.	$9 00	111 1-9
January 1, 1863	135	9 50	141
February 21, 1863	162¾	10 50	155⅛
August 1, 1863	129⅛	11 00	117¼
September 17, 1863	138⅜	12 00	115
January 1, 1864	152	12 50	121 3-5
April 1, 1864	167½	13 50	124
April 22, 1864	173¾	14 50	119¾
June 1, 1864	188½	15 00	125⅔
July 1, 1864	236	16 50	143
August 1, 1864	255	18 00	141⅔
January 2, 1865	228	18 00	126⅔
February 16, 1866	137¼	15 00	91½
September 17, 1866	145	15 00	96⅔
January 14, 1867	134½	15 00	89⅔
June 4, 1867	137½	15 00	91⅔
September 16, 1867	144¼	13 50	106⅔
April 1, 1868	138½	13 50	162½
July 1, 1868	138¾	13 50	102¾

mining, through the examination of all available data, a question of no little interest in connection with our future financial policy, viz: the relative amount of currency in use and required in the three commercial nations of Great Britain, France, and the United States. The detailed results of this investigation, which has been made at the request of the Commissioner, by Hon. George Walker, late bank commissioner of Massachusetts, are given in full in an appendix to this report, marked B, but in brief are as follows:

Popular estimates have fixed the circulation of France at $30, and that of Great Britain at $25 a head. These estimates are excessive; a careful comparison of the best and latest authorities tending to show that the circulation of France, in coin and bank notes, does not exceed $18 34, and that of Great Britain $15 50 a head; while that of the United States in 1860, before the suspension of specie payments, was about $11 49 a head of the population.*

But, in fact, population has very little to do with the question. The function of a circulating medium is to make the final exchanges of a country, and the amount required therefor, depends on the amount and mobility of the country's wealth, and upon the extent of its domestic and foreign trade. The wealth of Great Britain is estimated at $40,000,000,000; while that of the United States on the same gold basis cannot exceed $20,000,000,000. Thus on the basis of property, were there no difference in the nature of that property, Great Britain would be justified in using a circulation twice as large as that of the United States, while it is in fact only 31 per cent. larger. But there is also a marked difference in the kind of property which constitutes the national estate, Great Britain having much less locked up in lands in an unproductive or partially productive state, and far more moving rapidly through the channels of production and trade. This is made evident by the statistics of her foreign commerce; her exports and imports being nearly $2,000,000,000 a year, while those of the United States are only about $700,000,000. On the basis of trade, therefore, Great Britain would need three times as much currency as the United States.

The social condition of the British people also necessitates the use of much circulating money. Thus, out of 30,000,000 of people, Professor Levi estimates that 22,000,000 consist of workers for wages and their families.

France has a foreign trade of $1,400,000,000, or twice as great as that of the United States, while her circulating medium is only 55 per cent. greater.

But these data, striking as they are, fail to present all the elements of comparison. There are circumstances of national condition and habits which largely affect the question of currency. In England, above all countries, and in the United States next to England, contrivances have been adopted to economize the use of money. Of these bank deposits and clearing-houses are the most familiar examples; but all the instrumentalities by which the exchanges have been quickened tend in the same direction; so that the railroad, the express, the telegraph and cheap-postage, have all led to the economizing of money.

France, on the other hand, is backward in all banking facilities, and this, together with political disquietude, and the persistance in old habits, have led to an undue use of money, both as hoarded wealth and a ruder instrument of exchange than the manifold and rapid substitutes adopted in Anglo-Saxon countries. But even France is yielding to the influence of this kind of economies; so that, while the population, wealth, and trade of the empire have steadily increased, the volume of money has probably declined; and this is especially true of the circulation of coin. In Great Britain the circulation of bank notes is no greater than 25 years ago, and the coin has only moderately increased, while in the interval the national wealth has doubled, and trade has attained a threefold dimension.

This tendency to retardation in the growth of the circulation, when compared with wealth and trade, is fully established also by American statistics. An instinct of economy, more influential than any recognized economic law, leads society to use the least amount of money which will perform the needed exchanges with rapidity and convenience. Money is wealth in a state of barrenness. The capacity of reproductive investment does not belong to it so long as it remains money—its only function being to measure and exchange other wealth by which the world is enriched. The amount of money which any people requires to do its business will vary with their habits and notions; but no intelligent nation will keep any more of its capital in an unproductive state than is absolutely necessary to fructify the rest. The nation, therefore, which with equal efficiency does its business with the least use of money, is the best off.

Paper money has no higher property value than real money. It is never wealth in itself, though like all credit paper it is an instrument by which wealth may be exchanged. Promissory notes, bills of exchange and checks, have the same property in a lesser degree. It is entitled to be called money only so far as it represents actual reserves of coin held by the issuer for its own redemption; beyond this it is only circulating credit. It saves the use of money, but it is not the thing which it saves. The same rule of economy applies to the employment of this credit substitute which applies to money itself.

The paper circulation of the United States is obviously redundant, because it is at a dis-

* See note at end of Mr. Walker's letter in Appendix.

count as compared with gold. With the help of taxation it keeps prices above the world's level. It thus renders it impossible to sell abroad the products which have cost too much at home, and it invites from other countries the products of a cheaper labor paid for in a sounder currency. It exaggerates imports while destroying our ability to pay in kind. Until gold can be brought to par, and kept there, with a paper circulation duly protected and instantly convertible, the industry of this country cannot rest upon a healthy basis.

COMPARISON OF PRICES OF LABOR AND COMMODITIES, 1860–'61 AND 1867–'68.

The present abnormal condition and the recent fluctuations in the prices of labor and commodities also properly comes up for consideration in connection with the subject of an irredeemable paper currency—the chief agency to which the disturbances in question must be referred.

The investigations previously instituted by the Commissioner have established the fact, that up to the commencement of the year 1867, the general effect of the agencies growing out of the war had been to occasion an average advance in the price of commodities to the extent of about 90 per cent., while the corresponding average advance in wages was not in excess of 60 per cent.

He has now to ask attention to the conclusions which another year's experience and investigation have brought to us in relation to this subject. The result of long and careful investigations in respect to the retail prices of the leading articles of domestic consumption by operatives in the manufacturing towns of New England, the middle, and some of the western States, have afforded data for accurately estimating the increase in the prices of such articles in 1867 as compared with 1860–'61. They establish the following conclusions:

That the average increase in the price of groceries and provisions in 1867, as compared with 1860–'61, was 88 per cent.; or, calculated on the basis of the quantities consumed on an average by a number of workmen, a little in excess of 86 per cent.; of domestic dry goods, including clothing, 86½ per cent.; of fuel, 57 per cent.; of house-rent, 65 per cent. This latter average is, however, largely affected by the circumstance that in New England, where manufacturing companies or corporations very generally own the tenements occupied by their operatives, rents have not been advanced to any considerable extent. Excluding New England from the calculation, the average advance in rents for 1867, as compared with 1860–'61, must be estimated at a much higher figure. Thus in the smaller manufacturing towns of Pennsylvania the average increase in the rents of houses occupied by operatives is believed to have been about 81 per cent., and in New Jersey 111 per cent. In the cities of New York, Philadelphia, Newark, and Pittsburg, the increase has been from 90 to 100 per cent.*

The average of these results, proportioned to the ascertained varying ratio of expenditure under the several heads, shows that for the year 1867, and for the first half of the year 1868, the average increase of all the elements which constitute the *food, clothing, and shelter* of a family

* For 1868, the returns very generally indicate a large advance in rents, and also for the latter half of the year in fuel; the advance in these two items alone being estimated as sufficient to counterbalance any advantages accruing from a decline up to date (December, 1868) in the price of breadstuffs.

has been about 78 per cent., as compared with the standard prices of 1860–'61.*

The result, in general, of this large increase in the prices of commodities of domestic consumption to the laboring man becomes evident, by comparing such increase with the increase in the rates of wages during the period under comparison—which rates, for the year 1867 as compared with 1860–'61, were as follows: For unskilled mechanical labor, 50 per cent.; for skilled mechanical labor, 60 per cent.

In the case of unmarried men, the comparison is more favorable than as respects men with families; the average increase in the prices of the articles consumed by them having been only about 73 per cent.; as, for example, board in manufacturing towns, 71 per cent.; clothing, irrespective of domestic dry goods, 75 per cent.; ordinary boots and shoes, 60 per cent.

Skilled workmen, who are at the same time unmarried, and who are in the receipt of wages from 65 to 70 per cent. in advance of the rates paid in 1860, find their condition, as regards net income, approximately the same as before the war.

The returns to numerous and careful inquiries, instituted at the request of the Commissioner, by proprietors or superintendents of manufacturing establishments in the New England, middle, and some of the western States, also afford much interesting information relative to the average weekly earnings and expenditures of American operatives, grouped as families, in the years 1860 and 1867; and also in respect to the comparative opportunities enjoyed by such families at the two periods referred to, for the realization of a surplus over and above the expenditures absolutely necessary for shelter and subsistence.

The following table, based on indisputable and actual data, shows the average aggregate weekly earnings in 1867 of families of various sizes, in different sections of the country; one or more members of each of which were employed in some branch of manufacturing industry; their average weekly expenditures for provisions, fuel, house-rent, &c., and the balance remaining to them, over and above such expenditure, available either for accumulation and capital, or for the purchase of clothing, or articles of enjoyment and luxury.

---

* The above results are exhibited specifically in the following table:

Table showing the average increase in the prices of some of the leading articles of domestic consumption, and in house rent in 1867, *as compared with* 1860–'61, *in the manufacturing towns of the United States.*

Articles.	Per ct. increase of 1867 over 1860.	Remarks.
Flour aud other breadstuffs	92	Apparent average increase in price of provisions, 88 per cent.
Meats—fresh and salted	86	True average increase, 86 per cent.
Butter	91½	Average increase in price of fuel, 57 per cent.
Fish—dry and pickled	74	Average increase in price of domestic cotton goods and clothing, 86½ per cent.
Potatoes and other vegetables	79	
Beans	92	Average increase in house-rent, 65 per cent.
Sugar and molasses	8s	Average increase in price of board, 76½ per cent.
Tea	99	General average increase in cost of provisions, clothing, rent, &c., to men with families, 75 per cent.
Coffee	117	
Milk	61½	Increase in cost of clothing, board, &c., to men not keeping house, 73 per cent.
Fuel—coal, wood, &c	57	
Domestic cotton goods	98	
Clothing	75	
House-rent	65	
Board for men	71	
Board for women	81½	

Average aggregate weekly earnings in 1867 *of families.*

Size of families.	Average weekly expenditures for provisions, house-rent, &c.	Average weekly earnings.	Surplus for clothing, housekeeping goods, &c.
Parents and one child	$10 24	$17 00	$6 76
Three adults	8 35	17 52	9 17
Parents and two children	12 26	18 75	6 49
Parents and three children	15 02	19 50	4 48
Parents and four children	17 79	23 33	5 54
Parents and five children	15 23	17 11	1 88
Parents and six children	11 67	13 50	1 83
Parents and seven children	23 78	25 00	1 22
General average of the above	14 29	18 96	4 67

In order to obtain the data for further comparisons, and especially to determine whether the large increase in wages in 1867–'68, has brought any real net gain to the employés of manufacturing establishments, a careful investigation was instituted in respect to the earnings and expenditures of individuals and families in 1860, similarly situated in all respects with those whose average aggregate weekly receipts and expenditures were given in the above table for 1867; and in so doing it has fortunately happened, that through the earnest co-operation of several proprietors or agents of manufacturing establishments, the data in respect to 1860 have been obtained, in many instances, from the same specific individuals or families which supplied the information relative to 1867. These data, carefully verified by reference to contemporary price-currents and other evidence, have afforded the means of constructing the following

Table showing the average weekly expenditure of families of varying numbers in the manufacturing towns of the United States for the years 1860 *and* 1867, *respectively.*

Size of families.	Average weekly wages.		Average weekly expenditures for provis'ns, house rent, clothing, &c.		Surplus in 1860.
	In 1867.	n 1860.	In 1867.	In 1860.	
Parents and one child	$17 00	$12 17	$17 00	$9 96	$2 21
Three adults	17 52	12 00	17 52	10 31	1 69
Parents and two children	18 75	11 50	18 75	10 79	71
Parents and three children	19 50	12 41	19 50	11 33	1 08
Parents and four children	23 33	14 15	23 33	13 18	97
Parents and five children	17 11	10 37	17 11	9 46	91
Parents and six children	13 50	9 50	13 50	7 67	1 83
Parents and seven children	25 00	15 17	25 00	14 09	1 08
General average of the above	18 96	12 16	18 96	10 85	1 31

In constructing the above table it has been assumed for purposes of comparison, (and so expressed in the third column of the table,) that the total average weekly wages obtained in 1867, viz: $18 96, were entirely expended, and in the following proportions: $14 29 for provisions, rent, fuel, &c., and the balance, $4 67, for clothing, domestic dry goods, housekeeping articles, luxuries, &c. Now the same quantities and qualities of provisions, groceries, clothing, rent, fuel, and housekeeping articles, could have been obtained in 1860 and 1861 for the respective sums indicated in the fourth column; showing an average weekly cost of $10 85 in 1860, as compared with $18·96 in 1867; and leaving a balance in the former year of $1 31 (gold) per week in favor of the operative, as against no accruing surplus whatever in 1867–8; or, in other words, supposing the requirements for food, clothing and shelter to have been the same in 1867 as in 1860, the operatives referred to in the table, who received in 1867 an average of $18 96 per week, obtained in that year only sufficient to give them the actual necessaries and comforts of life; while the same men, whose average weekly wages in 1860–1 were only $12 16, obtained with such earnings at that time the same articles of comfort or necessity, and had in addition a surplus of $1 31 (gold) per week, or $68 12 (gold) per annum.

As already stated, it has been assumed in this comparison that the wages received by the operatives in question during the year 1867 were wholly consumed in their living. To a very considerable extent it has been found that this assumption is justified by facts; but if, in view of the constant increase of deposits in savings banks and other evidences of accumulation, it should appear that a margin on an average has been saved, the figures presented show with equal certainty that on the same scale of living, the margin in 1860 must have exceeded that of 1867 in the proportions indicated. The fact, therefore, is established by incontrovertible evidence, that the condition of working men and women in a majority of the manufacturing towns of the United States is not as good at the present time as it was previous to the war, notwithstanding that their wages are greater, measured in gold, in 1867–'8 than they were in 1860–'1.

It should also be noted that most of the persons whose wages and expenditures have been discussed, were classed* as skilled workmen, receiving an advance in wages of about 52 per cent. in 1867, as compared with the amount received in 1860. If their condition has not improved, the condition of the large class of unskilled workmen, such as day laborers, teamsters, watchmen, and the like, is even worse. Thus a careful examination and comparison of a large number of returns from the proprietors or superintendents of furnaces, mills, foundries, and factories of every description in almost all sections of the United States establishes the fact, that the average weekly wages of laborers and other unskilled workmen for the years 1860–'1 and 1867–'8, respectively, were as follows: 1860–'1, $6 04 per week; 1867–'8, $9 54.

Assuming now, as in the preceding table, that the laborers in question expended their entire earnings in 1867, viz: $9 54, the same necessaries and comforts could have been obtained in 1860–1 by an expenditure of $5 52 per week, leaving an available surplus of 52 cents per week; or, in other words, the unskilled workmen of the country, obtaining the mere necessaries, and none of the luxuries of life, were in a worse condition by $27 a year in 1867, with receipts of $9 54 per week, than they were in 1860–'1, with receipts of $6 04 per week. The following tables illustrate the above facts more in detail:

---

* The skilled workmen whose wages advanced 52 per cent, on an average, from 1860 to 1867, were only those whose weekly expenditures are given in the above table. The average advance, in the same period, in the wages of *all the skilled workmen reported*, was, as previously stated, about 60 per cent.

Table showing the average weekly expenditures of laboring men in the various manufacturing establishments of the United States in 1860–'1, *and in* 1867–'8, *respectively; also, their average wages in those periods.*

Articles.	1867–'8.	1860–'1.
Flour and bread	$1 40	$0 74
Meat of all kinds	1 50	81
Butter	45	24
Sugar and molasses	50	27
Tea	37	19
Coffee	10	05
Soap, starch, &c	22	14
Lard	18	12
Milk	32	20
Eggs	20	12
Salt and spices	05	03
Potatoes and other vegetables	50	29
Fruits, fresh and dried	10	07
Coal, wood, &c	50	32
Oil, or other light	08	10
Other articles	82	51
House rent	1 25	75
Clothing, housekeeping goods, &c	1 00	57
	9 54	5 52
Weekly wages	9 54	6 04
Excess in 1861	....	52

Although the foregoing data and conclusions, founded as they are upon the average actual experience of a large number of mechanics and laborers in different sections of the country, sufficiently illustrate the increased cost of living and the decreased purchasing power of money which has taken place since the commencement of the war in 1861, the adoption of another standard for comparison, viz: the price of a barrel of flour, also affords some conclusions of interest. The average price of this article before the war is known to have measured pretty accurately, throughout the country, the average weekly wages of unskilled day laborers; and in the case of one of the largest corporations in the middle States, the principle was specifically established, that the weekly wages of common laborers in their employ should always be made equal to the varying cost of one barrel of flour per week.

Now the average increase in the price of a barrel of wheaten flour throughout the manufacturing States has been, from 1860 to July 1st, 1868, in excess of 90 per cent.; while the increase in the wages of laborers and operatives generally, skilled and unskilled, during the same period, has averaged about 58 per cent. Measured, therefore, by the flour standard, the workman is not as well off in 1867 as he was in 1860, by at least 20 per cent.; or, to state the case differently, the wages which in 1860 purchased one and a half barrel of flour now pay for about one and a quarter barrels.

From a large number of returns made to the Commissioner, the following are selected as further illustrating, by specific examples, the above conclusions.

Very careful and exact tables prepared at one of the largest iron works in Troy, N. Y., return the price of the flour used by the workmen, and purchased by them at retail in close proximity to the works, at $6 50 per barrel in 1860–'61, and at $15 per barrel in 1867–'68. In the same establishment the weekly earnings of the operatives were increased during the same time as follows:

Laborers, $5 to $8 50; engineers, $10 to $15; shearmen, $6 to $12 75; puddlers, $13 40 to $21 90; general average advance in wages from 1860 to 1867–'68, 69 per cent.

In one of the leading machine shops at Buffalo, New York, the weekly earnings of a portion of the workmen, in 1860 and 1867, computed in flour, were as follows:

	In 1860.	In 1867.
Riveters and boiler makers	1½ bbl.	1½ bbl.
Best machinists	2 "	1½ "
Ordinary machinists	1½ "	1¼ "
Flangers	2 "	1½ "

In an establishment for the manufacture of agricultural implements, located at Brooklyn, N. Y., the weekly earnings of the largest class of operatives, in 1860 and 1867, also computed in flour, were as follows: Wood workers, in 1860, one and a half barrels; in 1867, one barrel.

At a locomotive establishment in Paterson, N. J., the weekly wages of ordinary machinists in 1860–'61 were $7 50; and were about 75 cents in excess of the retail price of a barrel of flour. In the same establishment the same operatives received in 1867–'68 $13 50 per week for the same labor; but this sum then lacked $1 50 of the price sufficient to purchase a barrel of flour in the same locality.

Cotton mills of New England.—Price of flour used by operatives: 1860, $7 25; 1868, $14 12; increase, 94.7 per cent.

Wages.—Fly-frame tenders—female adults working by the piece, 1860, 67 cents per day; 1868, $1 per day; increase, 50 per cent. Mule spinners—male adults working by the piece, 1860, $1 18 to $1 25 per day; 1868, $1 92 to $2 per day; increase, 61 per cent.

Board paid by the same operatives.—Males, 1860, $2 25 per week; 1868, $3 75; increase, 66 per cent. Females, 1860, $1 25 per week; 1868, $2; increase, 60 per cent.

These illustrations, from the data in the possession of the Commissioner, might be greatly extended; but enough of evidence, probably, has been adduced to prove; that whether we adopt money or flour as the standard for the comparison of wages and commodities, in 1860 and 1867, the result is not dissimilar; viz: the purchasing power of the irredeemable paper money now in use is not nearly equal to what it was in the immediate ante-war years of 1860-'61; and that the working men and women of the country do not now receive as much in return for their labor as before the war.

The discussion of this subject, which has been instituted and carried on for the Commissioner with great skill and industry by Edward Young, esq., of the Treasury Department, is further continued with more extended tables in the appendix to this report, marked D, to which reference is here made. And in respect to the statistics as thus submitted, both in the text and in the appendix, the Commissioner would add, that if the prices of commodities in different sections of the country as there given are found (as they probably may be) to differ somewhat from the commercial price currents of the period, it should be borne in mind that the former represent the average retail prices which careful investigation by a large number of observers has found to prevail in the manufacturing towns of the various sections of the country, while the latter, on the other hand, represents either wholesale prices or prices at certain market centers. In fact, the large difference between the prices paid by operatives and laborers for provisions and other commodities bought in small quantities at retail, and the prices of the same articles as obtainable in large quantities or at wholesale, has constituted a marked feature of attention in all of these investigations, and forcibly suggests the importance of inaugurating measures whereby so large a proportion of the avails of the most productive labor of the country may not be diverted to the profit of those whose business is that of merely exchanging. The remedy for this, in a very great degree, is undoubtedly to be found in the principle of co-operation, not as applied to manufacturing or producing, but to agencies with established stores, whose simple and sole object should be the purchasing and supplying of commodities without the intervention of the middle man, and at the minimum of cost. A personal and detailed examination of the management and working of some of the leading and most successful co-operative stores in Great Britain during the summer of 1867, abundantly satisfied the Commissioner of their utility and benefit to the employés of manufacturing establishments; and apart from any testimony which he may adduce, the evidence in general in possession of the public is sufficient to prove that co-operation, at least to the extent referred to, is no experiment. The subject is one which by reason of its importance commends itself alike to the employers of labor, and to the representatives of those who are employed, inasmuch as it offers a plan which practically amounts to increasing the amount paid to labor without increasing the cost of product; and for removing, in no small degree, the incentives which now exist for strikes, and the consequent waste of the only commodity, viz.: labor, which the operative has to sell, and which, moreover, unless sold and used at the instant required, can never to the same extent be again made available.

GENERAL INFERENCES.

Finally, from the results of investigation which have thus been presented, we may draw the following conclusions:

The aggregate wealth of the country is increasing, probably, as rapidly as at any former period; yet it does not follow that there is the same increase in general prosperity. The laborer, especially he who has a large family to support, is not as properous as he was in 1860. His wages have not increased in proportion to the increase in the cost of his living. There is, therefore, an inequality in the distribution of our annual product, which we must, in no small degree, refer to artificial causes. This inequality exists even among the working classes themselves. The single man or woman, working for his or her support *alone*, is in the receipt of a rate of wages from which savings may be made equal, or greater than ever before, especially in the manufacturing towns, where the price of board is, to a certain extent, regulated artificially by the employer. Unmarried operatives, therefore, gain; while those who are obliged to support their own families in hired tenements lose. Hence, deposits in savings banks increase, while marriage is discouraged; and the forced employment of young children is made almost a necessity in order that the family may live.

Now whence comes this inequality, and this unnatural distribution of the results of labor? The student of political economy would predict *a priori* that such must be the result of the enforced use of a fluctuating measure of value, viz.: inconvertible paper money. It would be predicted *a priori* that the use of such money involves a most oppressive tax, which falls heaviest upon the laborer and lightest upon the owner of capital. Antagonism is produced where none ought to exist; the capitalist is forced to charge an additional profit for the increased risk involved in the use of a false measure of value, and the consumer of the commodity is forced to pay for such risk. There is no dishonesty to be inferred, and no injustice which the honest capitalist can avoid, so long as the law is as it is; he must either cover all risks, or withdraw his capital entirely from industrial enterprise.

It has been well said that there can be no true theoretic conclusion which will not be proved by the facts whenever the theory can be applied. We have given the theory of the effects of inconvertible paper money, and we find that the facts prove it. *The rich become richer and the poor poorer.*

In addition, however, to an inconvertible paper currency, there are other agencies which are powerfully operating to the production of a like result; and the consideration of these brings us to a new department of our investigation, viz: *The influence of taxation*, direct and indirect, upon the cost of domestic production, and consequently upon the ability of the country to exchange with foreign nations upon terms of equality. Taxation as it exists in the United States may be classified under *three* heads:

1st. Taxation under the internal revenue.

2d. Taxation under the tariff.

3d. State and local taxation.

We propose to examine, in the order enumerated, the present influence of each of these forms of taxation upon the cost of production and upon national development.

1.—NATIONAL TAXATION UNDER THE INTERNAL REVENUE.

At the close of the war, taxation under the system of internal revenue had been extended, through the necessities of the government, to a degree wh ch probably finds no parallel in any recent history; and with the exception of land and the direct products of agriculture—other than cotton and sugar—had been made, so far as domestic production was concerned, all but universal. In the case of manufactured products, furthermore, the system had been made to embrace not only the finished and marketable product, but very generally also every constituent which entered into the composition of such product. But burdensome and complicated as the system was, its inception and organization must be regarded as one of the wisest and most successful measures of the war; and it is only to be regretted that recourse was not earlier had to so effectual a method of raising revenue, rather than to the expedients at first exclusively resorted to, of loans at a heavy discount and an irredeemable paper money. How successful the system as a means of raising revenue has proved is made clearly evident from the revenue actually collected, which, from the inauguration of the system in 1862 to the 30th of June, 1868, has amounted *to over eleven hundred millions of dollars.* So long, moreover, as the war continued and the demand for manufactured products—owing to the enormous consumption of the army and the withdrawal of labor from its accustomed avocations—was fully equal to, or in excess of supply, so long taxation under the internal revenue was not regarded, at least by the majority of producers, as at all oppressive; but, on the contrary, by reckoning taxation in common with labor and material as an element of cost, and profit as a *per centum* on the whole, it was very generally the case that the aggregate profit of the producer was actually enhanced, by reason of his taxes, to an extent considerably greater than it would have been had no taxes whatever been imposed.

The close of the war, however, soon demonstrated the truth of the economic maxim, that the productiveness of a system of taxation is not its first or most important consideration. The condition of affairs before described was reversed; the supply of manufactured products became equal to or exceeded demand; products fell faster than either labor or material, and taxation, which formerly had been paid wholly from profit, now fell mainly upon capital. Apart from this it was evident, that a system which violated every acknowledged principle of taxation; which, instead of being concentrated, was diffused; which brought with it constant official inquisitions and intrusions; which hourly provoked to concealment, evasion, and falsehood; which, by duplications and enhancement of profits, took far more from the pocket of the people than was ever received into the treasury, could not exist much longer among a free people than the necessity which called it into existence. Accordingly as the requirements for expenditure growing out of the war and the existence of debt have diminished, the system of internal revenue has been extensively and rapidly modified. Within the last three years all taxes which discriminated against prudence and economy—as the taxes upon repairs; against knowledge, as the taxes upon books, paper, and printing; against capital and thrift, as the differential income tax; against the transportation of freights by boats or vehicles, and against the great leading raw materials, as coal and pig iron, cotton, sugar, and petroleum—have been swept from the statute-book. No direct taxes, moreover, are now imposed upon any manufactered product, with the exception of distilled spirits, fermented liquors, tobacco, gas, patent medicines, perfumery, cosmetics, and playing-cards, all of which may be regarded in the light of luxuries, and as involving, in the main, an entirely voluntary assessment on the part of consumers.

These reforms, although they have necessitated a relinquishment of at least $170,000,000 of annual revenue, have, it is believed, brought nothing of permanent detriment to the national exchequer; for that this great relief from taxation has both stimulated and strengthened the productive interests of the country cannot be doubted; and if so, then the period within which the national debt can be discharged has been accelerated rather than protracted, inasmuch as it can be demonstrated that the power of contributing to the public revenue increases geometrically as the activity of production and circulation increases arithmetically.

As thus amended, and as it now stands, the internal revenue system of the United States approximates closely to that which the experience of more than three-quarters of a century in Great Britain has shown to be capable of yielding the maximum of revenue with the minimum of disturbance to the wealth-producing elements of the country. The changes, apart from those pertaining to administration, which are required to still further perfect the system, are not numerous, and with the termination of the large payments for the equalization of bounties, and with an economical administration of the government, can, undoubtedly, be made with safety at no distant period. They should unquestionably embrace the taxes now levied upon telegraph and express companies; upon the gross receipts of railroads, steamboats, and other common carriers for the transportation of passengers; and the percentage taxes on the sales of merchandise; the gross receipts from all of which is less than one-half the annual expenditures during the last two fiscal years for the equalization of bounties. When this has been accomplished, it may with truth be claimed that the entire internal revenue system has been made wholly subordinate to the more important end of creating national wealth; and that under it no direct obstacle whatever is imposed by the government, which can prevent the domestic producer from placing his product upon the market at the lowest possible cost.

In concluding this review of the present influence and condition of the national taxation under the internal revenue, the Commissioner is constrained to confess, that thus far the abatement of prices consequent upon the large annual reduction of taxes has not been what was anticipated, or what the large amount of revenue abandoned would seem to have warranted. In the case of not a few articles, as pig iron, manufactured lumber, and salt,* the prices since the removal of taxation have actually advanced, while in other instances, as in the case of agricultural implements, sewing machines, hoop skirts, manufactures of silk, newspapers, and in fact most articles which are the products of monopolies created by patents, established custom, or other circumstances, the repeal of the internal tax, through the maintenance of former prices, has been only equivalent to legislating a bounty into the pockets of the producer.

2.—NATIONAL TAXATION UNDER THE TARIFF.

We come next to the consideration of the influence of national taxa tion under the tariff on prices and the cost of domestic production—a subject, the discussion of which is attended with the embarrassment that it involves more of prejudice and of opinion founded on private self interest than almost any other which since the abolition of slavery has occupied the attention of the American people. Notwithstanding this, it is important to recognize the fact, that under the existing financial condition of the country, the old-time issues between the advocates of free trade on the one hand, and protection on the other, have ceased to be of any real practical importance—inasmuch as in the arrangement of a tariff with a view to revenue, the requirements of the government must certainly, for the present, necessitate so high an average of duties as to afford all that can be reasonably asked for on the grounds of protection; and with a given requirement, moreover, for revenue, in excess of what can be derived from the taxation under the tariff of acknowledged luxuries, there would seem to be no valid objection to distributing the additional taxation in such a manner as to favor those branches of industry most exposed to foreign competition.

RECOGNITION OF THE PROTECTIVE SYSTEM IN EUROPE.

Again, a careful study of the financial systems of the various commercial nations of Europe has led the Commissioner unhesitatingly to the conclusion—that whatever may be the state of European public opinion in respect to free trade, and whatever may be the claims preferred for it on the broad grounds of liberality and humanitarianism, the fiscal legislation of Great Britain, France, Germany, Belgium, Holland, Austria andRussia is now, and always has been, framed solely and exclusively with reference to one object, viz., the promotion of supposed national self-interest, and has never had the slightest regard to the interest of any other nation, or to any arguments other than those based upon specific national wants and specific national experiences.

Thus, the policy of Great Britain, which exempts capital employed in manufacturing and banking from all direct taxation under the excise, and all raw materials imported from foreign countries from all taxation

* The statistics of the Chicago Board of Trade show that the average price of domestic coarse salt per barrel in the Chicago market during the year 1865–'66, when the manufacture of this article was subjected to a heavy internal revenue tax, was $2 44; while for the year 1867–'68, when no tax was imposed, the price was $2 73 per barrel.

under the customs, although not so termed, is undoubtedly protection in its most subtile and effective form, and as such has been recognized and commented on by the French economists; inasmuch as it permits the British manufacturer to apply the largest amount of home labor to the smallest value of raw material under such conditions as enable him to place his finished product in all foreign markets at the lowest possible cost. Any other policy than free trade at present in Great Britain would, by enhancing the cost of food and raw material, inevitably swell the cost of manufacturing, and thus result to the direct benefit of the foreign competitor.

The above observation also holds true in respect to the unquestionably inhuman policy of Belgium, which refuses to restrict the labor of women and children in its coal mines and iron-works, for the openly admitted reason that such restriction by diminishing the supply and enhancing the cost of labor would expose too seriously its manufactures to British and other competition.

If we turn next to France, we shall find that protection, besides being recognized as a principle in the determination of taxes on imports, manifests itself even more conspicuously in other forms; as, for example, in the regulation by government of railroad freights on coal and iron, and in the obstacles which are officially placed in the way of operatives changing their employment without the consent of their employers.

In the new tariff of the Zollverein, (June, 1868.,) although its rearrangement on a very low percentage of duties is claimed as a triumph of free trade, it is to be noted that especial care has been taken to largely and progressively increase the rates on the importation of all articles the domestic manufacture of which it is considered by Prussia as desirable to promote and foster.*

Now, if these premises are correct, it is evident that however much regard may be professed by the nations referred to for philosophic theory, their fiscal legislation is essentially framed in accordance with what seems to them to be the dictates of self-interest; and, in fact, it may well be doubted whether in modern times any financial legislation, even under its most favorable conditions, can or ought to recognize any other principle than that of enlightened selfishness. Such selfishness, however, does not necessarily imply illiberality; for experience in both public and private transactions sufficiently proves, that exchanges are likely to be the most extended and most profitable when a mutuality of interest between the parties concerned is fairly regarded.

Furthermore, while it is undoubtedly true that the leading commercial nations of Europe do foster certain branches of industry and commerce and may be said to protect them, the method adopted is entirely different from what we call protection in the United States. The method of England, especially, is to remove burdens, to cheapen cost, and reduce prices. Our method, on the contrary, is to levy a tax, thereby increasing cost and reducing consumption. The one method may be called a bounty to the consumer, the other a bounty to the producer; one the method of abundance, the other of scarcity or privation; and as our main difficulty at present is excessive cost and high prices, we

* Raw materials are admitted free, or nearly so; and the rates of duty rise from this point towards the maximum, (10 per cent.,) according to the degree and fineness of manufacture. For instance, cotton carded, combed, or colored, is free; wadding, 1 thaler 15 silver groschen per hundred weight; cotton yarn, one and two threads, 2 thalers per hundred weight; the same, bleached or colored, 4 thalers per hundred weight; the same, three or more threads, 6 thalers per hundred weight. Again, wooden ships or boats are charged 5 per cent., but iron ships or boats 8 per cent.

should do well to consider this difference and study the lesson which it teaches.

A TARIFF IS A TAX.

In entering upon the proposed analysis, it is important that one fact in the nature of an axiom, but too often overlooked in the discussion of this subject in the United States, should be kept clearly in view; and that is, that a tariff on imports is, under all circumstances, a tax, which is paid, wholly or in part, by the consumer. If the tariff be imposed solely for revenue, then the consideration of most importance in connection with it is one mainly of comparison, viz., to determine whether the tax in question is superior or inferior to other taxes in respect to economy of administration, equality of assessment, and productiveness of collection. To this theoretical economists would undoubtedly return a negative answer; and would support their conclusions by the experience of the densely populated manufacturing nations of the Old World, where the inhabited area is limited, the distribution of wealth most unequal, and law, through the maintenance of the police and standing army, not easily evaded. In the United States, on the contrary, where the area is continental, the population sparse, wealth more equally distributed, and the carrying out of laws is made dependent on public opinion rather than on the representatives of force, all experience tends to establish the fact that, objectionable as may be in many respects a high tariff, we have thus far been able to devise no other system of taxation which brings to itself so much of certainty in its results and equality in its apportionments. An illustration of this is afforded in the case of the customs duties upon the three articles of tea, sugar, and coffee, which at present approximate to an aggregate of about fifty millions of dollars per annum. These duties are assessed mainly at five or six ports of the country, and, being wholly specific, are collected without delay and with little trouble. It is not probable, moreover, that the revenue derived from them is evaded to any great extent through smuggling, while under-valuation is practically impossible. Being, furthermore, of almost universal consumption, the duties levied on them are very uniformly distributed, and fall upon the consumer in small amounts at any one time; while, as they cannot be considered as necessaries of life in a sense so absolute as breadstuffs and clothing, the payment of the tax through their use is in a great measure voluntary. Through these circumstances, therefore, the conditions of effectiveness, economy, and equality, as regards collection and apportionment, are most perfectly secured.*

* In illustration of this point the following statistics of the annual consumption of tea, coffee, and sugar in the United States are presented:

Article.	Average receipts from duty per annum.	Ave'ge annual consumption per capita.	Ave'ge annual consumption by each consumer.	Amount of duty or tax.	
				Per year.	Per week.
Tea	$8,300,000	1 pound.	2.08 pounds.	52 cents.	1 cent.
Coffee	8,000,000	4.8 pounds.	15 pounds.	75 cents.	1½ cent, (nearly.)
Sugar	30,000,000	26 pounds.	26 pounds.	78 cents.	1½ cent.
Pepper	64,750	2 ounces.	4 ounces.	3¾ cents.	.072 cent.
	46,364,750			[illegible]	4 cents.

From the above table it will be seen that a sum in gold is annually received into the treasury from the above few articles sufficient to pay the interest on $740,000,000 of the national debt, and at a cost of *four cents per week to each consumer;* a tax which practically must be unfelt by even the most indigent of our population.

Let us next consider the conditions of raising an equivalent sum from internal taxation levied on the products of domestic industry. We select iron and its manufactures, boots and shoes, clothing, cotton and woollen fabrics in illustration, for the reason that these articles yielded by internal taxation during the fiscal year 1866 an amount very nearly equivalent to what is now obtained from the duties on tea, sugar and coffee. It must be obvious, in the first place, that the collection of this amount of revenue from the above enumerated domestic products must be an exceedingly complicated matter. In the place of five points of collection, the collection districts would extend over every furnace, rolling mill, foundry, machine shop, and over every cotton, woollen, and hardware manufactory, and over every factory or shop for the production of clothing, boots and shoes in the country, thus entailing an additional proportionate increase of expense and official inquisition.

Again: as iron, cotton, and woollen fabrics are the direct and essential component elements of a great variety of other products, the taxation which enhances their prices as raw materials in the first instance necessarily multiplies the price of all articles produced by their agency, thus restricting consumption and the extension of foreign commerce, and unfairly exposing great branches of domestic industry to a competition with foreign producers who are free from similar disabilities.

Another illustration of the superiority of the tariff as a means of raising revenue may be found in the acknowledged failure to collect a large proportion of the taxes assessed under the internal revenue, and in the great inequality which is known to exist in the distribution of the income tax; the amount which passed to the credit of this latter tax in a single district of the State of New York for the fiscal year 1867 having been more than double the collections under the same head in the same year from ten entire States of the Union.*

Following what appears to be a logical order, the Commissioner would next ask attention to two other points which have been made the subject of investigation, namely, *the direct effect of the tariff on the prices of imports; and the effect of the increase of tariff in checking importations.*

DISTRIBUTION OF TAXATION UNDER THE TARIFF.

In respect to the first point, namely, the direct effect of the tariff on the prices of imports, the influence is undoubtedly the same as is recog-

* The following comments by a recognized authority on the superiority of indirect as compared with direct taxation, as seen from a European stand point of view, will be read with interest in connection with this discussion:

"If all indirect taxes could be abolished it would undoubtedly be a great gain to mankind; but, unfortunately there are two great reasons why in this country, (Great Britain) at least, they cannot be abolished. The first is the great expenditure of the English government. Who that is acquainted with actual responsible finance would propose to raise that sum by direct taxation? A theorist on paper may propose a three shilling (15 per cent.) income tax and other such things; but no real finance minister, conversant with the wishes and charged with the finances of the country, would ever meet Parliament with propositions so disagreeable to the House, so disagreeable to the country, so little likely to yield the money. The poor man may or may not be benefitted less than the rich man by the existence of the civil government; but at all events, he is immensely benefited. But no system of direct taxation can make him contribute to its support without costing more than it brings in. An income tax on agricultural laborers would give the exchequer nothing; it would cost money rather than bring money. The effect, therefore, of raising our national revenue exclusively by a direct taxation, would be to exempt the great mass of the community from contributing to the national expenditure. And not only is direct taxation unjust and inexpedient; it is also subject to a greater defect, it is disagreeable. Human nature does not like it. A man would rather pay an unknown increment, an invisible addition to the price of some few things, than be asked point blank by the direct tax gatherer for a palpable conspicuous enjoyable sum. We do not say that men ought to feel thus, but that they do feel it, and they will always feel it."—*London Economist.*

nized in the case of the taxes imposed under the internal revenue. If the demand be constant and nearly equal to the supply, the consumer, through the enhancement of price, invariably pays the entire duty, and generally some small additional percentage in compensation to the importer for the advances made by him on account of the duties, or, as at the present time, in the way of insurance against fluctuations in the value of the currency. On the other hand, in case the supply of the imported article tends to exceed the demand, (especially if demand is checked by reason of an enhancement of price resulting from an increase of tariff,) the importer will often abate prices in order to retain his market; the practical effect of which is, that the payment of the duties is divided more or less unequally between the importer and the consumer. If the profit on the imported article is not sufficient to allow of such abatements of price, and the consumer refuses to pay an increase sufficient wholly to compensate for the duties, the importation ceases, or the products are entered with the avowed intention of being sacrificed.

A few examples in illustration of these principles may be given. Thus, in the case of the article of tea, in respect to which the demand is almost always equal to the supply, the price since 1861 has increased to fully the extent of the duties imposed since that period; the average wholesale price of a particular variety, having increased from 75 cents, gold, per pound, to $1 50, currency, in 1867. This increase has been made up as follows: importing costs 75 cents, gold; duty, 25 cents, gold—$1, gold, or $1 40, currency, (adding the average gold premium for the year, 40 per cent.,) leaving ten cents, currency, as additional profit, or, as currency insurance to the importer.*

Lumber offers another example of an article in which, owing to the relation of supply and demand, the duty imposed on the foreign import is undoubtedly paid wholly by the domestic consumer.

Fresh and dried fruits, fresh, dried, and salted fish, and many fancy articles, especially of German and French manufacture, are examples of importations on which the duty imposed is generally divided between the importer and consumer. It is also a noticeable fact that the wool tariff of 1867, by checking the importation of some varieties of wools and woollens, so increased the stocks of the same in foreign markets, that prices receded to an extent nearly or quite equivalent to the increase of duties.

Some forms of bar-iron, and of liquors, cigars, oats, butter, potatoes, cattle on the hoof, and fine wools, are examples of articles on which duties are imposed under the present tariff sufficient wholly or in a great degree to check importations.†

---

* The experience of Great Britain for the last 20 years in respect to tea, as a source of revenue under the customs, has established this curious fact, viz: that a decrease of the tariff on this article brings no corresponding benefit in the way of reduction of price to the consumer. Thus, for example, while the duty on tea, under the British tariff, was reduced to the extent of 77 per cent. between the years 1849 and 1866, (from 2*s.* 2¼*d.* in 1849 to 6*d.* in 1866,) the average price of tea "in bond," or duty free, during the same period exhibited a corresponding increase of about 50 per cent., (*i. e.* from 1*s.* 1*d.* to 1*s.* 7¼*d.*,) and this, too, notwithstanding the fact that the supply, through importation, had no way abated, but, on the contrary, increased during the years 1862–'63 to an extent sufficient to overstock the market. The explanation of this commercial phenomena is, that as there is practically but one tea-producing country, the trade partakes of the character of the monopoly to such a degree that a decrease of the duty inures mainly to the advantage of the producer, and an increase, conversely, to his disadvantage. The opinion, therefore, so often expressed of late that a reduction of the present duty on tea would result in advantage to the American consumer is not likely to be practically realized.

†The following table showing the prices of Turk's Island salt, in gold, from 1841 to 1862, under different and widely varying conditions of tariff, illustrates the difficulty which often

The general conclusion therefore of this investigation is, that while the imposition or increase of taxation under the tariff always occasions an increase in the price of imported articles to the consumer, it cannot be affirmed that such increase is always commensurate with the duties imposed, or that the duty is always *wholly* paid by the consumer.* On the other hand it not unfrequently happens, as will hereafter be shown, that the imposition of a tax in the form of a tariff on an imported article is made the occasion for very greatly and unnecessarily advancing the price of a corresponding domestic product, and thus taxing the community to an extent entirely disproportionate to any benefit which may accrue in the first instance to the national revenue.

INFLUENCE OF THE TARIFF IN CHECKING IMPORTATIONS.

We come next to the consideration of the influence of the tariff in checking importations; the practical interest in which question, at the present time, centres almost entirely in the fact, that an increase of the existing tariff has of late been persistently urged as a certain remedy for a present annual import, whose aggregate is regarded as excessive.

exists of tracing any definite or constant connection between the prices of the imported article and the duties that may be imposed upon it:

Prices of Turk's Island salt in New York and rates of duty thereon from 1841, *when it was free of duty, until* 1862, *when the present rate of eighteen cents per hundred pounds was imposed.*

Dates.	Average prices per bushel.	Dates and rates of tariff on salt in bulk.
	Cents.	
July 12, 1841	30½	Free.
December 20, 1841	27	Free.
Jan. 24 to Mar. 21, 1842	25½	August 30, 1842, 8 cents per bushel.
April 11 to July 6, 1842	22	
July 18, 1842	25	
Oct. 7 and Nov. 28, 1842	28½	
March 10, 1845	24	
January 12 to 19, 1846	29	August 6, 1846, 20 per cent., (equal to about 2½ cents per bushel.)
Feb. 9 to Mar. 16, 1846	45	
April 27 to Dec. 21, 1846	27	
March 15, 1847	33	
March 20, 1848	27½	
Average of the year 1855	33	
Average of the year 1856	32	
April 9, 1857	26	March 3, 1857, 15 per cent., (equal to about 1½ cent per bushel.)
May 14, 1857	25	
June 17, 1857	23	
July 4, 1861	20	March 2, 1861, 4 cents per bushel.
July 25 to Aug. 15, 1861	21½	August 5, 1861, 12 cents per 100 pounds.
August 22, 1861	23½	
July 9, 1862	29½	
July 16, 1862	30	July 14, 1862, 18 cents per 100 pounds.
October 1 to 11, 1862	32½ to 34½	

* Nothing can be more unfair than the practice which often prevails in discussing the tariff of comparing the prices of great staple articles of manufacture, as cotton fabrics, hosiery, iron, Bessemer steel, &c., at different periods, and then referring the decline which has taken place in their market values to the influence of legislation. In nine cases out of ten the slightest examination will show that the decline in question was due to what may be called the "world's progress," *i. e.*, to discoveries in mechanics and chemistry; to diminished cost and greater supply of raw material; to cheaper and quicker methods of transportation and to the general increase and diffusion of human knowledge; and that this progress has been in a very great degree independent of the United States, and would have taken place all the same if no tariff whatever had found a place upon the statute book of the country.

That the imposition or increase of a tariff does contribute specifically to diminish or prohibit importations cannot be doubted; as, to use but a single illustration, the experience under the increased tariff on wool, passed March, 1867, sufficiently demonstrates. Thus, the net import of foreign wool, which amounted to 86,969,987 pounds in 1864, and 67,065,386 in 1866, declined to 29,475,698 in 1867, and to 21,682,166 in 1868.*

But whatever may be the force of specific examples, it is equally certain that a consideration of the whole subject will show that no material reduction of importations—certainly none proportionate to the means employed—can be effected through any practicable increase of the existing tariff. This will appear evident when we reflect, that the articles which constitute a very considerable part of the value of importations are not articles of strict luxury, which can be dispensed with at will, but articles whose consumption the people will not relinquish except upon the pressure of extreme poverty or necessity; or others which are absolutely essential to the continuance of great branches of domestic industry. Thus, for example, the four articles of tea, coffee, sugar and molasses, constituted nearly one-third of the net value of the imports for the fiscal year 1867–'68, exclusive of bullion and specie. Their consumption, moreover, is not only constantly and rapidly increasing with every increase of wealth and population, but the whole drift of popular sentiment is unmistakably inclined to favor a much larger importation through a reduction of the existing tariff. Another large class of articles, as the various dye-woods and dye materials, crude India-rubber, soda-ash, bleaching powders, guano, lumber, sulphur, hides and horns, hatters furs, ivory, raw silk, gums, rags, jute, saltpetre, tin, &c., are so essentially the raw materials of great branches of domestic industry, that while any interruption of their importation could only be attained at the expense of national decadence, an increased importation would infallibly indicate an increase of national prosperity. On these two classes of articles alone, the increase in the value of imports growing out of perfectly legitimate and natural causes, will probably be sufficient during the next three years, to fully counterbalance any reduction in the value of imports which might be effected through any changes which it would be possible to make in the tariff in respect to all other articles of foreign growth and importation. Thus, for example, the increase in the consumption of imported sugars for the year 1868 is reported as full *sixteen per cent.* above the consumption of the preceding year, while for the year 1869 an increase of at least ten per cent. is anticipated. Again, all experience, and especially the experience of the United States within the last three years, shows that there is a point beyond which duties imposed on importations cannot be carried without rendering them practically inoperative. Thus, under the existing tariff, the duties on wines, liquors, and silks have been carried to such a degree that only so much of these articles are now imported as are necessary to meet a popular requirement that no law can prevent from being satisfied. If carried beyond this point, the requirement or necessity will still be met, but the smuggler and illicit dealer, rather than the regular importer, will become the agent of supply; for in no country can evasion of the excise or customs be carried out more successfully than in a republic where popular opinion is both the law-maker and the law-sustainer. If proofs in support of this position are demanded, they are most abundant.

* The diminution of the exports of woollens to the United States from certain of the great manufacturing centres of Europe was also very noticeable. Thus the exports from the town of Huddersfield, Yorkshire, England, which, for the quarter ending June 30, 1866, were of the declared value of £139,775 18s., fell off under the increased tariff on woollens for the corresponding quarter of 1867 to £41,025 12s.

We select first the article of champagne, the importation of which in accordance with popular demand is less subject to fluctuation than almost any other article of foreign growth or production. In 1864, with gold at from 200 to 250, as compared with currency, the importation was 103,158 dozen; while in 1866, with gold at 140, the importation was 102,341 dozen. In view of this uniformity, is it reasonable to suppose that in this the last half of the 19th century any enactment of law is likely to prevent the people of the United States from obtaining at reasonable prices so much of this article as they may be willing and able to pay for? We find the answer in the experience of the last few years in respect to cigars, on which a rate of duty most excessive and extravagant, and twice as great as that imposed on champagne, has been adopted. Thus, in 1859, with a moderate duty, the importation of cigars was returned at about 800,000,000 per annum; in 1867, with a duty of about 150 per cent. in gold, *ad valorem*, the imports are returned at less than 30,000,000; and yet cigars of foreign production continue to be used in such quantities as to make it clearly evident that the supply is much greater than the returns of the legitimate importation would indicate. Again, opium, with a duty of nearly 100 per cent. *ad valorem*, was sold freely in the New York market during the past year at lower prices in currency than the equivalent of the market value through legitimate sources in gold.*

Another agency which tends to counteract or render temporary the influence of increased duties, in checking importations, is due to the circumstance, that experience shows, that whenever an advance has been made in the tariff on an imported article which comes in competition with a domestic product, the price of the domestic product is often advanced to a degree proportionate to the increase of duty. Prices being thus restored to a common level, the foreign producer is again enabled to enter the domestic market, to a greater or less extent, as a competitor.

If any further evidence is required, to prove the almost utter impossibility of predicating anything whatever, respecting the amount of importations, from the rates of duty imposed, it will be found in a review of the experience and workings of the various tariffs that have been enacted since the year 1840.

Thus, in 1842, the average tariff being 23.1 per cent., the total importations were of the value of $100,162,087. Three years later, or in 1845, the tariff having been advanced to an average of 32.5, the total value of the importations was $117,254,564, or an increase of the average duty one third, having increased the imports one-sixth.

The following table shows the varying value of imports for a number of years, under comparatively the same average rate of duty:

Years.	Rate of duty.	Value of imports.
1842	23.1	$100,162,087
1849	23	147,857,439
1854	23.5	304,562,381
1855	23	261,468,520

* The following extract from the report of the controller of customs of New Brunswick submitted June 29, 1867, has much significance:

"The total value of all goods imported into New Brunswick in 1866 was $10,000,794, against $7,085,595 in 1865, showing a large increase on the year's importations, (41 per cent.) The principal increase was on goods from the United Kingdom, the value of which was $4,022,956, against $2,284,449 in 1865, an increase of over 76 per cent. Two-thirds of the value of the imports from the United Kingdom consisted of haberdashery. St. John being a central point for travelers from the States, a considerable quantity of our duty-paid haberdashery is annually purchased and taken away by them."

In 1866 the duty on spirits imported into New Brunswick was increased about 50 per cent., viz: to 35 cents per gallon and three per cent. proof. In face of this we have the commercial phenomenon of a largely increased importation, viz: 470,590 gallons, against 311,688 in 1864.

In 1860, the average rate of duties being 19 per cent., the returned value of the imports was $362,163,941. In 1866, the average rate of duties on total importations being 43.19 per cent., the returned value of imports was $437,640,354.

In short, it is other and far different agencies than the rates of duty which may be imposed under a tariff that determines the extent and value of importations.

For tabular statement showing the revenue collected each year, from 1789 to 1868, the amount of dutiable imports and free goods imported annually, and the average rate of duty on imports annually, reference is made to the appendix of this report marked F.

It is evident, therefore, that however desirable it may be, under the present financial condition of the country, to diminish the drain of the precious metals, or to avoid foreign indebtedness on account of importations, the way for the successful and practical accomplishment of the object does not lie in the direction of an increase of the existing tariff.

RELATIONS OF A TARIFF FOR REVENUE AND A TARIFF FOR PROTECTION.

But whatever of interest may attach to the discussion of a tariff, framed solely with a view to revenue, such discussion, except it refers to mere matters of adjustment, is at present of but little practical importance, inasmuch as there is no subject pertaining to our fiscal legislation in respect to which there is greater unanimity of public sentiment, than that which recognizes the advantage and necessity of making the tariff available to the greatest extent possible as a source of revenue. In this there is no essential difference in the policy of any party; and if there are any who can so far divest themselves of the conditions and necessities of the hour as to advocate a removal of all imposts and an abolition of all custom-houses, their expectation certainly does not extend to the immediate future. It is only when we pass to the consideration of a tariff imposed for purposes other than revenue, that essential differences of opinion manifest themselves and the embarrassments of the question are encountered.

In the consideration of a tariff for revenue the question at issue would, as already stated, appear to be one mainly of comparison, viz;, as regards the relative superiority of this or some other system, for the collection of a given and necessary amount of revenue.

In the consideration of a tariff imposed for purposes other than for revenue, the question at issue on the other hand would appear to be one of profit and loss, or rather of burden and advantage;—the burden being the tax and enhanced prices which the community consents to impose upon itself; and the advantage, the profit which is held to accrue from the resulting stimulus and development of domestic industry.

If these premises be correct, the essential point of interest in all this inquiry then is, simply to ascertain on which side of the account stands the balance; and this knowledge, in turn, is to be obtained so far as this investigation is concerned, through the analysis and determination of facts and through the experience alike of producers and consumers.—These facts and this experience the Commissioner, during the last three years, has sought, through his official position, diligently and impartially to obtain; not, as has been already stated, with a view of supporting the theory of free trade on the one hand, or protection on the other, but solely with a desire to know what policy hereafter is likely to prove most advantageous to the revenue and most certain to establish the credit of the whole country upon a sound and substantial basis. To the result of this investigation in particular he would next ask attention.

ESSENTIAL FEATURES OF THE EXISTING TARIFF.

The basis of the existing tariff is to be found in the act of March 2, 1861, which virtually repealed all former duties, by providing that upon all raw or unmanufactured articles and upon all articles manufactured in whole or part, not enumerated in said act, the rates of duty should be respectively 10 and 20 per cent. *ad valorem*. Since this date there have been eleven amendments essentially affecting rates of duty, some of which, like the acts of July 14, 1862, and June 30, 1867, were equivalent to almost complete revisions.*

The rate of duty imposed by the existing tariff on the invoice value in gold of the dutiable goods imported into the United States has averaged for the last three fiscal years about 48 per cent.†

If to these rates, freights, insurance and commissions, which in themselves constitute a natural and unavoidable tariff, be added, the average of duties will be still further increased to the extent of from 10 to 15 per cent.

Again, the requirements for revenue growing out of the war having necessitated the creation of an all-pervading system of internal taxation subsequent to the increase of the tariff in 1861, it became absolutely necessary, in order to prevent such increase from being neutralized by the taxes levied on the products of domestic industry, to increase at least correspondingly the rates of duty levied on the importation of competing products, which end was steadily kept in view, and in a great measure attained in the respective acts of June 30, 1864, and March 3, 1865. This statement is illustrated by the following table, which shows in respect to certain staple articles, the internal tax imposed by the act of June 30, 1864, and subsequent acts, and the increase of tariff allowed on the corresponding competing imported article.

---

* The number of articles taxed under the existing tariff and specifically enumerated in the unofficial catalogue generally referred to, (Ogden's compilation,) is upwards of 2,000; but as many separate articles are often embraced under one common designation, the specific number is undoubtedly much greater; of these, a very large proportion afford only a nominal revenue, and in not a few instances the gross receipts from specific articles will not exceed the sum of $50 per annum. That conclusion, however, would be most hasty and injudicious which would advocate an exemption from duty of all articles yielding an inconsiderable amount of revenue, inasmuch as many such articles constitute, as it were, the outworks which defend and make certain the most important sources of revenue. Thus, for example, the amount of the article of sugar-candy imported is very inconsiderable, (probably not sufficient to defray the costs of collection,) but if this article were to be exempt from duty or admitted at a lower rate than simple sugar, its importation as a substitute for sugar would probably increase to an extent sufficient to seriously affect the revenue.

† The following table shows the exact percentage of duties to dutiable imports, and the per centage to total imports for the three fiscal years 1866, 1867, and 1868, respectively:

	1866.	1867.	1868.
Percentage to dutiable imports	48.58	47.34	47.86
Percentage to total imports	43.19	42.85	44.04

Internal tax imposed by the act of June 30, 1864.

Articles.	Internal tax.	Duty prior to June 30, 1864.	Duty subsequent to June 30, 1864.	Increase.
Cotton, raw	$0 02½*	$0 00½*	$0 03	(†)
Bristles	‡5	10	15	$0 5
Blue vitriol	‡5	‡20	‡25	‡5
Brushes	‡5	‡35	‡40	‡5
Saltpetre	‡5	2	2½	½
Domestic cottons, jeans, bedticks, pantaloon stuffs, &c	‡5	3	6	3
Domestic bleached cottons	‡5	3	5½	2½
Axes, hay-knives, hoes, steel rakes, sheep-shears, scythes, shovels, &c	‡5	‡35	45	‡10
Iron castings, gas and water pipe	§3 00	¾	1½	‖¾

* Per pound. † Repealed. ‡ Per cent. § Per ton. ‖ Or $15 per ton.

Since the 13th of July, 1866, the internal taxes on the above and all other domestic products, with few exceptions, have been substantially removed, but without any corresponding alterations in the tariff. The practical effect of this action, therefore, has been to increase gradually, and as it were insensibly, the percentage of the tariff, which increase for the majority of domestic products will average five per cent. as a minimum. On some articles, however, the comparative increase has been much greater, as, for example, upon imported liquors, the increase of tariff upon which, by the reduction of the internal taxes, must be regarded as equivalent to at least 40 per cent.

Notwithstanding these extreme rates, higher than have ever before been levied by the United States, or by any civilized nation in modern times, and higher, as we have just shown, by a minimum of five per cent. than at the termination of the war, the tariff as it stands to-day, fails in a great degree to check importations, or to give that degree of protection to which persons engaged in almost all branches of domestic industry have represented to Congress that they are rightfully entitled.

The cause of this curious politico-economic phenomenon is undoubtedly due in the first instance to the toleration and use of an inconvertible paper currency, which always has and always will work to the prejudice and disadvantage of the industry of every nation which adopts it, in comparison with those nations who recognize only the standard of gold and silver in their commercial transactions. In addition, however, a careful and impartial review of the arrangement and workings of the existing tariff will not fail to satisfy that not a few of the evils which those who advocate a continued increase of duties seek to remedy, have really been occasioned by an indiscriminate and injudicious application of identically the same policy.

The avowed object of the tariff, as revised in 1861, was revenue to provide for the expenses of a great war. Subordinate only to this was the other principle of discriminating duties in favor of domestic or home industry—a principle which may be considered as the present policy of the great majority of the American people, and which, as we have already shown, is recognized and virtually acted upon by all the leading commercial nations of Europe. With the termination of the war, and with accruing receipts from the tariff in excess of the actual requirements of the treasury, the popular tendency, as expressed by legislation, accomplished or projected, has been to reverse the order of importance of these two principles, and to make the idea of revenue subordinate to protection rather than protection subordinate to revenue. And in carrying out, furthermore, the idea of protection, but one rule for guidance would appear to have been adopted for legislation, viz: the assumption that whatever rate of duty could be shown to be for the advantage of any private interest, the same would prove equally advantageous to the interests of the whole country. The result has been a tariff based upon small issues rather than upon any great national principle; a tariff which is unjust and unequal; which needlessly enhances prices; which takes far more indirectly from the people than is received into the treasury; which renders an exchange of domestic for foreign commodities nearly impossible; which necessitates the continual exportation of obligations of national indebtedness and of the precious metals; and which, while professing to protect American industry, really, in many cases, discriminates against it. But as it is facts not assertions that are wanted, let us examine the existing tariff and see if the facts make good the assertions. One of the first things that an analysis will show is, that every interest that has been strong enough or sufficiently persistent to secure efficient representation at Washington has received a full measure of attention, while every other interest that has not had sufficient strength behind it to prompt to action has been imperfectly treated, or entirely neglected. Thus let any one glance at the great departments of wool and iron, and he will find that the duties on all the leading products have been carefully increased, harmonized, and adjusted, in a great degree, in accordance with the wishes of those interested.

TARIFF ON DRUGS AND CHEMICALS.

Now, in striking contrast to these is another great department of the tariff, viz: the department of drugs and chemicals, which embraces nearly one-half of all the articles on the list of enumerations on which a duty is levied. In this department there is hardly an individual in the nation who is not more or less directly interested. It regulates the price of nearly all medicines and remedies from the expensive alkaloid that protects from malaria, to the material of the cheap infusion that constitutes the relying remedy of the humble housewife; the gums of the varnish-maker and paper-stainer; of all dyewoods, dye extracts, resists, and mordants; of sulphur and the nitrates that form the basis of the great commercial acids; of the salts of artificial manures; of all the reagents and tests of the chemist; of the materials which assist in the welding and polishing of the metals; of the essential oils that constitute the raw material of the perfumer, the soap-maker, and manufacturer of extracts; of the great alkalies, bleaching powders, and antiseptics; of all photographic salts and preparations; the enamels of the jeweller; the fluxes of the glass-maker; the astringents of the tanner and leather-dresser—upon all of these, and many other articles and products embraced in this department, the duties are discordant and often antagonistic alike to the attainment of either revenue or protection; ad valorems being mixed up in the most heterogeneous manner with specifics, and neither having in general the slightest regard to the cost or use of a product. On some articles, like opium and the alkaloids, the duties are so excessive that the chief import is already made through the agency of the smuggler; on others of corresponding use and cost the duty ranges from the merest nominal to the most excessive rates. On the drugs used as medicines the duties which might be made specific are generally ad valorem, and so high as to constitute in themselves a bounty for the importation of the worthless material which all other markets have rejected. In some instances a discrimination has actually been made against domestic and in favor of foreign industry, as in the case of lac and lac dye, where the raw material is burdened with a duty of 10 cents per pound, and the manufactured article admitted free. On some of the varnish gums, articles which compete in no degree with any domestic product, the duty is in excess of their prime cost in the London markets; while in respect to glass, the statement is made to the Commissioner by one of the leading manufacturers of the country "that more duty is paid to the government by the domestic glass-maker on the imported raw materials used by him in his business than is received from duties imposed on the importation of table glass ware of foreign manufacture." Now the reason of this unfortunate condition of affairs is to be found in the fact that it has never been made the special interest of intelligent and influential parties disconnected with the government to press this matter upon the attention of Congress; and whenever a partial effort to arrest the attention of the committees has been made, the claims of the great special interests have been too urgent and imperative to allow time for consideration. Two years ago the Commissioner, aided by the voluntary efforts of some of the best experts in the country and leading members of the American Pharmaceutical Society, prepared and submitted to Congress a complete revision of this important branch of the tariff. His work, however, was not only not accepted, but the very fact that it was performed has been made the occasion of complaints as involving unnecessary interference with pending legislation, and a useless expenditure of time and labor.

INDISCRIMINATE PROTECTION A CHARACTERISTIC OF THE EXISTING TARIFF.

Another characteristic feature of the existing tariff is that it attempts indiscriminate or universal protection, an idea which, if fully carried out, would render all protection a nullity; and to the extent to which it is carried out does more for foreign as compared with domestic industry than almost any other one agency.

This will appear evident when we consider that but few products, the result of applied labor and capital, come to the consumer as the result of one process, but nearly all involve several stages or well-defined points of progress, in which the finished product of the one becomes the raw material of the other. If a tax laid under the tariff, with the view of protection, were impartially and universally apportioned; as, for example, if all duties were increased by one act ten per cent., prices, after a little, would be affected uniformly; all raw material of foreign production, or those of domestic origin whose price is regulated by a partial foreign supply, would rise equally with the manufactured product, and the cost of production, though pushed to a higher level, would relatively remain as before. If, on the contrary, the distribution of the tax were not made uniform, it is evident that whatever was laid upon a raw material would be equivalent to a reduction of protection to the product which results from its manufacture. But the term raw material, as above shown, is only a relative expression; so much so, that it would be difficult to instance any article, the product of industry, to which it could be absolutely and unqualifiedly applied. Thus, coal is the finished product of the miner, but the raw material for the manufacture of pig iron; pig iron, in turn, becomes the raw material for the manufacture of bar iron; bar iron for machinery, machinery for textile fabrics, textile fabrics for clothing, and clothing for the laborer, whose efforts in the single department of agriculture determine the national prosperity, and indeed the very existence of all other forms of industry. It will be found, furthermore, on analysis, that the amount of labor or capital invested or required in the several stages of industry above cited is very disproportionate, and increases very rapidly in the order of enumeration; there being, for example, more individuals employed in the manufacture of clothing in the city of Boston alone than there are in all the woollen mills of Massachusetts; while the number of laborers employed in agriculture is far in excess of those in all other industries combined. Hence the necessity in the construction of a tariff, whether the object aimed at be revenue or protection, of the exercise of discrimination; which discrimination, in order that it may be intelligent, must be based, not on a consideration singly and separately of the interests involved, but upon a consideration and knowledge of the relations which the separate interests sustain to the whole, keeping in view at the same time the cardinal doctrine that all legislation approximates to perfection in the degree that it provides for the greatest good of the greatest number. And unless this course is recognized and adopted, it never can be known, whether the benefit that may follow from the imposition or increase of a particular duty will not be more than counterbalanced by the injury that the same duty may inflict indirectly. In fact, the industrial interests of a highly civilized country are as mutually inter-connected and inter-dependent as are the diverse parts of the human body, and growth in both cases must be natural, symmetrical, and uniform, or the result will be distortion, torpidity, and paralysis.

The following incident of recent tariff experience strikingly illustrates the difficulty and danger of attempting to base legislation upon the demands of single interests, even though such demands may in themselves appear, and within a limited sphere actually be, intrinsically fair and just:

In the year 1864, the manufacturers of spool thread ascertained that fine English thread was being imported as yarn under a 35 per cent. duty and afterwards spooled in the United States, thus evading the duty on spool thread, which was considerably higher. Accordingly, on proper representation of the facts, the tariff was so amended that a duty of four cents was imposed upon each skein or hank of unwound thread or yarn of 840 yards, and, in addition thereto, thirty per cent. ad valorem—a rate which practically amounted to prohibition. On the attempt being made to enforce the duty, it became clearly apparent for the first time that the fine cotton threads or yarns, ranging from numbers 100 to 200, which it was proposed to exclude in the unwound state, were needed for many other purposes than for sewing, and that some of them could not at that time be furnished under any circumstances in this country. The very best quality are especially needed for the manufacture of elastic fabrics, which was indispensable for the making of suspenders, gaiters, and other products; and their manufacture, for the time being, would have been utterly ruined, could the object aimed at in the duty have been practically carried out. The manufacture of lastings, coburgs, and other worsted fabrics to which these yarns were essential, was also then being for the first time entered upon, and in one known case was actually abandoned in consequence of the interruption of the supply of fine cotton warps caused by the attempt to enforce the duty.

After considerable difficulty, great interruption of business, and the reshipment to Europe of importations of yarn which had been ordered before the enactment of the tariff amendment in question, the matter was adjusted by a decision of the Treasury to this effect; that a cotton warp or yarn intended for use in the manufacture of elastic, worsted, or woollen fabrics was a manufacture of cotton not specially enumerated, and was therefore subject to the ad valorem rates imposed on articles of this kind, rather than on those specifically fixed on thread or yarn; and by this decision only, several branches of American industry, involving probably more of capital and labor than was represented by the article which it was originally intended to protect, were saved from absolute destruction.

As another incident to this transaction it may be stated, that it was subsequently found by experience to be impracticable to enforce the duty on the skein or hank, according to the arbitrary standard of 840 yards, the effect of which has been that yarn in the skein, bundle, or cop continues to be imported at the rate of duty existing previous to the enactment of the amendment referred to.

EFFECT OF THE TARIFF ON SHIP-BUILDING AND COMMERCE.

But it is in respect to the absurdity, as well as the utterly disastrous influence that flows from the carrying out of the principle of universal and indiscriminate protection that the illustrations are the most numerous and significant. What, indeed, can be more instructive than the lesson afforded by the present condition of the ship-building interest and the foreign commerce of the United States. There are three things, the importation of which is theoretically impossible, viz., counterfeit money, indecent publications, and ships. In addition to this measure of absolute prohibition of ships there has been superadded, for the benefit of American ship-builders and ship-owners, a bounty in the restrictions which the law imposes on all foreign vessels from engaging in the coastwise trade; and yet to-day, speaking generally in respect to ocean traffic, we can neither build, buy, nor sell an American vessel.

This result is obviously due in no small part to the fact that while protecting the ships, we have also protected to nearly an equal degree the separate constituents that enter into the construction of ships, viz., the timber, the iron, the copper, the cordage, and the canvas; and these two agencies have so far neutralized and counterbalanced each other that neither party, within this particular sphere of industry, has been benefitted; the ships not having been built, or the constituents of their construction created or applied, while the community at large, whose interest it is that all these branches of industry should prosper, has likewise received no benefit, but rather detriment from the suspension or diversion of labor and capital from its previous employments. The same system, moreover, of checks and balances growing out of the indiscriminate and universal taxation under the tariff which we have thus shown to exist in ship-building, has been also so far extended to every other branch of production, *that if ships available for foreign trade were to-day furnished to hand, without cost, their use must be exceedingly limited, for the reason that the high prices of all domestic commodities would effectually prevent that exchange with foreign countries which in itself constitutes commerce.*

The nation during the last few years has rapidly learned to appreciate the effect of an universal and indiscriminate system of internal taxation in the enhancement of prices and in the restriction of production, but it has thus far failed to recognize, to the same extent, the inevitable tendency which the adoption of a similar system of taxation under the tariff has to produce results corresponding and analogous. Examples of the working of the tariff in particular instances will, however, greatly assist this understanding.

TAXATION AND ENHANCEMENT OF THE PRICE OF LUMBER.

We select as our first illustration the article of lumber, on which the government levies a duty of twenty per cent. ad valorem; which rate, by the addition of the percentage which the importer almost invariably will add by reason of the payment of the duty, may probably be considered as equivalent at the present time to twenty-five per cent.

Now, the increasing necessity and use of this indispensable article is such, that the demand for the last few years has been fully equal to or has tended to exceed supply, which in turn has resulted in constantly augmented prices; the price, for example, of the cheapest varieties of lumber in the Albany, New York, market having advanced since 1861 about 100 per cent.*

A supply of foreign lumber (*i. e.*, from the British provinces) being absolutely essential to meet the requirements of the country—a fact generally conceded—two things follow as a matter of necessity; first, that whatever duty is imposed on the foreign product is paid wholly by the consumer, and is therefore equivalent to so much direct tax, and secondly, that the price of the imported article regulates and determines the selling price of the domestic product, at least for all that portion of the latter which is exposed to the competition of the foreign supply in the open and leading markets. Whatever, therefore, under these circumstances enhances the price of foreign lumber, be it a tax or some other agency, will from necessity augment the price of the domestic product to the same extent. Or, in other words, a tax on the importation of foreign lumber becomes also a tax upon the consumers of the whole domestic product; with this essential difference, that in the one case the proceeds of the tax results to the benefit of the national treasury; and in the other to the benefit exclusively of private interests.

Let us now see to what these respective taxes amount. The net invoice value of the importation of rough lumber, during the fiscal year 1868, was about seven and a half millions of dollars; while the value of the domestic product for the same period, or that part of it which entered into competition with this foreign import, may be approximately estimated at fifty-four millions. For every dollar, therefore, that is taken in the form of a direct tax, seven are taken indirectly through the increase of prices; or, in other words, $2,250,000 currency are received into the treasury at an indirect cost of about sixteen millions. And this is not all. 25 per cent. on the increased price of lumber means 25 per cent. in the increased price of houses, 25 per cent. in the increased price of vessels, of fences,

* Table showing the prices of the leadtng varieties of lumber in the Albany, New York, market, on the first of May, from 1861 to 1868, inclusive.

	1861.	1862.	1863.	1864.	1865.	1866.	1867.	1868.
Pine..............per M. feet..	$16 00	$18	$24	$30	$22	$29	$35	$31
Spruce ....do......	10 00	12	15	21	17	24	25	20
Hemlock ....do......	8 50	9	12	17	14	19	22	17
Black walnut ....do......	....	42	60	90	70	80	75	70

It will be observed that of the lumber most in demand for building purposes, the advance in prices from 1861 to 1867 was as follows:

Spruce, 150 per cent.; pine, 119, and hemlock, the most in demand for erection of the common description of dwellings, 158 per ceut. In May, 1868, the prices had fallen from $4 to $5 per M. feet, making the increase from the prices of 1860, on the above varieties, 100,94, and 100 per cent. respectively.

of railroad ties, and other constructions of which wood is the principal constituent.* All these find their expression in the increase of wages and of the cost of other forms of raw material; and these in turn augment the cost of manufactures; and thus the wave of taxation, emanating from a common centre, continues to extend and enlarge itself until no man can measure the breadth and power of its influence, but breaking ultimately with its full force upon two classes of society, viz.: those living upon fixed incomes and the day laborer, for it is not in the power of either of these to arbitrarily increase his income as a measure of compensation. And all this has been done in the name of protection to American industry!

But are not the producers of lumber, it may be asked, equally entitled to the same measure of protection against the cheaper labor and capital of foreign countries as is conceded to other domestic interests? We find the answer, in the first place, in the claim which the lumber producers themselves preferred during the continuance of the universal system of internal taxation, viz.: that their product, by reason of its importance as a fundamental raw material in almost all other branches of industry, should be exempted from all burden of an excise; and this claim was promptly acknowledged and acceded to by Congress. Again, it has never been pretended, even by those who advocate the most extreme rates in respect to protection, that protection, or what is the same thing, a bounty, should ever be given to any interest that is able otherwise to sufficiently sustain itself. Now, previous to the repeal of the reciprocity treaty there was no duty imposed on raw and unmanufactured lumber imported from the British provinces, and previous to that time no interest was in a more flourishing and stable condition than that engaged in the production of lumber. Since the commencement of the war, moreover, *the increase in the price of lumber has been far in advance of the average increase in the price of labor and of other commodities.*

The interest of lumber production, therefore, judged simply by comparison, does not stand on terms of equality in respect to a claim for protection with other products; and if it did, there can be no benefit shown to accrue from taxation levied on the importation of lumber that will, in any degree, compensate for the injury that is thereby inevitably entailed upon other branches of industry. To tax lumber, therefore, under the tariff, even to the slightest extent, is to discriminate against rather than protect American industry.

A wise foresight, furthermore, would indicate that the national interests are likely to be best subserved by restricting rather than stimulating the destruction of our forests, which, in consequence of the continually augmenting demand for lumber, are diminishing and receding with alarming rapidity. So certain, moreover, is the future advance in the price of lumber, owing to increased demand and diminished supply, that if it were possible to draw for the next ten years the whole domestic supply from foreign sources, the result would unquestionably be for the benefit rather than the detriment of the country; while in respect to private interests the increase in value of timber lands held in reserve during the same period would probably exceed any average interest that would be likely to accrue from a different employment of capital.†

---

* In the United States there were sixty-six trades reported in 1860 as dependant upon wood as their material for manufacturing; and 242,958 men employed in the simple trade of carpentry alone—or three times as many as worked in cotton, and thirteen times as many as worked in the production of flour and meal.

† That the views here presented are beginning to be entertained in those sections of the country at present most directly interested in this branch of business, is evident from the following extracts from a communication from an authority on this subject in the State of Maine, who takes the view that the State itself should not allow the manufacture of lumber

The increase in the receipts of lumber at some of the principal lumber markets of the country shows the remarkable increase in the demand and consumption of this article. Thus the increase at Albany of the quantity of boards and scantling received by the canals alone, in the two years from 1865 to 1867, was nearly 50 per cent., or 25 per cent. per annum; while at Chicago, in the four years from 1863 to 1867, the increase in the receipts were as follows: on lumber, 113 per cent.; shingles, 159 per cent.; and in laths, 251 per cent.

TAXATION OF SALT.

The Commissioner would next ask attention to the taxation imposed under the tariff on salt, a product which properly should be classed as an article of food.

The importing prices of salt at the principal foreign sources of supply range from 7 to 11 cents per bushel; the average price at Turk's Island being 10 cents, at Cadiz 7 cents, and at Liverpool 8 cents per bushel.

In 1841 the importation of salt was free; in 1842 a duty of 8 cents per bushel was imposed on salt in bulk, which was changed in 1846 to 20 per cent. ad valorem, or about 2 cents per bushel; in 1857 it was reduced to 15 per cent., or about 1½ cent per bushel; in March, 1861, it was increased to 4 cents per bushel; in August, 1861, to 12 cents, and in July, 1862, to 18 cents per 100 pounds. As the weight of a bushel of salt ranges from 56 to 85 pounds, it will, therefore, be seen that the existing duty is equivalent to an advalorem on the importing prices, as above given, of from 100 to 170 per cent., an average higher than is imposed under the tariff on any other article of primal necessity and consumption.

The relation between the duties and the importing cost of salt will, however, be rendered more apparent by the following statements, showing, in several specific instances, the results of actual experience:

No. 1.—Brig Goodwin, from Cadiz, arrived at New York, August, 1867:

Cost of cargo, 15,340 bushels, (gold)	$1,159 83
Duty paid on same	1,967 36
Percentage of duty to first cost	170

No. 2.—Brig Sarah Kennedy, from Bonaire, New York, September, 1867:

Cost of cargo, 16,740 bushels, (gold)	$1,500 00
Duty paid on same	2,160 00
Percentage of duty to first cost	144

to exceed its growth, and that "the sources of wealth represented by the forests of the State should not be wastefully drawn upon for the sake of present gain to the few at the expense of future profit to the public." "In the manufacture of the yearly growth of the forests of Maine," says the writer, "the lumber business would still be very extensive, and play an important part in increasing the wealth of the State. But as it is now conducted, business will soon begin to decrease in these places instead of increasing with the population as it ought to do." "Fifty years ago the immense tracts of woodlands on the banks of the Saco seemed almost inexhaustible; but with the mills that have been built, and the extensive manufacture of 'box shooks' and 'headings,' the lumber that now comes down is comparatively small, showing that the extent of the trade is beginning to cause an approximate exhaustion of the forest."

By a report made during the past year to the Foreign Office of Great Britain by the British consul at Stockholm, it would also appear that notwithstanding 91 per cent. of the area of the kingdom of Sweden consists chiefly of forest land, there is a general apprehension of approaching failure of the product of timber, and a reduction in the export of wood; all the forests in the populated parts of the kingdom and along the great lines of communication having been nearly or quite exhausted. It is also stated that no considerable compensation for this deficiency can at present be expected from the vast Norrland forests of that country, in consequence of their almost absolute inaccessibility.

No. 3.—Ship Ontario, from Liverpool, New York, September, 1867:

Cost of cargo, 5,429 sacks Liverpool ground salt...........	$2,531,40
Duty paid on same....................................	2,913 84
Percentage of duty to first cost..........................	115

In 1860 the actual cost of a cargo of salt of 18,330 bushels, imported into Boston from the port of Trepani, Sicily, was declared at $2,063 41. The duty on this import under the then existing tariff, (viz., 15 per cent. ad valorem,) was $309 45. The duty on the same quantity of salt imported from the same port, under the present tariff of 18 cents per 100 pounds, would amount to $6,089 58, (gold.) The freights paid (in gold) in 1868 were not essentially different from those of 1860, but the selling price of salt has advanced about 28 cents per bushel, or from 20 to 23 cents in 1860 to from 48 to 51 cents in 1868.

And yet, notwithstanding this experience, it is claimed that the duties as they now stand are not sufficiently protective, and a further advance of from 18 to 24 cents per 100 pounds is urgently demanded, and has been acceded to in the bill now pending. (House of Representatives, No. 1211.)

In considering this application the question which naturally suggests itself, is: Are such excessive duties necessary to the existence and development of the salt manufacturing industry in the United States? And, independent of all particulars, it may be said, in reply, that it would seem in the first instance, to stand to reason, that there must be something entirely abnormal and unnatural in the prosecution of a business of any kind which requires, as the primal condition of its existence, the imposition of a tariff ranging from 100 to 170 per cent. ad valorem, and a consequent average enhancement of its price to consumers greater than that paid by other commercial nations.

Coming down, however, to particulars, we find that the leading organizations engaged in the manufacture of salt in the United States are at Syracuse, in the State of New York, and Saginaw, in the State of Michigan. Now, in order to the attainment of a full understanding of the relation which the duty on imported salt sustains to the manufacture and cost of the domestic product, we propose to ask attention briefly to the condition of these two companies, and to allow each one of them to submit the statement of its case through the medium of the sworn testimony of its principal officers.

The association at Syracuse, New York, obtains its brine or raw material from a State reservation, and pays to the State as a remuneration for a free supply of brine and for inspection, weighing, branding, and for keeping in order the conduits, buildings, and machinery, a toll of one cent on each bushel of salt manufactured.

Previous to 1860 the Commissioner finds that the manufacture of salt at this place was the result of independent individual, rather than of associated enterprise, and was lacking in such a systematic management, both as regards the manufacturing and selling, as was essential to continued and uninterrupted prosperity. In 1860, this result having become apparent, the various individual interests were consolidated into one association, an enactment having previously been obtained from the State legislature (viz., in 1859) which forbade the superintendent from furnishing brine to any other, or to new works, "until the quantity raised and distributed by the State shall be sufficient for fully supplying all the existing works through the manufacturing season." As the supply of salt water was not then nor has since been in excess of demand, the effect of this law was obviously to restrict the production of salt to the then existing manufacturers or their representatives. In the organization of the association, each individual manufacturer leased his salt property to the company at a yearly rental of 12½ per cent. on an appraised valuation, which valuation was considerably greater than what at that time was undoubtedly the actual cost. About five per cent. of the aggregate valuation, or about $160,000, was paid in to furnish a working capital, and the stock pro-rated to the manufacturers leasing their property.

With this preliminary explanation, attention is invited to the following abstract of testimony:

SYRACUSE, NEW YORK, *October* 24, 1867.

John W. Barker, secretary of the Onondaga Salt Company, being sworn, testified:

Question. What has been the average quantity of salt made during the last ten years on the Onondaga reservation?—Answer. In round numbers, 6,895,000 bushels. The present production is above the average of this period, and for the present year (1867) it will be from seven to seven and a half million bushels, (actual production, 7,595,565.)

Q. Is the quantity of brine obtained sufficient to work all the blocks and covers?—A. There is not a sufficient quantity raised, but we think there is an inexhaustible supply.

Q. What is the lowest strength of brine that you can work economically?—A. About 60 degrees by the salometer.

Q. Are you in the habit of working brine of less strength than 60 degrees?—A. We have several wells which furnish brine of less strength, and this we use, to some extent, with the stronger.

Q. Please state the nature of present organization of the Onondaga Salt Company?—A. It is an organization which was originated in 1860, and is to continue for ten years from that time. Previous to 1860, the manufacture of cover or solar salt was mostly carried on by separate companies, and block salt by individuals. In 1860 these separate companies were consolidated.

Q. Under what conditions was the individual property consolidated?—A. The property was appraised by the parties in interest. The original valuation of the property was $3,200,000.

Q. What interest was guaranteed on the property thus stocked?—A. We pay on that valuation 12½ per cent. as rent.

Q. Was that valuation a real valuation, or was it a price above cost?—A. It might be considered, on a general average, as a high valuation at that particular time.

Q. Was it not, in fact, 33 per cent. above the cost at that time?—A. No; it was not.

Q. Was it not 20 per cent above cost?—A. The general average of a salt block is $5,000.

Q. Was the actual cost of making a salt block in 1860 in excess of $3,000?—A. I think it was considerably. I can speak more definitely in regard to coarse salt.

Q. What is the working capital of your company?—A. It was originally $160,000, contributed by the parties to the block in the proportion of five per cent. on each share.

Q. Will you state what dividends the company has declared on the stock thus paid in?—A. Well, I don't know as I can do that. I shall have to refer to my books for the exact figures. The company has in some years paid very heavy dividends. The first year they incurred a loss. That was in 1860. They did not make enough in that year to pay expenses. In 1861 they made a small dividend. In 1862, 1863, and 1864 they made very large dividends. The price of salt was enormously high, owing to the state of the country at the time.

Q. Will you state how large the dividends were?—A. On the 14th of December, 1861, the first dividend was made. It was a dividend of seven per cent. The next dividend was made in March, 1862, of 12½ per cent. The next was made April 23, 1862, of $1 25 per share. The next was September 13, 1862, also $1 25 per share. The next, September 27, 1862, also $1 25 per share. Salt was then selling at $5 per barrel. The next was October 4 of the same year, of $1 25 per share, and again on October 11, of the same month, of $2 50 per share. The last extra dividend was made February 20, 1864. Since then the average annual dividends have been seven per cent.

Q. Has the stock of the company been increased since that time?—A. It has been doubled. [Making the present working capital of the company $320,000.]

Q. Have you divided since 1864 your full profits, or have you carried any considerable amount to a surplus fund?—A. We have a surplus on hand of about $600,000. Since the organization of the company in 1860 the whole amount paid in dividends is about $2,000,000; but of the profits made by the company since its organization, two-thirds at least have been made in coal and coal mining. The property of the company is now absolutely worth $4,498,969.

Q. What is the largest amount of government tax which you paid in any year?—A. Nearly $200,000.

Q. What legislation do you think is necessary to insure the continuance and prosperity of your company?—A. Well, I think it would be for the benefit of the salt company, and mankind generally, if we could have a market in New York at the same profit as in the west.

We are obliged to send from a million to a million and a half or two millions of bushels to New York per annum, and upon this we make no profit.

Q. What, in your opinion, would be the effect on your works if the tariff should be reduced? —A. It would take us out of the market as a matter of course. We could not sustain ourselves there for a moment. We ought to have a higher duty. All the business we now do in New York is without profit. It is, in fact, a loss.

Q. What is the freight on a barrel of salt to New York?—A. It will average about 12½ cents per 100 pounds, or 37½ cents per barrel.

Q. Are your salt wells and works worked up to their fullest capacity?—A. Not the wells, but the works are. We are making all that is possible under the present condition of things.

Q. What proportion of your salt do you export to Canada?—About 100,000 barrels a year, (518,904 bushels in 1867.) The quantity has not materially differed in the last few years.

Q. Please state the present range of prices for your salt?—A. Our price here (at Syracuse) is $2 35 per barrel. At Buffalo our nominal price is $2 50; further west, $2 40. In New York city it sells at from $1 75 to $1 80.

Q. Why should you sell your salt at a less price at tide-water than at Buffalo and other western markets?—A. Because we have not the same competition to encounter in the west.

Q. Then I am to understand that you regulate your prices by the competition?—A. Yes; and the comparatively large amount which we dispose of in the chief cities is another consideration for lowering the price. Our first business is to take care of our home trade, on which we require only a fair profit.

In submitting this testimony it is but simple justice to state that it was not only claimed by the Onondaga Salt Company, but that figures in support of the claim were also submitted, showing that a very large proportion of the great profits realized since 1861 have been due to the possession and control of cheap coal, and that if the average market price had been paid by them for the coal used under their furnaces, the cost of manufacturing salt would have been greatly enhanced. But allowing all this, it is difficult to see what bearing the fact has upon the claim of this particular company for an increase of the tariff, inasmuch as in determining the question we are to look at the circumstances as things actually are, and not as they might have been if less of foresight and good management had been exercised. To maintain the contrary would be, in fact, to assume that the amount of protection to be awarded to a particular industry should be in proportion to the incompetence displayed in its prosecution.

The next witness, to whose testimony attention is invited, is Duncan Stewart, esq., of Detroit, president of a salt manufacturing company at Saginaw, Michigan, who, being sworn, (October 15, 1867,) made answer to the following questions:

Question. Will you please state the present condition of the business of producing salt in the Saginaw salt district?—Answer. For the first few years that the business of manufacturing salt in Saginaw was carried on, there were very few people engaged in it who knew anything at all about the business, as to how it ought to be managed. This left the salt interest laboring under a very great disadvantage. I should say that at least one half of all the money that has been invested in the salt business there has been squandered uselessly and extravagantly, and that the business up to last year has paid little or no profit. This has not been owing to any disadvantage or defect in the business itself, but is mainly owing to the competition which has existed among the manufacturers, there being a large number of manufacturers, and each of them competing in the same market with all the others. Nineteen-twentieths perhaps of all those engaged in the business, not having the requisite capital to carry it on, have to throw their salt into the market as soon as it is produced. This has, however, been remedied to some extent. About 75 per cent. of those engaged in the business now are associated into companies, called the Saginaw Bay Company, and the Saginaw Valley Salt Company. I think there is but about one quarter of the whole interest outside of these associations now. The result has been better management, greater unity of action, less competition and better prices. I submit a table of the cost of making salt in the years 1864, 1865, and 1866, with the average rate of sales and profit and loss:

Cost of making salt by the Saginaw Valley Salt Company in 1864, 1865. *and* 1866.

Year.	Wood.	Barrels.	Taxes.	Wages.	Repairs.	Material.	Incidental.	Total.	Sales.	Profit and loss.
1864....	$0 90.5	$0 48	$0 12.5	$0 54.3	$0 16.5	$0 05.2	$0 03.5	$2 30.5	$2 18.5	$0 12 per bbl. loss.
1865....	71.5	42.5	20	41.5	12.5	6	2¼	1 96¼	1 83¾	12.5 Do.
1866....	59	38.7	10.5	41.3	11.2	6.3	1.5	1 68.5	1 82	13.5 per bbl profit.
1867*...	....	....	....	....	....	....	....	1 50	1 78	28 Do.

* Estimated.

I will state that the loss exhibited in this table was entirely brought about by bad management.

Q. Has there been any essential reduction of freights from the Saginaw district to the various lake ports?—A. The average freights this season to the Lake Erie ports will not exceed 50 per cent. of the average rates of last year. Freights to Toledo are about 25 cents against 75 for the early part of the season, and a dollar for the later part of the season. The Detroit freights ran from 35 cents to $1 50 in former years—this year 20 cents. The diminution of freights has, of itself, converted the manufacture of salt in the Saginaw valley into a fair success, where, without it, it would have been an absolute failure.

Q. What is the average price per barrel of Saginaw salt in the lake ports?—A. It has sold at an average of $2 18, as nearly as may be.

Q. To what extent does the salt manufactured at Syracuse compete with salt manufactured in the Saginaw district?—A. It competes with it in all the lake ports, the Syracuse people selling their salt in the larger ports at a rate very much below what they charge in New York; for instance, for the same kind of salt which they sell in New York for $2 50 they sell in Buffalo for $2 20, making a difference of 30 cents a barrel. This is done for the purpose of damaging the interests of the Saginaw manufacturers, the present high tariff giving them nearly the entire control of the seaboard markets, where they make large profits, enabling them to throw their salt into the western ports at, sometimes, much below the cost of product at Syracuse. This they do for the purpose of destroying the Saginaw interest.

Q. Have you any knowledge of the profits derived from the business of manufacturing salt during the last few years.—A. Yes, sir; I should say that our own experience, according to the statement I have handed in, shows a loss in the year 1864, without counting the loss of interest on investments, and in 1865 also. The profit made in 1866 is profit on manufacturing without counting anything for interest on investments; so that on the whole it has been a losing business.

Q. Have you any knowledge as to what have been the profits derived from the manufacture of salt in Syracuse during the last few years?—A. Not further than the prices quoted in the eastern markets; and judging from those prices, they must either have made enormous profits there or else have made an enormous loss at the west. My own opinion is that they made very large profits in the seaboard trade, from the quotations given.

Q. Are the present high rates of duty on foreign salt necessary, in your opinion, to encourage our domestic production of this article?—A. I think not.

Q. Will you state the reason why?—A. Because we have the entire benefit of the cost of transportation, which must be added to the cost of the foreign article; this of itself is a sufficient reason why we ought to be able to compete successfully with foreign salt at a less rate of duty than is now paid. The tariff inures almost entirely to the advantage of the Syracuse manufacturers, giving them almost the entire control of the seaboard market, enabling them to realize large profits; enabling them to lay the salt which they send to the western markets at a rate so low as to be ruinous to the interests of the Saginaw manufacturers.

Q. You have no doubt that this system has been pursued by parties engaged in the salt interest at Syracuse?—A. I have no doubt whatever that it has been pursued systematically and constantly since the commencement of the manufacture of salt at Saginaw.

Q. Do you look for an increased production of salt in the Saginaw district during the coming year?—A. Not with the present results of the trade, but a fall in the price of labor and material would probably largely increase the quantity of salt produced. With present prices there will be no increase, very many of the works having, even under the favorable circumstances of this year, not run at all. There is another matter connected with the tariff that I would like to call attention to, and it is the duty of 50 cents per cord that is levied upon cord wood imported into the United States from Canada. It would be a great boon to have this repealed; there being a short supply of wood in the Saginaw valley, which could be remedied by imports from the Canadian shores where the supply is abundant. And it would also diminish the cost of living of the laboring people. It operates not as a general, but a purely local tax, and is creating a great deal of dissatisfaction in the laboring community. They look upon it as an oppression. Cord wood has become extremely scarce in all the frontier States; and while its consumption is largely increasing, its source of supply is diminishing.

The next witness is James Oakes, of Boston, dealer in salt, who being duly sworn, testified as follows:

Question. Will you state the prices at which Syracuse salt is sold in the Boston market, October, 1868?—Answer. When sold to fishermen, who have the right to use foreign salt in bond, that is, to salt fish on board their vessels, the price is made to compete with foreign salt, say from 33 to 35 cents per bushel; but when sold to those fishermen who salt their fish on shore, and therefore have no right to use salt in bond, the price is from 15 to 17 cents per bushel higher. In other words, the Syracuse salt is sold to fishermen at 15 to 17 cents per bushel less than when sold for salting meat. Besides this difference in price the manufacturers of Syracuse salt employ agents to go to the different large fishing towns to solicit the patronage of the fishermen, and will deliver salt alongside of the fishermen's vessels at the different places free of charge to the consumer; the expense of which cannot be less than ten cents per bushel, including "fall short in measure," and in transporting from one port to the other. If a large profit did not arise even when selling to the fishermen at 33 to 35 cents per bushel, it is presumed that the manufacturers would not employ agents to go among the fishermen to solicit their custom, and then deliver the salt alongside. In view of these facts it seems to me evident that if the selling of salt to the fishermen be a remunerative business, and I think it is, from the vigor with which the agents of the manufacturers promote it, then the profits on salt sold for curing meats and other purposes, on which 15 to 17 cents per bushel additional is charged, must be exorbitant; and it should also be borne in mind that the expenses of conducting the latter branch of the business are much less than when the salt is delivered alongside the fishing vessels.

Q. Was any reduction made in the price of domestic salt, in consequence of abatement in 1867, and the entire removal in 1868 of the internal revenue tax on the manufacture of salt?—A. I think not. The price of domestic salt, when sold for salting fish on board vessel, is fixed so as to compete with foreign salt in bond, without regard to tax of any kind.

With this exposition of facts and testimony the question of the necessity or expediency of further increasing the present high duties on salt may well be submitted without argument. On the other hand, however, when we consider how, through the indispensable use of this article, an increase of its price (from 23 cents per bushel in 1861, to 48 cents in 1868) has come home to the whole people; how such increase affects the great industrial interests involved in the packing of beef, pork, fish and butter, and consequently the distribution and price of food at home and its exchange for foreign commodities abroad; and especially when we consider that the internal tax on this article—which in 1865 was collected from one company to the extent of about $200,000—has been entirely removed;* in view of all these circumstances, may we not well ask, whether protection to American industry and a regard to the interests of the whole people does not demand, not only that there be no further increase of the tariff and the price of salt, but that a reasonable and moderate reduction of the existing duties be promptly conceded.

One further illustration of the effects of the existing duties on salt may be presented. In the Gulf of California, just north of the 26th parallel, there is an island—Carmen—where salt of remarkable purity is deposited by natural agencies in inexhaustible quantities. The situation and condition of this island are such, that it would seem as if it were intended to be the natural and cheap source of supply of salt for the whole Pacific coast of our country; and yet by the agency of men, and in the name of protection, this free gift of God, and this great source of national wealth, has been rendered practically of no account, inasmuch as the royalty exacted by the Mexican government, the United States

* As has been before shown, the price of coarse salt per barrel in Chicago ruled higher during the years 1867–'8, subsequent to the removal of the internal revenue tax, than in the year 1865, when a heavy tax was imposed.

tariff added, and the expenses of collecting and transportation, in the aggregate amount so nearly to the price of salt obtained from other sources in San Francisco, as almost completely to eat up all profits, and thus close in a great degree the only market to which it can be taken.*

The result of all this is, that capital and labor, in a section of country where capital and labor are of all things most in demand, are withdrawn from other employments and diverted to doing that which nature herself has already done much more perfectly, viz: making salt from sea-water in the bay of San Francisco, at a cost of from $7 to $10 per ton.

The character and results of this unnatural industry may be inferred from the following extract from a report made to the Commissioner by one of the best recognized authorities on this subject on the Pacific coast:

"The bay salt produced at San Francisco is frequently of an inferior quality, and is mixed with a large proportion of Carmen island salt before it can be made suitable for many of the purposes for which salt is required. The high price of labor, the absence of all reasonable facilities, and the inferior quality of the salt produced at the works, all combine to make the industry one of no importance on this coast, and not one that deserves special protection. At present the duty on Carmen island salt amounts almost to prohibition, and but from 3,000 to 4,000 tons are yearly consumed. Could it be admitted free or at a lower rate of duty, the consumption of this one variety would amount to at least 15,000 tons per annum. It is now utterly impossible to make money in many parts of California and Oregon by packing beef and pork, owing to the high price of salt, occasioned by the excessive duty: which upon the Carmen island product amounts to more than 300 per cent. of the original cost, exclusive of freight by steamers. I say nothing about the mining interests which would be advanced by cheap salt, but these will be ultimately very important, as the sulphurets containing gold are being worked with great success by chlorination in California, and salt in this is one of the principal items of expense."†

TAXATION ON PIG IRON.

Again, the article of pig iron affords a striking illustration of an instance where a duty originally levied for revenue and protection, or as an offset to internal taxes, has been continued long after its object has been fully attained, for the interest of the few, but to the detriment of the many.

The existing duty on pig iron is $9, gold; equivalent to over $12 currency. The average expenditure requisite to produce a ton of pig iron

* The items which make up this cost, as reported to the Commissioner, are as follows:

Cost of collecting and delivering on board a vessel, per ton of 2,000 pounds	$1 16
United States duty, (over 300 per cent.)	3 60
Freights	5 00
Mexican royalty and incidentals	2 74
Cost of Carmen island salt laid down in San Francisco, August, 1868, (gold)	12 50

† The following analyses, made during the past year at San Francisco, show the superiority of Carmen sisland salt as compared with that manufactured in the bay of San Francisco:

	Carmen's island.	Bay salt.
Water	3.320	5.959
Sulphate of lime	1.416	0.157
" " magnesia	0.000	0.742
Chloride of calcium	0.402	0.000
" " magnesium	0.066	1.016
" " sodium	94.796	92.135
	100.000	100.009

in the United States to-day may be fairly estimated as not in excess of $26 per ton, currency; and in the case of furnaces favorably situated as regards cheap coal or ore, and under good management, the actual cost, could it be truly ascertained, would not probably be found in excess of $24. Now, the selling price of Nos. 1 and 2 pig iron in the markets of the United States at present, and for the last year, has ranged from $37 to $42 per ton, with a demand continually tending to exceed supply.*

Under these circumstances the manufacturers of pig iron have, to the detriment of the rolling-mill interest, and to the expense of every consumer of iron from a rail to a ploughshare, and from a boiler plate to a tenpenny nail, realized continued profits which have hardly any parallel in the history of legitimate industry, the returns of one set of furnaces in one of the middle States, communicated to the Commissioner, showing a yearly product of 35,000 tons, on a capital of $450,000, sold at a profit of from $10 to $13 per ton.

The Commissioner, as he writes, (November, 1868,) has before him letters from the representatives of the bar and sheet-iron interests in nearly all sections of the country, to this effect: "Our works are busy, but not remunerative. The profit of the iron manufacture is all absorbed by the manufacturers of pig metal. Our only hope is in equalization, and in a fair increase of protection by Congress at its next session."

Now, it would seem that if the manufacturers of pig iron had really at heart the great interests of American industry, they would of their own accord memorialize Congress to this effect: "Our profits being far larger than is necessary for the prosperity and rapid extension of our business, we desire and can have no more efficient protection than what would of necessity be guaranteed to us by the prosperity and extension of the rolling-mill interest; and this protection can be readily attained, with benefit alike to producers and consumers, by affording under the existing tariff to the manufacturers of rolled iron cheaper raw material. We therefore request that the duty on pig iron, so far as it has heretofore been imposed or maintained for our benefit, may be relaxed or wholly abolished in the interest of the associated branches of the iron industry, which are less prosperous." The Commissioner has not, however, heard that any such movement has been contemplated, but on the contrary it is apparent from an inspection of House bill No. 1,211, now pending, that the manufacturers of pig iron propose to allow the representatives of the bar iron interest

* Thus we quote from recent price currents of recognized authority:

July, 1868.—Furnaces are still running on hard iron, and there is not enough No. 1 iron to meet the demand. Prices are nominally $42 for No. 1 extra; $36 to $38 for No. 2 extra for American, and $42 to $45 for Scotch. The latter is also becoming scarce.

August, 1868.—American, No. 1 extra and 2 extra irons continue scarce, and prices rule from $41 to $43; the offerings few and stock exhausted. The demand for 1 extra and 2 extra pig iron is increasing, without at present an adequate supply.

September, 1868.—American pig iron has not materially changed in price, and we do not alter our quotations. No. 1 continues very scarce, and the demand is in excess of the supply. No. 2 extra is also hard to find. Bar iron is very firm, and holders are indisposed to make concessions. The mills are fully occupied, and in most instances considerably behind their orders—in some cases four to six weeks. The stock they have on hand is unusually small.

November, 1868.—American pig is unchanged, with scarcely enough in market to make any business. We quote No. 1, $42 to $43; No. 2 extra, $38; No. 2, $36 to $37. Furnaces are more firm in their deliveries. Scotch pig is held at higher figures, and holders are not anxious to sell. Bar iron is unchanged, the demand from store being light, but the mills continue fully occupied, being in many cases a month or six weeks behind their orders.

December 24, 1868.—Since our last report there has not been any especial change in the market. American pig is very scarce, and lots, when wanted, are sometimes hard to find. No. 1 is generally held at $41, though there have been sales at $40 50 for prompt cash. By the manufacturers of pig iron it is contended that during the coming year prices will range higher than they have been.—*Iron Age.*

to ask from Congress at this session such further legislation as will, without reducing the present unduly enhanced cost of pig iron, guarantee to the latter at the expense of the consumers such additional profit as may render their business remunerative.

ADDITIONAL EXAMPLES.

The Commissioner has thus selected lumber, salt, and pig iron as illustrations of the working of the present tariff, because these articles, in their production and application, are widely and familiarly known. He might, however, have selected many others whose example would have been equally pertinent; but he believes enough has been said to fully prove the necessity of a revision of the existing tariff, with a view of increasing domestic production by removing obstacles which now obstruct the path of national development. A few illustrations derived from House bill No. 1211, now pending, may, however, be given to prove the danger of a partial revision, which may appear to be a change in the direction of greater freedom.

He would first ask attention to the article of quinine, which ought to be admitted free, or at a low rate of duty, unless it shall be admitted that it is the policy of the government to attempt to collect a revenue from an article upon which the health of the people in large sections of our country depends. The duty on quinine was raised, in 1862, from 30 per cent. to 45 per cent., at the time when a duty of 20 per cent. was imposed on the raw material of its manufacture—cinchona bark—(before free,) and when, in addition to a direct internal revenue tax, a heavy tax was also imposed on distilled spirits, which is indispensable for the manufacture of this alkaloid. Now, although the internal revenue tax on quinine has been entirely removed, and the tax on spirits greatly reduced, it is proposed in House bill No. 1211 to entirely remove the duty on cinchona bark, without making any corresponding reduction in duty on quinine, the practical effect of which is to afford an additional and very large protection on quinine, under the specious pretext of an abatement of duties, and thus place it in the power of a few manufacturers to unduly enhance the price of an article whose use is almost indispensable to existence in certain sections of the country.

Again, referring to the same bill, it will be seen that it is proposed in like manner to afford indirectly a large additional protection on glue by removing all duties from the raw material of its manufacture, but allowing the present high duty on the finished product to remain unaltered. The Commissioner submits that there is nothing in the condition of the glue manufacture of the United States that warrants the imposition of such an additional tax upon every carpenter, cabinet-maker, book-binder and wall paper manufacturer in the country; and he does not believe that the representatives of the quinine and glue interest would have been bold enough to have asked openly from Congress for that increase of 20 per cent. and 10 per cent. respectively on their products which they now propose to obtain indirectly through an act of apparent liberality.

The Commissioner also fails to see the protection to American industry involved in the proposition made in the same bill to impose new and heavy burdens of taxation upon the great industrial interests of paper, soap, glass, calico printing, and bleaching by increasing the duty now levied upon the importation of the crude carbonates of soda (*i. e.*, soda ash) 100 per cent. How important these products are to the industries above referred to, and how extensive would be the taxation to the whole community, arising from even a small increase in their price, may be readily inferred from the single fact that the annual industrial consumption of the common salts of soda in the United States is at present in excess of one hundred and fifty millions of pounds.

It is apparent that the questions here raised by the Commissioner have really nothing whatever to do with either the theory or the practice of free trade or protection. Protection implies help and defence to the weak; but in the instances cited the help has been given to the strong at the expense of the weak; and in this the proverb of old is as true in respect to nations as it is of individuals, viz., "he that giveth to the rich shall surely come to want."

RESULT OF EXISTING INFLUENCES ON NATIONAL DEVELOPMENT.

Let us, however, briefly consider the influence and tendency of the state of things we have described, whether such a state of things be the result of our irredeemable currency, or injudicious and indiscriminate taxation.

All commerce is in the nature of barter or exchange. The men who bring to us coffee, sugar, tea, hides, silks, dye-stuffs, and the like, are not the men whose labor or capital has been directly concerned in the production of these articles, but men whose simple and sole business is to exchange these products at a profit, for the products of other nations. What the exchanger desires most to receive is product in kind, which he may further exchange with additional profit elsewhere, and at the same time realize a profit both ways on the agencies employed by him in transmission, viz., on his vessels, by their freights. What he desires least to receive is gold or silver, inasmuch as the intrinsic value of these articles is nearly the same in all countries, and their movement and transmission, instead of being a source of profit, is rather a source of expense.

Now, the condition of things in the United States is just this. We have so raised the cost of all domestic products that exchange in kind with all foreign nations is almost impossible. The majority of what foreign nations have to sell us, as already shown, we must or will have. What foreign nations want and we produce—cotton and a few other articles excepted—they can buy elsewhere cheaper. We are therefore obliged to pay in no small part for such foreign productions as we need or will have, either in the precious metals, or what is worse, in unduly depreciated promises of national payment. And yet there are men who are so far unable to realize this condition of affairs, that they severally desire and honestly think they can remedy the evils in question by measures which, like the increase of the currency, the increase of the tariff, or other forms of taxation, will inevitably make prices and the cost of production still higher, and thus aggravate the very difficulties which are already so serious.

HOW THE UNITED STATES TRADES WITH THE ARGENTINE REPUBLIC.

As a practical illustration of the above proposition, let us subject to analysis the commercial relations existing between the United States and the Argentine Republic of South America, (Buenos Ayres.) The necessities of trade between the two countries belong in the first instance to the United States, which does not afford a supply of domestic hides sufficient to meet more than 58 per cent. of its domestic consumption of leather; and has, in addition, practically no domestic supply whatever of either goat skins or horse-hair. Now the Argentine Republic has these articles especially to sell and export, and if she is willing to dispose of them on terms equally advantageous with other nations, it is not a matter of choice on the part of the United States whether she will trade, but a matter of necessity.

It is also worth while to diverge for a moment from the discussion of the immediate subject under consideration, and see how important is the relation of this supply of foreign hides to American domestic industry, and how good a thing the United States makes of it. The estimated value of all the domestic hides manufactured in the United States during the year 1866, at $5 50 each, was $19,250,000. The estimated value of the foreign hides received at the principal Atlantic ports of the United States during the same year was about $14,000,000, (values in both instances being reduced to currency with an assumed gold premium of 40 per cent.,) making a total of $33,250,000 as the value of the raw material hides for the year in question. Now during this same year there was received in the city of Boston unmanufactured leather of domestic taninng to the value of $17,463,998; and there was sold and shipped from the State of Massachusetts alone, boots and shoes of an estimated value of $55,000,000—total $72,463,998, which large sums represent very imperfectly, but yet most strikingly, the extent to which the value of the hides became enhanced by the process of manufacturing, and also the remuneration which, through such enhancement, necessarily accrued to labor, inasmuch as the increased value in question represents to a greater degree than in most manufactures the amount paid directly to labor.

As might be inferred from this showing, the United States continues to purchase hides from Buenos Ayres, and continues to add to her wealth and to the sources of employment for her people by so doing; but in thus purchasing we find that the United States stands on a different footing from other commercial nations; or, in other words, has a way of doing things peculiar to herself. Let us see how this is:

The Argentine Republic, in sending hides, goat skins, and horse-hair to the United States, requires an equivalent. It has no forests, few manufactures, and an insufficient supply of breadstuffs. It therefore requires lumber, flour, textile fabrics, especially coarse cottons and calicoes, ready-made clothing, furniture, wagons, hardware, saddlery, paints, paper, &c , all products which the United States is capable of producing in unlimited quantity, and is desirous of selling. The people of the Argentine Republic, furthermore, do not desire payment for these products in the precious metals, and if obliged to receive them must immediately exchange them for the above-named commodities, which are absolutely essential to their existence as a civilized people. Now, as the United States stands to the Argentine republic in the relation of almost their best customer, and as the two nations are further assimilated through continental position and a common form of government, and as the former is capable and desirous of supplying those commodities which the latter especially needs, it might naturally be supposed that the trade between the two would be reciprocal. The exact contrary is, however, the case. The United States, year by year, increases its purchases from the Argentine Republic, while the amount of domestic products which the latter, in turn, purchases from the former increases very slowly, or remains altogether stationary. Thus, during the year 1866—the latest of which we have exact returns—the United States increased the value of its imports from the Argentine Republic to the extent of 20 per cent. over the values of any preceding year, but increased its exports during the same period to the same country only two per cent.* During the same year, however, Great Britain increased her exports to the Argentine Republic 46 per cent., France 65 per cent., and Germany 26 per cent. Now this result is due, not to any unwillingness on the part of the people of the Argentine Republic to purchase of the United States, but simply and solely to the fact that the prices of all commodities in the United States are so much higher than in all other markets of the world that reciprocal trade is disadvantageous and impossible. The United States, therefore, unable, as before shown, to dispense with the productions of Buenos Ayres, and unable to pay for the same in the products of its own industry, settles the balance of trade, not by sending gold and silver directly to Buenos Ayres, but by purchasing, in the first instance, bills of exchange on England, paying a banker's profit, and probably effecting such purchase to a greater or less extent by selling at a discount the nation's obligations of indebtedness. The debt thus transferred to Great Britain is settled by the exportation to Buenos Ayres of British manufactures, paying another profit, and in British vessels, paying freights and commissions. And this process goes on month after month and year after year, until the continued and unnatural drain of the precious metals and the continual exportation of bonds having become startling, it is gravely proposed to reverse the order of things by making the taxation a little higher; or, coming down to particulars, having as a nation the most perfect machinery for manufacturing boots and shoes, and the most skilled workmen for the management of such machinery, we propose to continue to neutralize these benefits and prevent the people of other countries from supplying themselves in our markets; first, by imposing a tax of 10 per cent. on the imported hides, of which we cannot produce a supply sufficient for our requirements for leather; 20 per cent. on the lumber of which we build the shoemaker's shop, thereby augmenting his rent; 2½ cents per pound on the hammer with which he drives his pegs; 40 per cent. on the thread with which he sews; $1 25 per ton on the coal with which he warms himself; 20 per cent. on the flour from which his bread is made; 25 cents per bushel on his potatoes; $2 per barrel on the fish which he may eat on Friday, if perchance any of these articles are imported; and then, when the shoe is completed, let the shoemaker charge back, in turn, all these taxes, and something additional as a consideration for paying them, to the sailor, the lumberman, the carpenter, the iron-worker, the weaver, the spinner, the farmer, and the fisherman, and if any profit on the transaction is realized, let him then convert this into a certificate of national indebtedness, and exchange it at a discount with the Chinaman, the Cuban, and the Brazilian, for his tea, his sugar, and his coffee. If the country does not prosper and increase in wealth under this condition of things, it is not because it has not fully tried the experiment.

INFLUENCE OF STATE AND LOCAL TAXATION ON THE COST OF PRODUCTION.

In reviewing the several causes which, through the enhancement of the cost of production, and consequently of prices, tend to prevent the products of American industry from exchanging on terms of equality in foreign markets with the products of competing manufacturing and commercial nations, the influence of State and local taxation should not

* It may also be noted that no small part of what is credited at Buenos Ayres to exports from the United States was really lumber shipped on board of American vessels at ports of the British provinces, and was not, in any sense, American product.

be overlooked. The space available in this report is, however, too limited to allow of much discussion on this subject, further than to point out and illustrate the fact that while in Great Britain, France, Belgium, and Prussia, especial care is taken that the incidence of local taxation shall not increase the cost of manufactures, or of the commercial transactions involved in the movement of the finished products of industry to a market; in the United States, on the contrary, up to the present time, it has been considered desirable rather than otherwise to impose upon the capital especially employed in manufacturing as large a proportion of the burden of local taxation as practicable. It is, therefore, conclusive that to the extent of this difference the American producer must enter the foreign market at a disadvantage, for which there can be no direct compensation; and that as regards the home market he has need and claim for a corresponding measure of protection, to which there cannot, in fairness, be any legitimate opposition. How this condition of inequality operates as a bar to national progress and development may be practically shown by an example.

Let us suppose the projection of a new line of steamships to run between New York and Europe in competition with existing lines, now controlled by foreign capitalists and registered under a foreign flag. If the nationality of the company is to be American, and its location New York, the State, county, and city of New York would have levied during the past year on the whole accessible capital of the company—in the form of vessels, wharves, machine-shops, offices, and floating capital—a tax of 2.62 per cent. Beyond this the national government would impose an average duty under the tariff on all articles of foreign growth and importation used in the vessels of the line of 48 per cent.; on the gross receipts from passengers, of $2\frac{1}{2}$ per cent., and on the profits or dividends of the company, (if perchance there should be any,) an income tax of 5 per cent. If now, on the other hand, the status of the company is made foreign, and its location be fixed at Liverpool, the whole amount of local taxation to which the company would be subject would be merely an assessment to the extent of from 10 to 25 per cent. on the rental value of the premises occupied either as offices, storehouses, or machine shops. Beyond this the British government would have levied, in the year 1867, an income tax on the profits of the individual stockholders or owners, of four pence on the pound sterling, equivalent to $1\frac{2}{3}$ per cent.; and omitting all other forms of direct taxation would have allowed all articles of foreign growth and production, such as sugars, tea, coffee, wines, and tobacco, which might be required for use on board the steamers in question to be taken from bond free of duty. The difference in the return on the investment, therefore, growing out of the difference merely in the fiscal systems recognized in the different localities specified, would be of itself sufficient to afford to the foreign capitalist a dividend on his stock nearly or quite equal to the ordinary rate of European interest on the capital employed, while to the American investor the disadvantage would have an expression two-fold greater, through the increase of expenses and the diminution of profit. With competition, therefore, with foreign nations on terms of equality, being thus from the very outset, by our own acts, rendered impossible, the failure or slow growth of American steamship enterprizes becomes no longer a mystery.

If we select as another example the manufacture of cotton in Great Britain and the United States, respectively, we find that in the former country the incidence of all local or other direct taxation extends only to the rental value of the buildings for the reception of machinery or the promotion of other details of the business, and does not in any way regard the value of the machinery which may be placed in such buildings, or the capital employed in its workings. On the other hand, in the United States the incidence of local taxation falls on everything connected with the business of cotton manufacture that is accessible, viz., buildings, land, and machinery; and is, moreover, not unfrequently duplicated in the following manner: thus, factories are often built in this country under acts of incorporation in one State, while the stock is held or owned chiefly in other States. The municipality in which the factory is located taxes the building and machinery, and collects the tax of the corporation; the municipality, on the other hand, in which the stockholder resides taxes the stock to him at its market value as personal property, thus duplicating the tax on identically the same property, and leaving its owner no remedy. In one instance, (and that not an exceptional one,) brought to the notice of the Commissioner, the aggregate of these local taxes imposed on a particular corporation amounted, in 1866, to $4\frac{9}{10}$ per cent. upon the capital invested, and in 1868, to over four per cent. But vicious as this system is upon its face, its effect, especially in a national point of view, cannot be realized until we take into consideration the fact that the capital required in the United States to build a cotton mill is about double the amount required for a similar purpose in Great Britain. Four per cent., therefore, on the capital of a cotton mill in the United States represents eight per cent. on the same productive power in Great Britain, or a rate which is almost double the average rate of interest in the latter country. It is, therefore, clear that American manufacturers, engaged in cotton and other industries similarly affected, absolutely need a measure of protection in respect to this one item alone, in order to enable them to compete successfully even in the domestic markets against these foreign competitors.

Now, if the United States proposes to maintain and extend its foreign commerce, an attainment indispensable to national greatness, and to hold and exert that influence throughout the civilized world which its continental dominion, its population and wealth should entitle it, it must place itself on an equality as regards the conditions of production with other competing nations. And a timely consideration of the influence of this local taxation on prices and national development is therefore most important. The remedy for the objectionable features which characterize the existing system is probably to be found in a re-adjustment, rather than in a reduction of taxation, although in respect to this latter point much can undoubtedly be accomplished by the exercise of economy and wise administration.

The burden, in any event we may be certain, will be heavy, but in proportion as it is so, it is all the more important to consider, whether we will place it squarely on the back rather than hang it to the neck or suspend it from the extremities.

Furthermore, it must not be imagined, that the local taxation of England or France is inconsiderable. On the contrary, it is heavy. Thus, for the year 1867, the aggregate amount of local taxation for England and Wales was £18,367,773, sterling ($89,610,000,) which amount, if we except such anomalies as the taxation of some of our large cities, that for the city of New York the present year being in excess of $22,000,000, will not prove unfavorably disproportionate to the average of the United States.* This amount in England and Wales is raised almost wholly by

* Recent parliamentary returns show that the local taxation of England and Wales has increased since 1837 nearly 100 per cent., the taxes for the relief of the poor having increased from $20,220,000 in 1837 to $32,595,000 in 1867, while the county rates, which in 1837 were $5,840,000, had advanced to $16,715,000 in 1867. The total local taxation of the city of Lon-

a system which makes the rental value of real estate the basis of taxation, it being assumed that the rental value of houses occupied affords a better measure of a man's income and ability to pay taxes than any other standard which can be adopted.*

In France the revenues for local and municipal expenditures are derived in a great degree from what is termed the personal and property tax. The first of these is in the nature of a poll tax, and is estimated at the average value of three days' labor, which cannot, however, be rated under 50 centimes, or above 1 franc 50 centimes; in other words, this annual tax varies from 1 franc 50, (30 cents,) the lowest, to 4 francs 50, (90 cents,) the highest. It is the only tax levied on the individual in France, and includes every inhabitant, native or foreign, male or female, not a pauper.

The French property tax falls on "tenant occupancy," and is usually fixed at about one-twentieth part of the rent paid by each resident, but only for the portion of the building which serves as a residence. It has regard to the rent really paid, and if the individual resides in his own house he is taxed to the amount which would be payable if the apartments he occupies were leased to a tenant.

It is also curious to note that, going back to the commencement of the 17th century, we find the same system of indiscriminate State, local and municipal taxation at present existing in the United States was recognized both in France and Great Britain. Experience, however, has gradually brought to them that reform which probably at no distant day will also be entered upon in this country. It would be difficult, however, to find in the ancient records referred to anything of greater inconsistency than is exhibited in the existing legislation of some of our States; as, for example, in the State of New York, in which the statute holds, as respects its own citizens, that personal property follows personal residence, and exactly the reverse in respect to foreigners and citizens of other States. A citizen of the United States not a resident of New York is therefore liable to double taxation in respect to all capital invested in business or banking in New York: first, by virtue of the location of the property; and secondly, in virtue of the residence of the owner in some

---

don is reported at $17,500,000, made up of the following items: Poor rates, $6,250,000, local rates, $5,000,000, drainage, fire brigade, lighting, &c., $3,750,000 and police, $2,500,000.

The yearly expenses of the city of Paris for municipal purposes are reported to be at present about $50,000,000, of which $20,000,000 is raised by what are known as *octroi* duties. It should, however, be remarked that this enormous taxation is due in a great measure to a reconstruction, as it were, of the city under the auspices of the Imperial government. The rental taxes, moreover, are in all cases paid by the "occupier as owner or tenant."

* As showing the working of this system of taxation, we present herewith the local taxes actually levied for the year 1866 in St. Marylebone, one of the largest of the parishes of the metropolitan district of London:

	£	s.	d.	
Poor rate	0	2	2½	on the pound of rental value.
General rate, (street lighting, watering, paving, &c.)	0	0	11	on the pound of rental value.
Sewer rate,	0	0	4	on the pound of rental value.
Church rate	0	0	1	on the pound of rental value.
Metropolitan main draining rate	0	0	4	on the pound of rental value.
		3	10½	

These rates, which are probably among the highest levied in Great Britain for municipal or local purposes, would in the aggregate be equivalent to nearly twenty per cent. (19 37) of the annual rental value of the real estate liable to taxation. It will be observed that the highest single item in this account is that known as the "poor rate."

It should also be stated that in this system of rental taxation *the rate is levied only on real estate occupied and having a rental valuation;* and that government property also of certain descriptions does not enjoy the privilege of exemption, as in the United States, from local taxation.

other State. One suggestion, in view of these facts and circumstances, may be pertinent, which is, that if any State should determine to adopt a system of local taxation analogous to that recognized in Great Britain or France, it might confidently anticipate a very large influx of capital and manufactures from beyond its borders, thereby rapidly increasing its wealth and development, and possibly as an ultimate result, compelling other States to adopt the same liberal and enlightened policy as a measure of defence and protection.

FUTURE FINANCIAL POLICY.

Having thus presented, in part, the evidence which demonstrates the rapid development of the country, and having also endeavored to determine and analyze the causes which at the same time tend to check of interfere with such development, we are now prepared to take up and intelligently consider the lesson to be deduced from these investigations relative to the inquiry proposed in the outset, viz., what policy of legislation is likely to prove hereafter most advantageous to the revenue, and most certain to establish the credit and industry of the whole country on a sound and substantial basis.

It seems clear that whatever fiscal policy may be proposed for adoption, it must not only recognize and be based on the existing condition of affairs, but must be also in the nature of an amendment which shall to the smallest extent possible partake of the character of an experiment. Violent change, uncertainty, and instability are, of all things, what the business interests of the country have most reason to dread, while, on the other hand, the determination and recognition of a clear, well-defined, and practical issue, to be attained to by a certain progressive, even though slow, movement, is sure to bring with it stability, hope, and confidence in the future—the elements which constitute in no small degree the basis of both private and national prosperity. Can such a policy be determined? Can such an issue be consummated?

The ends to be attained are, mainly, three: *first*, *full restoration of the national credit and resumption of specie payments; second, refunding the national debt at a lower rate of interest; third, reduction of the cost of national production, with a view of enabling the products of American industry to compete on terms of greater equality with the products of foreign nations than is now possible*, thereby establishing a system of national protection and insuring stability, increased product, and a redevelopment of American commerce and ship-building.

Let us now inquire what elements are ready at hand for the accomplishment of these results. The nation at present is excessively in debt, and is further embarrassed with the volume of its matured and suspended paper. To free itself from embarrassment and to redeem its suspended paper, there would seem to be but the one method, which is alone available to individuals under similar circumstances, viz., to manage in some way to receive more than is expended, and to apply the surplus of receipts over expenditures to the payment of debts and to the restoration of credit.

The determination of the probability of obtaining such a surplus, and also its possible extent, involves the consideration of the national finances, present and prospective, and to this attention is next invited.

NATIONAL RECEIPTS AND EXPENDITURES FOR THE FISCAL YEAR ENDING JUNE 30, 1868.

The accounts of the national treasury for the fiscal year ending June 30, 1868, show an aggregate of receipts of $405,638,083 32, and of expenditures of $377,340,284 86, leaving a balance to the credit of surplus income of $28,297,798 46. In this statement the bonds issued to the Pacific railroads are not included, such issue, at least for the present, being regarded as a loan of credit, rather than a direct expenditure.

For a more detailed statement of the receipts and expenditures of the treasury of the United States for the fiscal year ending June 30, 1868, together with the general result of the payment or refunding of the various species of national indebtedness during the same period, reference is made to the balance-sheet submitted on page 57.*

* The expense of collecting the revenue, both "internal" and "customs" for the last three fiscal years, is shown by the following statement:

The percentage of entire expenditures of the Internal Revenue Bureau, including cost of assessment, collection, office expenditures, &c., to net receipts, during the fiscal year ending June 30, 1866, was 2.49 per cent.; 1867, 3.41 per cent.; 1868, 4.94 per cent.

The expenses attending the collection of the revenue from the customs during the same years were as follows:

Fiscal years.	Custom receipts.	Cost of collection.	Percentage of cost to receipts.
1860	$53, 187, 512	$3, 324, 431	6. 25
1864	102, 316, 153	4, 146, 585	4. 05
1866	179, 046, 652	5, 356, 458	2. 94
1867	176, 417, 811	5, 738, 971	3. 25
1868	164, 464, 599	a 7, 615, 675	4. 63
Total	675, 432, 727	26, 182, 120	3. 88

a The increase in expenditures for the collection of customs for the fiscal year 1868, was due mainly to the reorganization of the custom service at the south, to the increase of salaries of officers, and to the increase of expenses incurred for the prevention of smuggling.

RECEIPTS AND EXPENDITURES OF NATIONAL TREASURY FROM JULY 1, 1867, TO JUNE 30, 1868.

RECEIPTS.

Balance in the treasury, agreeably to warrants, July 1, 1867		$170, 146, 986 47
From customs (gold)	$164, 464, 599 56	
internal revenue	191, 087, 589 41	
puplic lands	1, 348, 715 41	
direct tax	1, 788, 145 85	
miscellaneous sources, premium on gold, &c., (including $7, 078, 203 42 for premium on 5-20 and 10-40 bonds	46, 949, 033 09	
		405, 638, 083 32
Total receipts		575, 785, 069 79

EXPENDITURES.

For civil service	$53, 009, 867 67	
For pensions and Indians	27, 883, 069 10	
For war including bounties	123, 246, 648 62	
For navy	25, 775, 502 72	
		$229, 915, 088 11
For interest on public debt	140, 424, 045 71	
For premium on treasury notes	7. 001, 151 04	
		147, 425, 196 75
Total expenditures		377, 340, 284 86
For redemption of public debt, exclusive of interest	692, 549, 685 88	
Less received from loans	625, 111, 433 20	
		67, 438, 252 68
Balance in treasury, agreeably to warrants, June 30, 1868		131, 006, 532 25
Total expenditures		575, 785, 069 79

The receipts from internal revenue were derived from the following sources:

From taxes on raw cotton	$22, 500, 947 77		
taxes on distilled liquors, (including $871, 638 from apples, peaches, and grapes)	14, 280, 730 98		
taxes on fermented liquors	5, 685, 663 70		
taxes on tobacco, cigars, and snuff	18, 644, 091 03		
taxes on manufactures of iron	2, 674, 364 93		
taxes on other manufactures	36. 488, 709 81		
		$100, 274, 508 22	
taxes on sales	4, 837, 900 33		
taxes on watches, carriages, silver plate, billiard-tables, &c	1, 140, 370 35		
sales of stamps	14, 852, 252 02		
special taxes, (licenses)	16, 364, 547 28		
taxes on income of individuals, including salaries	33, 071, 172 18		
taxes on income of banks, railroad and insurance companies, &c	8, 384, 426 18		
taxes on gross receipts of railroads, telegraph, and express companies, &c	6, 280, 069 34		
taxes on bank circulation and deposits	1, 866, 745 55		
taxes on legacies and successions	2, 823, 411 24		
taxes on passports, &c	28, 280 00		
fines, penalties, &c	1, 256, 881 59		
		90, 906, 056 06	
		*191, 180, 564 28	

* This amount, as given by the Commissioner of Internal Revenue, shows a difference from the figures reported by the Treasurer and given above, and is due to the fact that the same receipts are not entered upon the books of the two offices on the same day.

NATIONAL RECEIPTS AND EXPENDITURES FOR THE CURRENT FISCAL YEAR ENDING JUNE 30, 1869.

For the current fiscal year ending June 30, 1869, the Commissioner estimates the receipts of the national treasury as follows:

From customs	$170,000,000 00
From internal revenue	155,000,000 00
From public lands	1,700,000 00
From miscellaneous sources	30,000,000 00
Total	356,700,000 00

The total expenditures for the same period, including $7,200,000 gold paid for Alaska, are estimated by the Secretary of the Treasury as follows:

Civil and miscellaneous, (including $7,200,000 for Alaska)	$61,227,106 00
War Department, (including bounties)	93,219,117 00
Navy Department	21,604,785 00
Pensions and Indians	30,358,648 00
Interest on public debt	129,742,814 00
	336,152,470 00

The estimates of total expenditure for the above period as made by the Commissoner are somewhat less than those presented by the secretary, viz: $326,300,000, (a reduction of about ten millions,) and indicating a surplus of receipts over expenditures for the fiscal year ending June 30, 1869, according as one or the other of the above estimates is accepted, of from *twenty* to *thirty* millions. And it is especially to be noted that the surplus actually attained during the last fiscal year, and the one predicated for the current year, are on the basis of a system of revenue administration, which, to use a very mild expression, has been exceedingly imperfect.

NATIONAL RECEIPTS AND EXPENDITURES FOR THE FISCAL YEAR ENDING JUNE 30, 1870.

Let us now look forward to the fiscal year commencing July 1, 1869, and ending June 30, 1870, the first complete year of a new administration; and starting with the relation of receipts and expenditures as above shown to exist, inquire what it is further possible or practicable to accomplish. Such a basis allows us to anticipate a surplus of thirty millions for the year under consideration, with the law and the administration of the law in relation to the collection and expenditure of revenue remaining unaltered; and this surplus, the Commissioner has reason to believe, may be increased through the following agencies:

First. *From the certain and continued gain which will undoubtedly accrue to the national revenue, under any circumstances, from the continued increase of the wealth and population of the country.* The amount of such increase in Great Britain, for the six years prior to the year 1865–'66, is estimated to have averaged £1,780,000 ($8,900,000) per annum. The data for arriving at this estimate in Great Britain, viz., a comparison of annual receipts, are not, however, at present available in the United States, as the aggregate of taxation in the latter has been materially affected by legislation for nearly every year since the inauguration of the internal revenue system. Nevertheless, it cannot be doubted that the yearly gain from this source is very considerable, inasmuch, as in no year since the commencement of the reduction of the internal revenue taxes have the aggregate receipts of revenue been diminished to an extent commensurate with the corresponding reduction or abatement of taxation. Taking this fact into consideration, and also the fact established by the census returns of the two countries, viz., that the annual rate of increase in the value of real and personal property in the United States is considerably greater than that of Great Britain, the Commissioner believes he is warranted in assuming that the gain of revenue likely to accrue from the increase in the wealth and population of the United States will, for the present, be at least $10,000,000 per annum.

Second. *A gain to the credit of the treasury from the discontinuance of payment through settlement of the claims of soldiers and sailors for arrears of pay and bounty.*

This gain, as predicated on the payments actually made under these heads during the last and current fiscal years, may be estimated at $25,000,000.*

Third. *A gain from a further general reduction of national expenditures.*

This gain for the next fiscal year through a continued reduction of the army, reconstruction and pacification of the southern States, and a greater economy in civil expenditures, and in the appropriations annually made for fortifications, ordnance stores, rivers and harbors, and private claims, ought to aggregate at least $30,000,000; especially if the amount paid during the current fiscal year for the purchase of foreign territory ($7,200,000, gold) be carried to the credit of this account.

If we should adopt the estimates of reduction of expenditures which the Secretary of the Treasury has stated in his last report (December, 1868) to be practicable, the amount to be carried to the credit of surplus income from a reduction of expenditures would be nearer $50,000,000 than $30,000,000, as above assumed by the Commissioner. Under this head the Secretary says:

"There is no department of the government which is conducted with proper economy. The average expenses of the next 10 years, for the civil service, ought not to exceed $40,000,000 per annum. Those of the War Department, after the bounties are paid, should be brought down to $35,000,000, and those of the navy to $20,000,000. The outlays for pensions and Indians cannot for some years be considerably reduced, but they can doubtless be brought within $30,000,000. The interest on the public debt, when the whole debt shall be funded, at an average rate of interest of five per cent., will amount to $125,000,000, which will be reduced with the annual reduction of the principal."

Pensions.—In looking forward, furthermore, to the relation which in the future the national receipts are to sustain to the national expenditures, it should be borne in mind that although the amount now annually paid by the government for pensions is very large, (approximating $25,000,000 per annum,) and may possibly for a year or two longer continue to increase, yet there is nothing more certain than that the expenditure under this head will soon begin to diminish. In proof of this we have only to refer back to the past experience of the government in regard to this matter.

---

* The total amount disbursed to soldiers and sailors for arrears of pay and bounties since July 1, 1866, is believed to be approximately as follows:

For fiscal year 1866–'67, bounties	$11,382,859 83
For fiscal year 1867–'68	43,476,549 48
First four months of fiscal year 1868–'69	13,410,142 77

The balance of claims for back pay and bounties yet unsettled (December, 1868) are estimated at, approximately, $15,000,000, but it is not probable that claims will be allowed to this amount.

Thus we find that in 1816, immediately after the close of the war with Great Britain, the amount annually disbursed for pensions was $188,804; which increased in four years, or in 1820, to $3,208,000; and decreased in the next eight years, or in 1828, to $850,573. Again, at the close of the Mexican war the annual pension expenditure, which was $1,226,000 in 1848, rose in 1852 to $2,431,000, and declined in 1861 to $879,000. If we argue, therefore, from the past experience of the government, it will be safe to predict that in the course of the next six or eight years the annual amount disbursed for pensions will be reduced 50 per cent., thus effecting a reduction of national expenditures to the extent of from $10,000,000 to $12,000,000 per annum.

Fourth. *Gain from reform of revenue administration.*—But in addition to whatever of surplus may accrue to the national treasury through the agencies above cited, a very large increment of receipts can also, undoubtedly, be secured by means of a thorough and effective reform of the administration of the internal revenue. It is useless here to enter into any discussion as to the extent of the losses to which the government is annually subjected, through the positive dishonesty or gross inefficiency of great numbers of the subordinate officials intrusted with the management of this branch of the public service; but that such losses are very great no one who has given the subject attention can have the slightest reason to doubt. Assuming $155,000,000 as the annual average of receipts from internal revenue, as the law and its administration now stand, the Commissioner believes that an increase of $75,000,000 in the receipts as a minimum could be obtained without any practical difficulty.

On the other hand, as an offset to these estimates, we may have a reduction of treasury receipts from miscellaneous sources—which are largely derived from the premium on sales of gold—and also from certain unforeseen expenditures. But allowing for all these contingencies it seems possible for the treasury to have at its command at the close of the next fiscal year an available surplus of from $100,000,000 to $125,000,000; and with such elements of strength there is not a single fiscal problem of our immediate future which will not be greatly aided in its solution. The Commissioner, furthermore, maintains that the realization of such a surplus involves nothing impractical, and nothing which partakes of the nature of an experiment.

It requires, however, that there should be unity of purpose on the part of the Executive, of Congress, and of the people, and a full realization of the fact that the work to be accomplished is of such paramount importance that nothing else should be allowed to interfere with it. It requires that the agents who are to be intrusted with the collection and disbursement of the revenue shall be appointed on some other grounds than the devotion to party service, the length and number of their campaign speeches, or the amount of money contributed to aid in elections. It requires that Congress shall exercise the most rigid economy in respect to appropriations, and that the sums heretofore expended for fortifications, rivers and harbors, coast survey, new buildings, the manufacture of arms, for private claims and war damages, and as *subsidies to railroads*, shall constitute no precedent for the immediate future. It requires that no more money shall be disbursed for the purchase of foreign territory, and that no reciprocity treaty shall be negotiated like that proposed with the Sandwich Islands, the operation of which is calculated to immediately impair the revenue.* It requires that there shall be a broad

* The present cost of the ratification of the proposed treaty with the Sandwich Islands, through a diminution of the current receipts from imports, will not be less than five hundred

distinction made between the promotion of mere private and selfish ends, and the true protection of American industry. It requires that we shall stop talking about the letter of the contract in respect to the payment of debts, but in the spirit of the same honesty determine that the debts shall be paid. With these requisitions supplied, the extrication of the nation from its financial embarrassments and the attainment of great national prosperity becomes within a limited period a matter of no uncertainty. To disregard and refuse them is to protract but not to prevent the attainment of a like result, for the nation, even under bad management, will in the course of time certainly drift out of its difficulties; but this will be through the honesty and economy of its individualism, and through the development of its great national resources, and not because the government either wills or directs it.

RESTORATION OF NATIONAL CREDIT, AND RESUMPTION OF SPECIE PAYMENT.

The Commissioner does not feel that it is his province to present any plan in detail, whereby a surplus like that anticipated can be best used for facilitating a return to specie payments; but he does feel convinced that if one-half of such surplus, or from two to two and a half per cent. on the whole debt, were applied regularly, month after month, and year after year, to purchase in the open market, and to the cancellation of the gold interest-bearing obligations of the government, so long as those obligations can be obtained at a discount from their par value in gold; and if, at the same time, the legal-tender notes were, under certain restrictions as to time and quantity, made convertible at the pleasure of the holder into interest-bearing bonds, that the value of both bonds and currency might be so greatly and so rapidly enhanced as to make a resumption of specie payments a matter of much less difficulty than it now appears.*

If it be objected that this measure involves contraction of the legal-tender currency, the Commissioner would reply that he is in favor of such contraction. Resumption of specie payments can be commenced at any time; but the question is not one of commencement, but of continuance; *and in order that there may be continuance, there must be a certain proportion or ratio first established between the amount to be redeemed and the agency (coin) which is to redeem.* This ratio, considering the amount of legal-tender and national bank currency in existence, could not probably with safety, at the existing premium on gold, be assumed

thousand dollars, gold, per annum; which amount in a comparatively short time, through the profit assured by the treaty to the sugar-growers of the Islands on the one hand, and to the sugar refiners of San Francisco on the other, will undoubtedly be increased three or four fold, or from a million to a million and a half, gold, per annum. The Commissioner submits that there can be no advantage shown to accrue to the United States at the present time from the ratification of this treaty, which will at all compensate for the detriment which it will surely bring to the treasury.

* The Commissioner would again invite the attention of Congress to the fact that the legal-tender notes issued under the acts of February 25 and July 11, 1862, are, by the terms of their issue, convertible into United States 5-20 bonds, the pledge of the government having been engraved upon each one of said notes. It is true that Congress attempted, subsequently to the issue of the notes, to revoke this privilege by declaring that the right of conversion should cease on a certain day. The right of the government to alter the terms of the issue without the consent of the holders of the notes has recently been called in question, and the Commissioner is advised that these notes have, within a few months, been sorted and hoarded in the reserve fund of the banks to a very large extent, under the impression that the government will be compelled ultimately to convert them into bonds.

at less than the total amount of United States notes now outstanding. At present the treasury has no such amount of gold at command, and for the future but two methods present themselves for its obtainment, viz: either to hoard and accumulate gold out of the national surplus revenue, or to reduce the volume of the currency, either by direct payment, or by funding, (which is in one sense also payment,) to a point where the ability of the treasury will be sufficient to compass the end desired. The first is a work of time, and dependent upon many contingencies. The second can be effected more rapidly—perhaps as rapidly as may be desirable. But this is the problem to be worked out sooner or later, and if the Commissioner has rightly stated its conditions, much of the discussion which is continually taking place respecting the necessity of currency, and the desire of the people for its continuance, is of comparatively little moment.

As bearing upon the proposition to accumulate gold in the treasury with a view of resumption, it is important to consider the exact position of the United States in respects its its foreign commercial relations and exchanges.

Thus it appears from the statistics of commerce and navigation, that the imports and exports of merchandise—exports reduced to gold values, and exclusive of the movement of bullion and specie—for the fiscal year 1868, were as follows:

Net imports of merchandise	$347, 549, 209
Net exports of merchandise	269, 042, 041
Apparent balance against the United States	78, 507, 168

To settle this treasury balance and for other purposes, there was sent out of the country during the fiscal year 1867–68, specie and bullion to the value of $83,746,161, and national bonds and other evidences of indebtedness to an estimated amount of $100,000,000; and that this additional amount was needed to pay an indebtedness of the United States to foreign countries over and above what the returns of imports would indicate, is evidenced by the fact that exchange during the whole period in question was in favor of Europe and against the United States. This indebtedness was undoubtedly created through the following agencies: *first*, freights, which are in a great degree carried by foreign vessels; *second*, expenses of Americans travelling in foreign countries; *third*, interest on public and private securities held abroad; *fourth*, undervaluation, and smuggling.

With a drain of gold out of the country from legitimate causes, therefore, in excess of the annual product of our mines; and with influences at work which tend to increase rather than diminish such a movement for the future, the practicability of accumulating within any reasonable time a quantity of coin in the treasury sufficient to insure the continuance of resumption, without at the same time producing great disturbances in business, appears to the Commissioner to be altogether problematical.

Again, as bearing upon the proposition of contraction as a method of arriving at resumption, the Commissioner believes that no man can look back to the period when a moderate contraction was authorized by Congress, and put his finger on one single bad result assumed to have flowed from such contraction, which was not due, in the first instance, to a wholly imaginative influence; and furthermore, the Commissioner asserts that no one can review the history of prices when contraction was authorized and in operation, without feeling convinced that there was, during such time, *i. e.*, from March, 1866, to January, 1868, a tendency to a gradual and healthy shrinkage of values and prices; and that the shrinkage in prices which actually did occur was equivalent, through an increase in the purchasing power of the money in use, to a practical increase and not to a diminution of the power of the currency to effect exchanges. This increase was estimated by the Commissioner in his last report to have been equal, during the year 1867 alone, to at least $100,000,000.

The Commissioner sees no economical objection to an increase of the national bank circulation equal to the proposed decrease of the United States notes, inasmuch as the banks are required to resume specie payments whenever the government shall do so. The authority for such increase of national bank notes would be immediately availed of in the event of monetary stringency, but not otherwise. If we assume that the aggregate paper circulation is not to be increased until specie payments are fully restored, the Commissioner cannot conceive of any better mode of giving flexibility to the currency than this. It is alleged that an undue proportion of the existing circulation issued under the national banking law is held in the eastern States, and that the west and south are entitled, by virtue of their population, to a greater ratio than they now have. If this be true, as the Commissioner believes, the additional amount here contemplated might properly be assigned to those States where the alleged inequality is complained of, thus restoring the equilibrium contemplated by law without taking from the eastern States any privileges which they now enjoy.

REFUNDING OF THE NATIONAL DEBT AT A LOWER RATE OF INTEREST.

The national bonds and the legal tender notes being once brought to par with gold, and the national credit thus fully restored, the gradual refunding of the debt at a lower rate of interest becomes then, for the *first time*, really practicable. We use the expression "the first time," because a principle should be kept clearly in view which heretofore has not always been done in the discussion of this subject, viz., *that the rate at which governments can borrow is indicated not by the nominal rates of interest which they may offer, but by the price of their stocks.* They may indeed, as has been expressed by a recent foreign writer, "fix once for all in issuing a loan the interest of which they will have to pay, but the interest which the individual fund holder will derive is, of course, entirely determined by the price at which he buys his stock." Whoever, at this moment, buys in Europe our bonds, nominally yielding six per cent. interest, for 75 gold, practically expresses the fact that the rate at which it suits him to lend money to the United States is eight per cent. gold per annum; and there is no possible way in which the United States, or any other government, can help itself, with advantage in this matter, except to so far elevate its credit as to render the purchase of its securities at a higher figure desirable, or, what is the same thing, induce a loan to itself from the capitalist at a lower rate of interest. So long, therefore, as the government credit is depreciated, any advantage to be derived from the issue of bonds bearing a lower rate of interest, will be fully compensated by the reduction in price which such bonds must sustain in the open market; or, in other words, the only method available alike to nations and individuals for the attainment of a low rate of interest is to offer perfect security. Furthermore, with the elevation of the national securities to par, the issue of national bank currency, based upon bonds, will be equivalent, or nearly so, to the issue of currency based upon specie, and with a system of redemption, either in specie or treasury notes, (legal tenders redeemable in specie,) which could be easily provided for, the government might then safely remove all restrictions from free banking, and allow the demand for currency to regulate its issue.

CONTRACTS ON A GOLD BASIS.

One of the most wholesome measures, in the judgment of the Commissioner, for smoothing the way to specie resumption would be an act legalizing gold contracts. A much larger share of the business of the country than is generally supposed is now transacted in gold, the parties relying upon the rules of commercial integrity for the fulfilment of contracts when the law fails to provide for their enforcement. These transactions relate principally to foreign goods, the cost of which is always computed in coin. Under existing laws the citizen may make any contract for the disposition of his property or services, payable in anything except the recognized money of the world, and the government stands ready to enforce it. When he bargains for gold or its equivalent he becomes practically an outlaw. Under the operation of this policy we are, to a large extent, cut off from the money reservoir of the world, *i. e.*, the aggregate amount of gold and silver coin and bullion in use among all nations. Gold will go where it is appreciated, and will refuse to stay when there is no use for it. It is idle for us to expect to retain the product of our own mines if we refuse to give it as good employment and character as other nations do.

The question whether the introduction of two standards, possessing unequal value, into commercial transactions would be deleterious to the business of the country, seems to be sufficiently answered by the fact that no harm has come from the employment of gold as the standard in reference to articles imported from abroad. Reasoning *a priori* it can hardly be supposed that the introduction of a better currency will have the effect to deteriorate the whole mass. The immediate effect of an act of Congress legalizing gold contracts might be to advance the price of gold by creating a sudden demand without adding to the supply. But this effect (if it should take place) would be only temporary, for the demand would be answered by unlocking hoarded gold, by checking the exportation of bullion, and by calling in as large a supply from abroad as might be needed for legitimate business.

It has been objected that an act legalizing gold contracts would cause the holders of promissory notes, mortgages, &c., to call in their loans and require borrowers to make new contracts with them on a gold basis, thus practically increasing the rate of interest. The Commissioner believes that this objection is fallacious. The lender of money will always charge the borrower for the risk of depreciation of the currency in which the loan is payable. Such risk must always be greater in an irredeemable paper currency than in the precious metals; therefore the rate of interest must be higher. Usury laws may aggravate, but cannot overturn this principle, which is as well established as any fact in economical science. The rate of interest depends, in general, upon the demand and supply of loanable capital, and in particular upon the nature of the security offered. An act of Congress legalizing gold contracts will not alter the demand or supply of loanable capital, but it will furnish a higher security for loans. Payment cannot be demanded upon outstanding notes, mortgages, &c., until they become due. When they fall due the payers will settle with the payees according to these principles, and if new loans are necessary the rate of interest will not be higher by reason of the security being better.

To conclude this branch of the discussion the Commissioner would remark that a government ought not to deny to its citizens, in time of peace, the right to put their business upon a substantial basis. If it is impolitic for government to *encourage* a gambling spirit among men, it is still more impolitic to compel them to resort to games of hazard and chance in their daily transactions. Under existing laws each man is required to take into his calculations the probable fluctuations of the currency, and these are dependent upon circumstances so numerous and complicated that nothing short of omniscience can foretell them. We have recently witnessed the unhappy results of what is called a "currency corner," or the sudden locking up of a large amount of legal-tender notes at the financial centre of the country, the apparent purpose and actual consequence of which were to create a panic and cause an artificial decline in the prices of property. We are justified in denominating this procedure not only as gambling, but gambling with loaded dice. So long as we are cut off by law from participation in the gold supply of the world, which constitutes the balance wheel of human industry, we are subject to these and similar cheating devices. The aggregate amount of gold and silver coin, and bullion, in the world is too large and too widely distributed ever to be made the subject of an artificial "corner."

It is now nearly seven years since gold and silver disappeared from circulation among us. During this time a large proportion of the young men and women of the country have come upon the stage of active life. They have grown up without any practical knowledge of the virtues of a metallic currency. Their ideas and habits have been formed in the most vicious school of economy; and it is exceedingly desirable that specie should reappear among us before this baneful education shall have ripened into its natural fruit of universal extravagance and insolvency.

REDUCTION OF TAXATION, WITH A VIEW OF REDUCING THE COST OF PRODUCTION.

In the application of a moiety of the anticipated surplus to the reduction of taxation, the especial object sought to be accomplished should be the reduction of the cost of national production; with a view of removing those impediments which now so greatly restrict and, in many instances, prevent the free exchange of the products of American industry with the needed products of other nations; and thus bring to the country a more favorable balance of trade than now exists. In using the expression, balance of trade, the Commissioner does not wish to be understood as recognizing in any way the old exploded ideas in respect to this subject, viz: that a nation gains in proportion to what it sends abroad, and loses in proportion to what it receives back; but he does mean to clearly express the opinion, that a condition of affairs like that now existing in the United States, whereby gold and silver and certificates of national indebtedness continually tend to flow out of the country in payment for foreign commodities, in preference to the products of domestic industry, is both unnatural and injurious, and is a condition of affairs exactly the reverse of what prevails in Great Britain, France, and other prosperous commercial nations.

The Commissioner believes that he has already sufficiently indicated the course he would recommend in reference to the application of the anticipated surplus to the reduction of taxes. In the department of internal revenue, the removal of the taxes on the transportation of passengers, the receipts of telegraph and express companies, the manufacture of gas, and possibly upon sales, would reduce that branch of our revenue system to almost the simplest form that can be devised for the collection of the requisite amount of money which the requirements of the treasury may necessitate.

In the matter of the tariff, the Commissioner trusts that the government will not allow itself to be diverted from the consideration of the real questions at issue, through any prejudices which may be evoked, either on behalf of free trade or protection. There is no considerable proportion of the people of the United States in favor of the adoption of free trade in the European sense, even were the necessities of the treasury for revenue far less urgent than at present. There are none worthy to bear the name of an American citizen who desire that the industry of foreign countries should prosper and be extended at the expense of our own.

Since the Commissioner entered upon his official duties in the spring of 1865, he has made it his special business to inquire into the condition of American industry, in all its departments, and acquaint himself with its necessities and deficiencies. He has for this purpose visited the principal seats of the most important branches of industry in the country, conferred with their most intelligent representatives, and personally inspected the detail of many manufacturing operations. He has, also, during this period, been afforded an unusual opportunity of observing the manufacturing systems of Europe, and acquainting himself, through personal and local inquiry, in respect to the cost of European production, and the condition and wages of European laborers. He has sought in all this to promote the interests of his country, to know only the truth, and when found he has not, thus far, in his official communications, hesitated to speak it boldly; and the general conclusion of his investigations in this department is, *that the policy of moderate and judicious protection under the tariff is certainly, for the present, the policy best suited to subserve the industrial interests of the whole country.*

Thus, it cannot be doubted, that, so long as the existing systems of national, State, and local taxation continue to impose heavy burdens upon the American producer, such burdens should not be allowed to work to the advantage of the foreign competitors in the domestic market.

So long, moreover, as a system of diversified manufacturing industry is recognized as desirable in the United States, so long it is the duty of the national government to guarantee to that interest the conditions of stability. Such stability is not, however, posssible, if undue facilities are offered to the European manufacturer of using the American markets for temporary realization to meet emergencies through the forced sale of commodities; or for the disposal, at any sacrifice, of stock which may have happened to constitute an unsalable surplus in Europe. The argument that if foreigners are willing to sell goods under cost it is our interest to receive them, loses in a great measure its force, from the fact that such a trade is not regular and legitimate, but spasmodic and exceptional, and renders success in many branches of industry dependent upon accident rather than upon the exercise of skill, foresight, and prudence. In short, such trade is a perpetual menace to the domestic market without producing any commensurate good.

During the period of commercial depression throughout Europe, in 1867, it is known to the Commissioner that it became a question with many of the continental manufacturers whether to close their mills and allow their operatives to disperse, or to continue their manufacturing operations at a loss, retaining thereby their supply of skilled labor; and in many instances the latter alternative was decided to be the most advantageous. In such cases the American market was regarded as the most available for the disposal of the commodities thus manufactured, not only without profit, but with an absolute loss, even under the most favorable condition as regards European prices for labor and material. Now, how far it is for the interests of this country to allow itself to be made the means of assisting foreign manufacturers to tide over a period of financial embarrassment, may be an open question, but the Commissioner has no doubt that even the temporary gain which might result to the United States, from the opportunity to purchase cheap commodities under such circumstances, would be more than compensated by the disturbance which would be occasioned thereby to legitimate domestic industry. It should, however, be remarked, that the condition of things as here described must be necessarily of short duration in any particular instance.

There is furthermore another view of this question which cannot be overlooked in this country—its social aspect. Free trade looks only to the increase of wealth. It takes no account of social results; it does not even regard the distribution of property. Even English economists admit that its axioms lead to sameness of occupation, and sameness of occupation means a tardy development of society. But in this country every man is a citizen and nearly every citizen a voter. As the possessors of power we cannot afford to have any class of the people ignorant or socially degraded. To insure a safe standard of education and of domestic comfort, there must be a certain scale of wages, and these must be relatively higher than are paid to the competing laborer of Europe, to whom power is not intrusted and education is denied. These degraded laborers constitute the "dangerous classes," but no dangerous classes ought to be suffered to exist in America. Whatever discrimination, therefore, may be necessary to keep up the social status and the self-respect of the American voter, is a tax imposed by our political system, and it is a tax which the enjoyment of that system amply repays.

COMPARATIVE WAGES IN CERTAIN LEADING BRANCHES OF INDUSTRY IN THE UNITED STATES AND EUROPE.

As the data in respect to this matter heretofore accessible to the public have been very vague and indefinite, the Commissioner, through his assistant, Mr. Edward Young, has made the collection of such information a specialty; and although the work of comparison is extremely difficult, and often most unsatisfactory, by reason of differences in the nomenclature, division, and hours of labor in the different countries, yet some exceedingly interesting results have been arrived at. These in detail will be found in the appendix to this report, marked E, but in brief are substantially as follows:

Manufacture of cotton.—Average excess of wages paid in the United States in 1867, over those paid for corresponding labor in Great Britain, (gold being taken as the standard in both cases,) 35½ per centum.

A reduction having been made in the wages of some operatives in cotton mills during the present year 1868, amounting to a general average of five per cent. on the aggregate wages paid, the excess over the average rates paid in Great Britain, is thereby reduced to 28.7 per cent.

In Belgium, from an examination of less complete data, the average depression in wages, as compared with the United States, appears to be about 48 per cent. The following are specific illustrations of the wages in leading specialties of labor in the cotton manufacture in the United States, Great Britain, and Belgium:

Average weekly wages or earnings (in gold.)

Occupations.	In the United States, (gold.)	In England.	In Belgium.	Excess of wages in United States over England.	Excess of wages in England over Belgium.
Drawing frame tenders	$3 44	$2 75	$2 10	25 per cent.	31 per cent.
Roving frame tenders	3 54	3 38	3 00	5 per cent.	13 per cent.
Mule spinners	7 24	5 36	5 00	35 per cent.	7 per cent.
Weavers	6 06	4 54	3 60	33 per cent.	26 per cent.

In France the average weekly earnings of persons employed in manufactories of cotton are as follows: men, $4 27; women, $2 57; boys, 87 cents, and girls, $1 04. Taking the 467 men and 1,446 women employed in that branch in Paris, the average weekly wages of adults is 14.93 francs, or $2 98; and including the children the average is 13.82 francs, or $2 76.

Manufactures of wool.—The average excess of wages paid in woollen mills of the United States in 1867–'68, over those paid for similar labor in Great Britain, would appear to be about 25 per cent. (24.53 per cent.;) and in carpet and other worsted mills 58 per cent. The following are specific illustrations of the average weekly wages paid in the woollen mills of the three countries above referred to:

Occupations.	In the United States (gold.)	In England.	In Belgium.
Carders	$4 37	$3 85	$3 00
Spinners, (males)	8 23	6 05	....
Spinners, (females)	3 91	2 75	2 00
Drawers	5 89	4 13	2 40
Weavers	5 73	4 67	3 20

Fire-arms.—The average weekly wages of all employés in the manufactories of fire-arms in the United States, Great Britain, and France, in the year 1867, were as follows:

In the United States, (Colt's, Sharp's, and Remington's)	$12 22
In England, (Birmingham)	7 79
In France, (Paris)	5 94

In this branch, therefore, the rates of wages in the United States are 56 per cent. more than in England, and 105 per cent. more than in France; while the rates in England are 24 per cent. in excess of those in France.

Iron founding and machine building.—Average excess in wages paid in iron foundries and machine shops in the United States in 1867–'68, over those paid for similar labor in England, 58 per cent. The following are specific illustrations of the average weekly wages paid to the following enumerated employés in this branch of industry in the countries above referred to:

Occupations.	In the United States, (gold.)	In England.	In Belgium.	In Saxony.
Moulders	$11 52	$8 00	$5 40	....
Machinists	11 54	7 00	3 60	....
Boiler-makers	12 64	7 50	4 20	$4 50
Blacksmiths	12 32	7 12	4 12	3 75
Engineers	11 40	7 50	....	....
Laborers	7 03	4 50	2 40	1 80

Iron manufacture.—In this department we select the price paid for puddling as an indication of the entire average of wages in this branch of industry in the different countries, although the work performed under this head is not always the same in every establishment. The following data are submitted:

Price of puddling iron per ton in New England $5 00; in New York $5 50; New Jersey $6; Eastern Pennsylvania $6; Western Pennsylvania $6 75; in western States $7 50; average price in currency $6 12½. Average price in gold, United States $4 37½; England $2 37½; Belgium $1 20.

The average weekly earnings of puddlers in the leading iron producing countries are as follows:

United States, (gold) $16 54
England.................................. 8 75
France 8 00
Belgium.................................. 6 00
Russia, (at the Vicksa iron works) 1 93

Unskilled labor.—The following are the average rates of weekly wages paid for unskilled labor in the manufacturing establishments of the countries below enumerated:

In the United States, general average, (in gold) $6 81
In Great Britain, general average.................. 4 50
(Sheffield $5 25, Hull $4 50, Wigan $4 25, Bradford $4 00, Glasgow $3 75.)
France 3 60
Belgium—Liege $2 40, Ghent, in cotton mills, $2 52, Mayence $2 40.
Saxony, (Dresden) 2 25
Prussia, (Berlin) 3 10
Russia, (at the Vicksa iron works) 1 33

COMPARATIVE COST OF PRODUCTION IN THE UNITED STATES AND EUROPE.

Now while the American producer, in these and doubtless in some other respects, labors under great and serious disadvantages as compared with his European competitor, it seems equally clear to the Commissioner that these disadvantages are not and cannot be compensated for by the adoption of an indiscriminate, arbitrary rule of protection, and that it is not for the interest of the country that such indiscriminate protection as has heretofore been granted, and seems likely to be further asked for, should be continued.

Thus in most of the tariff discussions that have taken place of late in the United States, the question of the necessity and extent of protection is made to turn almost wholly upon the difference in the cost of labor employed in domestic as compared with foreign industry—which differences, as already shown, are certainly very considerable. And it is also very generally taken for granted in such discussions, that the nominal rate paid for wages, of itself alone, or at least in a very great degree, determines both the cost of production and the social condition and prosperity of the laborer. It is difficult, however, to conceive of a more egregious fallacy than is involved in such assumption; inasmuch as it is not the nominal rate paid for wages, but rather what the labor employed actually produces, and what the wages paid are able to purchase, that determines both of these questions.

A striking illustration of the truth of the first proposition is to be found in the circumstance that while the wages paid in Great Britain in almost every branch of industry are uniformly much higher than those paid for the purchase of similar labor upon the continent—the rates, for example, paid for female labor, in the cotton manufacture, ranging from 12*s.* to 15*s.* per week in Great Britain; 7*s.* 3*d.* to 9*s.* 7*d.* in France, Belgium and Germany; and 2*s.* 4*d.* to 2*s.* 11*d.* in Russia—the one thing which is the most dreaded by continental manufacturers everywhere is British competition; and this feeling of apprehension manifests itself most strongly, and the demand for protection becomes the loudest, in those very districts of continental Europe, as, for example, in France, Austria and Russia, where the average of wages reach their minimum, and moreover, at those times especially when through commercial depression and the scarcity of employment a supply of labor becomes available to the continental manufacturer at rates even below the general average. The recently manifested opposition in France to the continuance of the Cobden treaty, and the demand on the part of the French manufacturers for its abrogation and for a renewal of high duties, is in itself also a further proof and confession of the truth of the proposition we have submitted.*

It is also worthy of note that notwithstanding the many statements which have been made of late respecting the interference of the cheaper labor of the continent with the industry of Great Britain, there has been up to this time, taking the average of the last five years, no decrease whatever, in any of the great leading products of British industry, or in the quantity of such products exported and sold to foreign countries; but, on the other hand, the commercial returns show, for the period specified, a rapid and continual increase of such products and of such exports. The markets and the character of the product may change, but the aggregate of production increases in defiance of all competition.

The explanation of this curious politico-economic phenomena is undoubtedly to be found in the fact that whatever of increased price Great Britain pays for her labor, as compared with the price paid for similar service upon the continent, is far more than compensated by

* "Addresses are being signed in the manufacturing districts of Moravia and Lower Austria, petitioning the Reichsrath not to sanction the treaty of commerce concluded between Austria and England. As according to the provisions of the treaty, the woollen and cotton of English manufacture may, instead of paying by weight, pay 15 per cent. *ad valorem*, which, no doubt, is a signal advantage for the cheap goods, of which the chief import in woollens and cottons from England consists. According to the calculations of the petitioners 15 per cent. *ad valorem* is tantamount to reducing the duty, which they think in itself low, to about one-half. As it is they complain that English goods are inundating the country, and if the treaty takes effect, the native manufacturers in those articles will be ruined."—*Correspondence London Times, November* 1868.

And yet the wages of Austria in the woollen manufacture are probably full 35 per cent. less than the corresponding wages in Great Britain.—*Commissioner.*

the greater corresponding product of British industry, and also to some extent by the gain which results to the British manufacturer by the command of cheaper and more abundant fuel.

As an illustration of this we quote from a recent report of the inspectors of British factories,* the following statement showing the average number of persons employed to spindles in the cotton manufactories of Europe:

"In France, one person to 14 spindles; in Russia, one person to 28 spindles; in Prussia, one person to 37 spindles; in Bavaria, one person to 46 spindles; in Austria, one person to 49 spindles; in Belgium and Saxony, one person to 50 spindles; in Switzerland and the smaller states of Germany, one person to 55 spindles; in Great Britain, one person to 74 spindles."

And the inspector further adds that this comparison "is unfavorable to Great Britain, inasmuch as there is so large a number of factories in the latter country in which weaving by power is carried on in conjunction with spinning, while the factories abroad are chiefly spinning factories."

Now, if the above statement is correct, it follows that although the British cotton manufacturer pays on an average from 200 to 300 per cent. more for his labor than is paid by the cotton manufacturer of Russia, the labor of Great Britain is really, of the two, the cheaper labor, and the Russian manufacturer acknowledges it by asking and receiving a high protective tariff.†

The report above referred to also furnishes a comparison of the working of a cotton factory located at Oldenburgh, Germany, with the average results attained in Great Britain, which shows "that the German machinery, superintended by British overlookers, turned off weekly the same weight of work with hours of labor extending every day from 5.30 a. m. to 8 p. m., (including Saturdays,) as would be turned off in an average British factory during a like period, with the hours of labor extending from 6 a. m. to 6 p. m., and not including the whole of Saturday; and further, that if German, in place of English overlookers, were employed the product would not be nearly so much." To show, furthermore, that these differences in the results of British and other European production are not confined to the department of textile manufactures, we submit the following data in respect to the manufacture of iron. Taking puddling as the representative process in this department of industry, we find the average daily wages paid in Staffordshire, England, in France, and in Belgium, to be as follows:

England	7*s.* 6*d.* to 7*s.* 10*d.* per day.
France, (Sireuil)	6*s.* 4*d.* per day.
Belgium	4*s.* 2*d.* to 5*s.* 0*d.* per day.

Now, with these differences in favor of production in France and Belgium, as compared with England, the average price of merchant bar-iron,

* Report of Alexander Redgrave, esq., inspector of British factories, to her Majesty's principal secretary of state for the home department, London, 1867.

† From what appears to be entirely reliable evidence submitted in the report of the inspectors of British factories, above referred to, we present some further details of interest derived from a comparison of results of labor in Russian and British cotton factories, respectively. The estimate of relative production shows "that the same machinery in England would produce half as much again either yarn or cloth as in Russia." "Mules in Russia seldom make above two and a half draws per minute when spinning 32s twist, while in England they do not run at less than three and a half." "In Russia looms on 32s run at therate of 145 picks per minute; in England, 220 is not considered too fast. No weaver in Russia ever minds more than two looms; in England it is not unusual for hands to keep four looms running without any assistance.'

the product of the respective industries at the works, is returned on the best authority to be as follows:

In England.................................... £6 10*s*. per ton.
In Belgium.................................... 7 0*s*. per ton.
In France..................................... 8 0*s*. per ton.

But it may be said "these facts are all very curious and very interesting, but what have they to do with the questions at issue?" Just this: they show first that the mere differences in the nominal wages paid in the great leading branches of industry in the United States, as compared with Europe, constitute in themselves no fair standard for determining the degree of protection to which American manufacturers may be entitled, unless it is conceded in the outset that the results of American industry are in no way superior to the results of the least productive, which, as above shown, is also the poorest paid labor of Europe. They also show, secondly, that, in many respects, it is not with the pauper labor, but with the best paid and highest skilled labor of Europe that the United States comes most in competition, and therefore has the most reason to apprehend and consider. And, finally, the above facts make it clear that there is a method by which a more stable protection can be made available to the industry of nations other than through the medium of the continued imposition and piling up of duties under a tariff; a point which we believe is the most important that can to-day occupy the attention of all interested in the future of American industry, inasmuch as upon its proper consideration and recognition depend the settlement of the question whether production in the United States shall continue as now, to be dependent upon the artificial support which Congress is annually called upon to administer; or whether the nation, in this respect, availing itself of the greatest resources and opportunities ever granted under Providence to any people, shall hereafter go forward in the full strength of its manhood to command such a share of the commerce and the markets of the world as its population and wealth would rightfully entitle it.

In touching this subject we touch alike, in a great degree, the secret of the commercial and industrial supremacy of Great Britain, and the deficiency and weakness in the same respect of the United States. As we have already shown, Great Britain is at a disadvantage in point of wages to every other commercial and industrial nation, with the single exception of the United States. She enjoys, furthermore, no pre-eminence in the natural supply of any of the great raw materials, except coal; while her manufacturers know that they have nothing to expect from their own government, except non-interference, and a careful exemption from all unnecessary burdens of taxation, either on raw material, processes, or products. In the competition for the trade of the world, with the advantages generally against them, in respect to cheap food, cheap labor, and most raw materials, they further know that the only protection available must be the protection which results from sagacity, energy, cheap capital, economy, and the utilization to the greatest possible extent of every natural opportunity; and knowing this they exercise these qualities, planting the furnace and the rolling-mill in the closest proximity to cheap ore, coal, and transportation, and not in the locality where the principal stockholder happens to reside; conducting manufactures by private rather than corporate enterprise; and subjecting the same when once established to the continued supervision of principals rather than of agents. Production in Great Britain, therefore, based on these and other similar conditions, commands succes, defies and crushes foreign competition, and renders the whole world tributary to itself.

Now on the other hand we maintain, and are prepared to establish our assertion with the most abundant proof, that the whole course of recent legislation in the United States—national, state, and local—has been to establish a policy and results exactly the reverse of that of Great Britain. What has it done?

First. It has neutralized every benefit that can flow from the possession of cheap raw material from cotton and pig-iron down to ice. Take a single illustration: go on to the continent of Europe and ask any manufacturer the cause of British supremacy in production, and one reason always assigned will be the possession of cheap and abundant fuel; and yet to-day the price of coal in the United States, raised and ready for delivery at the pit's mouth, will average, in most localities advantageously situated for industrial purposes, less in United States currency, than the price obtainable, expressed in United States gold, at the pit's mouth of many of the leading mines of Great Britain and of Belgium.* When, however, the coal reaches the American consumer the case is entirely reversed, the advantage as measured in price accruing to the foreign consumer to the extent of very large differences.

Second. It has offered a bounty on incompetence and bad management, rather than a stimulus for the exercise of increased skill and economy. During the three years that the Commissioner has been engaged in his official investigations relative to the national revenues, he has been afforded the opportunity of conferring with the representatives of nearly all those branches of industry that have, from time to time, come to Washington for the purpose of procuring additional protection through an advance of the tariff; and he avers, through his own knowledge, that in very many, perhaps a majority of instances, when it was represented that ruin or curtailment would follow the failure to obtain specific legislation, other persons, in different sections of the country, were prosecuting the same branches of industry with success, and with the realization of fair if not large profits. These latter, when consulted, almost invariably replied, "We do not desire any additional protection unless a gradual advance of the tariff on the constituents of our products render it necessary; and what we would most prefer would be that Congress take off the internal revenue taxes, give us our raw materials as cheap as possible, and then let us alone."

We appeal, furthermore, to the members of the thirty-ninth and fortieth Congresses, or to any one else, to name the industries that have been ruined or materially crippled through the failure, as an immediate and principal cause, to pass any one of the bills that have been matured and reported since the termination of the war, granting increased protection. The Commissioner, on the other hand, were he at liberty to state what has been communicated to him confidentially, could name not a few that have paid larger dividends since the failure of such bills than at any former

* The following are the prices of coal at the pit's mouth, returned to the Commissioner from various localities, in the United States and Europe, for the year 1867:

UNITED STATES.—Eastern slope of the Alleghanies, anthracite $1 50 to $1 75, currency, per ton, (including royalty;) bituminous and semi-bituminous, 1865, $1; 1867, $1 30. Western slope, Westmoreland, $1 50; Pittsburg banks, $1 68; Brazil, Indiana, $1 25; La Salle, Illinois, $2. Previous to the war, coal at the pit's mouth in the United States was much cheaper. In 1858 the Philadelphia and Reading Railroad Company mined and delivered anthracite coal on cars, per contract, for 87½ cents per ton; while the details of the workings of one of the best conducted iron furnaces in the middle States for the year 1860-'61, exhibited to the Commissioner, show the average cost of the best coal at the furnace mouth to have been but little in excess of 60 cents per ton.

EUROPE.—Newcastle, best, $1 75 to $2, gold, per ton; Wigan, $2 12½; near Liverpool, $1 62½; Gartsherie, Scotland, $1 37½; Belgium, Mons, $2 07; Charleroi, $1 94; Westphalia, $1 50.

period; and many others that have not achieved a fair measure of success through the excessive enhancement of the price of the constituents of their products by the existing tariff.

The members of the Finance Committees of the thirty-ninth Congress will remember full well the earnest appeal made to them in the spring of 1866, to increase the duties on piece silks from the present high rate of 60 per cent. *ad valorem*, to 70 per cent.; and the predicted destruction of the industry in question in case the request should not be granted. Let them contrast with this recollection the following advertisement of recent extensive publicity:

AMERICAN SILKS.—Messrs. —— and ——, of Boston, take pleasure in announcing that they have contracted with Messrs. —— for the entire production of their celebrated mill in American silks. * * * The price of the silks is only — per yard at retail; the extraordinary cheapness of which is accounted for by the fact that 85 per cent. of the raw material of which they are made comes into the country absolutely free from impost duties; and we confidently assert that at this price we are giving to the public a silk which could not be imported from Lyons for a much larger sum.

The Commissioner could also name an article of hardware to which, after hearing and earnest solicitation, increased protection was, in 1866, granted in committee, (but through the failure of the bill not eventually obtained,) that since the period referred to has, it is claimed, not only driven the imported competing article entirely out of the domestic market, but is also now constituting an article of export. To have granted increased protection, in any of these instances, would, therefore, have been equivalent to imposing an unnecessary tax upon the public, or of supplementing, through legislation, that increase of skill and economy which the failure to obtain additional protection subsequently compelled the manufacturer to exercise.

The Commissioner will submit but one further illustration of this subject from the many that have fallen under his observation:

In the summer of 1867, while studying the industries of Europe, he visited a factory the products of which had for many years found an extensive market in the United States. The product being staple, and the industry one that it was exceedingly desirable should be extended in the United States, the Commissioner studied the process of manufacture with great care, from the selection of the raw material to the packing of the finished product; the rates of wages; the intelligence of the operatives, and the hours of labor. When his investigation was completed, the Commissioner said to the foreign manufacturer—a man whose name is a household word in his own country for integrity and philanthropy—"the duty on the import of these articles into the United States is, respectively, 35 per cent. ad valorem, and 30 per cent. ad valorem and 20 cents per pound; if you have given me your prices, products of machinery, and cost of labor correctly, I do not well see how you could export your fabrics to the United States, even if there was substantially no duty, as the advantage of raw material is mainly upon our side." "I am sometimes at a loss myself to account for the course of trade," was the reply; "but perhaps it will help you to a conclusion if I tell you that some time ago, finding ourselves pressed with German competition, we threw out our old machinery and replaced it with a new and improved pattern; and the machinery by us rejected was sold to go to the United States." To complete the story, it is only necessary for the Commissioner to add that the owners of this second-hand machinery have since its importation demanded and received an increased protection on its products.

Third. In further enumeration of the effects of the national policy under consideration, we assert that it has largely contributed to the destruction of our foreign commerce by rendering an exchange in kind, for most articles of domestic production, an absolute impossibility. The proofs already submitted under this head are believed to be conclusive.

Fourth. It has contributed to repel the immigration into the country of skilled labor, and has not improved the condition of the working man at home. Thus, instances are not infrequent where skilled workmen from Europe have visited the United States within the last three years with the view of engaging permanently in their special industries, and have returned with the feeling that the inducements offered were not sufficient to render a change of residence on their part desirable; and the Commissioner is assured by manufacturers that, at the present time especially, the tendency among skilled workmen, brought from Europe in pursuance of special arrangements for the extension of special branches of industry, is rather to return to the Old World than remain in the United States. The explanation of this is, that although the wages paid at present in the United States for skilled labor are nominally much greater than in Europe, their purchasing power, as respects commodities and rents, are so much less as to leave either no balance whatever in favor of the industry of the United States or one that is comparatively trifling. We will adduce a few facts in proof and illustration:

In a leading establishment in central New York, manufacturing an article of hardware in competition with Sheffield products, the present advance in wages for skilled workmen, as returned to the Commissioner, calculated on a gold basis, is about 11 per cent. on the established Sheffield prices—an advance not sufficient to compensate for the difference in favor of the foreign workman, in respect to rents, to clothing, and some other commodities. In an establishment in the vicinity of New York city, manufacturing the same products, the difference in wages is even still less.

By reference to tables of prices of commodities, of rents, &c., &c., in the United States, (given in Appendix D to this report,) it will be seen that the average rent of six-roomed tenements in the United States is $84, gold, per annum; and for four-roomed tenements, $63. Compare, now, these rents with those of tenements in the manufacturing districts of Great Britain. In the cotton districts, according to official returns, the average rentals of the houses occupied by operatives are £8 16*s*., or $43 per annum; while in Sheffield 56 per cent. of the houses rented by operatives are under £7 ($35) per annum, and only 26 per cent. command a rental of £10 ($50) and upwards.

At the celebrated iron-works of Le Creuşot, France, a small, ordinary, but comfortable house, with a garden, rents for $16 per annum; but this latter price is believed to be exceptionable.

The Commissioner believes that the mischief wrought to the laboring classes in the eastern sections of the United States during the last two years, by the high prices of food, which have in part resulted from the repeal of the reciprocity treaty, has far more than counterbalanced any advantages which have otherwise accrued to the country through this specific legislation; for although the quantity of food supply which is capable of being imported from the British provinces is, as compared with the national aggregate most trifling, yet it has been sufficient during the period referred to to constitute the difference between "enough" and a deficiency; and such deficiency or tendency thereto, combined with the uncertainties of an irredeemable paper currency, has placed the consumer almost entirely at the mercy of the speculator.*

*A striking illustration of the disproportionate ratio in which a deficiency in the ordinary supply of an essential commodity increases prices is afforded by the experience of Great Britain in reference to her supply of wheat for the years 1863 and 1867. The present average yearly consumption of wheat in Great Britain is about 20,800,000

That the existing policy brings prosperity to certain branches of domestic production cannot be questioned; but like the vigor of the tropical parasite, which eventually paralyzes the tree on which it leans for support, such special prosperity is most antagonistic to the normal and healthy growth of the State. Thus, under the influence of an almost prohibitory tariff, the business of manufacturing pig iron enjoys a high degree of prosperity, and furnaces continue to be multiplied; but if the community at large has been compelled to pay an unnecessary profit of from $7 to $10 per ton on a present annual product of 1,500,000 tons, and has therefore been subjected during the past year to a tax of from $10,000,000 to $15,000,000, the prosperity of the pig iron manufacture in question has cost the country a great deal more than it is worth; and further, it is only necessary that a few more such waves of commercial prosperity should sweep over the land in order to necessitate the enactment of an average tariff of 100 per cent. ad valorem in order to enable the great mass of less favored producers to effect the sale of any product even in their own markets.* And furthermore, that such prosperity as is continually pointed out to prove the beneficial effects of the existing tariff does tend to produce such a result, is proved by the fact that although the tariff has been constantly and largely advanced since 1861, and although the internal revenue taxes, which neutralized in part its protective influence, have been substantially removed during the last year, the demand for still further advances is at present as urgent as at any time previous. As offering some explanation of this circumstance, we mcomend to the careful consideration of all interested the following significant answer given under oath to a question propounded by the Commissioner to the largest and most successful manufacturer in a special department of the iron and steel industry of the United States:

Question. What, according to your experience, was the effect of the increase of the tariff in 1864 on the industries with which you are specially connected. Answer. The first effect was to stimulate nearly every branch—to give an impulse and activity to business; but in a few months the increased cost of production, and the advance in the price of labor, and the products of labor, were greater than the increase of the tariff, so that the business of production was no better, even if in so good a condition, as it was previous to the advance of the tariff referred to. That was the effect on most articles with the manufacture of which I am practically acquainted.

Now, what the country needs is a tariff looking first to the attainment of public revenue, and not primarily to the furtherance of mere private

quarters. The domestic product being insufficient to meet the requirements for domestic consumption, the purchase of an additional supply from foreign countries is every year a matter of necessity, which purchase varies in amount in accordance with the abundance or deficiency of the home crop. In 1863, the home crop being good, the requirement from foreign countries was 4,500,000 quarters, while the total cost of the wheat consumption of Great Britain for that year was £40,000,000 ($200,000,000); of which £6,100,000 ($30,500,000) was paid for foreign purchases. In 1867, on the other hand, the home crop was deficient and necessitated a supply from foreign countries of 11,100,000 quarters, as compared with 4,500,000 in 1863; which deficiency, and the necessity for purchasing 6,600,000 additional quarters from abroad, carried up the cost of the total home consumption from £40,000,000 ($200,000,000) in 1863 to £70,000,000 ($350,000,000) in 1867; and that, too, notwithstanding the total home consumption, by reason of enforced economy, was undoubtedly considerably diminished, or supplemented by the consumption of other and cheaper articles of food. To obtain the additional supply needed in 1867 there was furthermore paid to foreign countries the sum of £33,500,000, ($107,500,000,) as compared with £6,100,000 ($30,500,000) paid for the necessary foreign supplies in 1863.

*It should be especially noted that this enhanced price of iron enters into the cost of every article made of iron or steel; that is to say, it increases the cost of every tool and implement of production and transportation. Upon this enhanced cost must be predicated the necessity of greater capital in other manufactures of iron, more loss of interest, decreased consumption and increased risk. No tax can be more vicious than one imposed upon tools, implements and machinery—upon the processes rather than the results of labor. The enhanced cost of iron beams, ceilings, cornices and stairways for fire proof buildings, may also be mentioned as one of the unfavorable results of a high price of pig iron.

interests. Government can add nothing to the capital of the country by legislation. It can only prescribe the channels into which capital already created shall flow.

It is time, furthermore, that the United States should have a broader and more liberal policy, in respect to its industrial development, than is at present made the basis of legislation; and that this policy should not be, as it were, self-defensive, and looking merely at the retention of our own markets, but aggressive.

THE POSSIBLE FUTURE OF AMERICAN INDUSTRY.

The Commissioner prefers no claim to the possession of any extraordinary insight into the future, but he believes that it is possible to look forward to the attainment of results, in respect to a development of national industries, which shall find no parallel in the history of our former experience. Now, is this mere fanciful writing, or has it a basis of substantial reality?

Let us see. By the recently published mineral statistics of Great Britain, it appears that the mean market price of pig iron for the year 1867–'68, taking Welsh pig as the standard, was £4 *3s.* *9d.* ($20.38.) But, as has been already stated, the present average cost of producing pig iron in the United States under favorable conditions and good management is not in excess of $26 per ton currency; and as respects some of the furnaces of Pennsylvania and Maryland, the Commissioner is assured that the present cost of production is little in excess of $23, which price, reduced to gold at 36 per cent. premium, $16 91, is $3.47 per ton less than the market price of the cheapest and standard supply of this article in the markets of Europe. It is evident, therefore, that it is possible for the United States, at the present time at least, to compete on terms of equal advantage in the markets of the world for the partial supply of an article that is even more essential to civilization than cotton; and this advantage which has accrued to the country under the most unfavorable circumstances, is capable of being rendered still greater and more preeminent, by the attainment through legislation of results which, by increasing the purchasing power of wages, shall render labor less costly and more available, and thus decrease the present cost of production and transportation. And if the representatives of the industrial interests of Pennsylvania and Maryland, instead of interesting themselves to prevent a natural distribution of cheap coal, would devote themselves to the full solution of the problem referred to, ten furnaces would speedily spring up within their territories where one now exists, and the commerce of the world would become tributary to their products.

Again, let us consider the condition of the manufacture of cotton. It is well known that before the war American coarse cottons were obtaining a preference over all others in the markets of the east and of South America, and that their export was rapidly increasing. The war interrupted, and in a great degree destroyed this business; but the Commissioner, after a careful examination and comparison of all the elements of the cost of producing coarse cottons (No. 25 and under) in the United States and Europe, in which examination he has had the assistance of experts in both countries, has come to the conclusion that if the American manufacturer could be put upon the same basis as his foreign competitor as regards direct and indirect taxation, cost and excellence of machinery, and would bring to his business the same skill and economy, he would be enabled to produce cotton goods and yarns, of the number specified, at a cost which would enable him to undersell all other similar producers. The attainment of such a result, which involves nothing that is impracticable, nothing that is visionary, would determine the exportation of no small part of the cotton grown in the United States in a manufactured, rather than in an unmanufactured condition; would erect two cotton mills where one now exists; would largely increase the demand for agricultural produce in the home markets, and would bring back four-fold that commerce of the ocean which now wanes almost to annihilation, in great part through want of legitimate occupation in effecting exchanges.

And what has been said of the possible future of the coarse cotton manufacture is equally true of the manufacture of medium table cutlery, common locks, axes, spades, shovels, agricultural implements generally, and many other articles of hardware; the advantage in the production of which, growing out of the application of superior skill and the greater use of machinery, is already so far on the side of the United States, that to go from one of our first-class establishments, manufacturing many of the above articles, into similar ones in Great Britain, France, or Germany, is like going from the 19th century back to the middle ages. Now, if we will but give to the American manufacturers in these departments, who have already established their business on a basis of sufficient skill and capital, an opportunity to produce cheaper, a result clearly within the reach of legislation, we shall also afford an opportunity for the extension of production which can have no limit, except the ability of three-quarters of the population of the globe to purchase and consume; and the skilled labor of other nations must either come to the United States to pursue their special avocations or seek other employments.

But a prospect of industrial development, which far transcends all others in importance, awaits the Pacific coast of our country when reason and common sense, rather than prejudice, shall exercise control over its population and the enactment of its laws.

No one can study the industrial elements of Great Britain and of western Europe without becoming impressed with the fact that an adequate supply of intelligent and cheap labor, to meet the increasing demands of the world for manufactured products, is one of the most difficult problems of their future. Already in France and Germany the drain of labor from the rural districts, to engage in manufacturing industry in towns, has become a cause of complaint by reason of the embarrassment which it entails upon the planting and harvesting of the crops, and the continuance of a further supply of labor from this source can only be effected by the offer of higher wages.* Increased wages, in turn, tend to increase the price of agricultural products, and other like raw material; and also contribute directly to largely increase the capacity for the consumption of domestic manufactured products, inasmuch as the cost of all articles, which are in great part the result of the application of

*"The demand for labor in France, consequent on the impetus given to manufacturing activity, has tended to drain it from the rural districts and congest it in the great towns. The consequences have been very seriously felt in the agricultural districts, where a dearth of labor has at times entailed great embarrassment and heavy losses on the farmers. On the other hand, large numbers of foreign workmen, chiefly Belgian, German, and English, are employed in the manufacturing towns. In the town of Mulhouse alone there are more than 8,000 German workmen, and the number of Belgians employed at Roubaix is stated to be nearly 15,000."—[Correspondence with her Majesty's ministers abroad, regarding industrial questions. Mr. Fane to Lord Stanley, London, 1867.]

"Increased industrial activity, in Belgium, has naturally produced a corresponding increase in wages as well as in the price of raw materials. Several establishments could yield a greater produce had they but a sufficient amount of hands at their disposal. The demand for workmen, particularly in the coal districts, has raised great pretensions on their part and has led to several strikes, which, however, have fortunately lasted but a short time, owing to concessions usually made by the masters."—[Ibid. Lord Howard de Walden to Lord Stanley, Brussels, 1867.]

natural forces through machinery, does not even increase in the same ratio as the wages of manual labor that attend such machinery. Thus, Saxony, in 1866, is reported to have produced six million dozen pairs of stockings, and of this product to have exported some two million dozen to the United States, equivalent to about three-quarters of a pair of stockings to each man, woman, and child of our population per annum. But to effect this result Saxony has already drawn upon her rural population to an extent sufficient to produce a marked diminution of labor available for agricultural purposes, so that if she should propose to double her product of stockings and supply the population of the United States with one and a half pairs, instead of three-quarters of one pair per head per annum, she must provide herself with such an additional supply of labor, as will require an additional supply and probable importation of food. But such an additional supply of labor can only be obtained through such an inducement of increased wages as will enable the recipients to purchase and use more largely machine-made domestic products; or, in other words, to wear stockings, or some other equivalent article of clothing, in place of dispensing with them as they may at present. It is, therefore, obvious that there is a limit beyond which Saxony cannot go in supplying stockings in competition with other countries where food is cheaper and labor more abundant. And this illustration in respect to Saxony holds good in respect to all the other manufacturing countries of western Europe.

Again, an examination of the present condition of the production of pig-iron will show, that of all the countries of Europe, Great Britain is the only one that has any resources adequate for meeting the future greatly increased demand of the world for this article, or, possibly, of even supplying their own future requirements for domestic consumption; and in Great Britain the prospect of future increase is dependent altogether upon her ability to supply coal on a scale of consumption that already is in excess of the rate of 100,000,000 tons per annum. How great this prospective demand is likely to prove, may be inferred from a comparison of the present average per capita consumption of iron in different countries, which ranges from about 189 pounds in Great Britain and Belgium, to 100 pounds in the United States, and 69 pounds in France.

If we turn now to the Pacific coast of the United States we shall find the fundamental conditions for an unlimited extension of manufacturing industry supplied to a greater and more perfect extent than in any other country, viz: an unlimited supply of cheap and fertile land, thereby entailing a supply of cheap food; great natural resources in respect to valuable minerals, lumber, and the product of the seas; and finally, but above all in importance, a practically unlimited supply of cheap, docile, and sufficiently intelligent Chinese labor. Under these circumstances there is, really, nothing wanting but capital, which will speedily flow, in accordance with a demand that can offer both security and profit, to rapidly develop an industry which, favored with the means of rapid and cheap intercommunication, shall be able to supply to the markets of the east all that its immense population shall need of the products of a higher civilization. And the proposition is as true now as in the great days of Alexandria, Venice, Constantinople, and Genoa, that the people and the country which controls the trade of the east, controls in great part the wealth and the dominion of the world.

At present, however, the people of the Pacific repel rather than attract the labor which can alone make their natural resources and wealth available, and fail to afford it adequate protection either as respects life or the possession of property. How suggestive a commentary on the existing state of things is embodied in the following statement recently made to the Commissioner by the president of one of the largest mining properties on the Pacific coast: "*The hostility of our miners, which is sustained by public opinion, will not allow us to avail ourselves of cheap Chinese labor. Could we do so, the profits on our business would be increased from ten thousand to fifteen thousand dollars per month.*"

CONCLUSION.

In what has thus been submitted the Commissioner believes that he has sufficiently indicated his views in respect to the tariff. He cannot resist the conclusion that, as it now stands, it is in many respects injurious and destructive, and does not afford to American industry that stimulus and protection which is claimed as its chief merit. He believes that to grant, in the main, the advances asked in the bills now pending before Congress would be but to aggravate the very difficulties under which the country now labors to impair the revenues and hinder the return to specie payments.

In fact, our present tariff is in many particulars apparently based upon the old fallacy that, in the exchange of commodities between nations, which constitutes commerce, what one gains the other loses. It needs but a moment's thought to be convinced that there can be no permanent trade or commerce unless it is for the gain of both nations; all trade is based upon the mutuality of services, and it is one of the evidences of the progress of modern thought, that the inter-dependence of nations is beginning to be recognized. This is eminently true in England, France and Germany, true in China and Japan, true even in Spain, but not yet recognized in the United States, if our laws are to be taken as the evidence of our thought.

With these feelings and convictions he would therefore prove untrue to his trust did he not here enter his most earnest protest against any further general increase of the tariff, but would, on the contrary, recommend—

First. An enlargement of the free list.

Second. A reduction of some rates of duty, and, as an exception, an increase of a few others, with a view to the increase of the revenue.

Third. A reduction of some rates of duty with a view to an absolute abatement, on the simple ground that the reduction of a duty is the reduction of a tax, and that the most efficient method of protecting home industry is by the removal of obstacles in the form of taxes.

Fourth. The conversion to the utmost possible extent of the present *ad valorem* duties into specifics, as the only practicable method of insuring certainty and equality in the assessment of duties and the prevention of undervaluations and the abrogation of the privilege which enables returning tourists to import free of duty an amount of goods corresponding to their real or supposed social position.

In behalf of the conclusions thus expressed the Commissioner confidently appeals to the true friends of American industry for countenance and support; for nothing can be more certain than that if unnecessary and iniquitous burdens of taxation under the tariff continue to be laid upon the people, the day is not far distant when a reaction of public sentiment will compel either a sweeping reduction of duties, or induce through agitation such an instability in legislation as will in itself prove most injurious and destructive.

The Commissioner does not believe it expedient in this, a general report, to enter upon the specific details of a tariff revision, but the precise changes required in his judgment will, if called for, be presented in the form of an additional report, or be submitted personally to the finance committees of Congress. As a bill proposing a change in the existing warehouse system is, however, now pending before Congress, some recomendations in respect to this topic are herewith appended in the form of a supplement.

I have the honor to be yours, very respectfully,

DAVID A. WELLS,
Special Commissioner of the Revenue.

Hon. HUGH MCCULLOCH,
Secretary of the Treasury.

SUPPLEMENT.

THE BONDED WAREHOUSE SYSTEM.

The frequent complaints and controversies in regard to our present system for warehousing and bonding foreign merchandise have induced the Commissioner to make a special examination of the subject.

In a recent report submitted to the House of Representatives by the Committee on Manufactures, the practical abolition of the whole system was recommended, and bill reported, carrying the above recommendations into effect. With these recommendations the Commissioner cannot concur; but would rather suggest certain important modifications to the warehouse system as at present constituted.

The objects of the system are two-fold:

1st. To facilitate the importation of the products of one country for re-export to another; or, in other words, to make our ports depots for the distribution of foreign products.

The course of trade of late years has however been so far modified by the use of the telegraph and of steam, as partly to render unnecessary the large stock of merchandise which it was formerly considered necessary to hold in transit at intermediate points between the producer and consumer.

The cumbrous system of oaths, bonds, landing certificates, &c., required of the merchant before he can avail himself of the privilege of re-export, tends also to discourage this branch of commerce, and the warehouse system may be condemned as a failure, so far as this object is concerned. The proof of this is to be found in the fact that out of a gross importation during the last fiscal year, exclusive of bullion and specie, of $359,706,000, only $12,157,000 was re-exported; of which the greater portion consisted of tropical or semi-tropical productions.

2d. Another object of the warehouse system is to facilitate imports, and to reduce the necessary expense of importation to the lowest point. In considering this branch of the subject, our importations must be divided into two classes:

1. Those which are essential to the comfort and prosperity of the people, including articles from which we expect to derive the largest portion of the revenue collected by means of the tariff.

2. Those which are non-essential, and are dependent upon style or fancy for their sale. To importations of this character it seems clearly not desirable that any undue facilities should be afforded; the tendency of which will be to induce the sending to the United States of the refuse which foreign markets will not receive; or to encourage needy or weak merchants or manufacturers in Europe to avail themselves of such exports as a means of raising money, by sending to our markets large quantities of goods on consignment, and out of season; and the sale of which, while ultimately benefiting the domestic consumer little or nothing, seriously injures the domestic manufacturer.

To the first class of commodities, the Commissioner is of the opinion that we should offer every possible facility to induce their importation with the least risk or expense; and should rather enlarge our warehouse system, and extend it by abolishing the additional duty of ten per cent. now imposed upon goods not withdrawn from bond within one year; while the privilege of warehousing the second class may be safely withdrawn, with probable benefit to all and injury to none.

In the first class should be included all articles of necessity or comfort—especially tropical and semi-tropical productions—such as tea, coffee, sugar, cocoa, raw silk, jute, hemp, drugs, dye-stuffs, and the like, most of which are needed in our various branches of manufacture; and also articles from which we expect to derive a large revenue, and therefore desire to facilitate importation, such as spirits, wines, spices, and tobacco. The more of the former of these commodities we have, provided they are obtained in exchange for our own surplus productions of cotton, oil, wheat, or even for our gold, the richer we are; and if our warehouses groan under the weight of them, it is a true sign of our prosperity, provided they are paid for.

Most of them are bulky; require for their importation large capital; and not unfrequently can be obtained or imported only at certain seasons. It seems expedient, therefore, that we should afford to the importer of this class of commodities every facility for storing them, and, furthermore, not require the payment of the duty on such importations any faster than they are withdrawn for consumption. We shall thus be able to obtain from them the largest revenue, and at the same time impose the least additional cost upon the consumer.

To the second class of commodities, which the Commissioner is of the opinion that it is inexpedient to extend the benefit of warehousing, belong textile fabrics, fancy goods, and such articles as depend mainly on fashion or fancy for their sale. Since the establishment of the Atlantic telegraph it has become much more the custom of manufacturers to work upon orders taken in advance, and with all our facilities for procuring what we need of these articles, which can be ordered almost at a day's notice, there need be no special facilities extended to merchants to aid them in carrying a heavy stock in warehouse. Such facilities rather tend to promote fluctuation and uncertainty than to establish uniformity of prices.

Investigation renders it probable that at least 60 per cent. of the textile fabrics and fancy goods which are entered in warehouse are consigned goods, and not *bona fide* purchases.

Investigation further shows that needy manufacturers in Europe, or often commercial adventurers in the possession of goods, often very undesirable articles, apply to the numerous foreign houses, who have agents in the United States, for advances, and then consign them to this country, where they are sent to bonded warehouse—often at a gross undervaluation—and finally sold to pay advances and duties. Now, such a trade is clearly detrimental to the *bona fide* merchant, and rarely a benefit to the consumer, inasmuch as the goods which are sold at auction if desirable are retailed at regular prices, and if undesirable are no benefit to any one. Yet it is for the interest of the banker and the consignee to stimulate this trade to the utmost, as they are the constant gainers from its continuance. If the bonding of articles of the character referred to were disallowed, the entire machinery of this undesirable trade would be given up; inasmuch as an immediate cash payment of the duties would involve the use of an amount of capital on this side of the Atlantic which foreign bankers would probably consider undesirable; and with such change, furthermore, this unnatural trade itself would also undoubtedly, in a great degree, be discontinued.

APPENDIX A.

TABLE *showing the aggregate receipts of internal revenue for the several fiscal years* 1865, 1866, 1867, *and* 1868; *the amount derived from the principal specific sources; and the percentage of the amount derived from each specific source to the whole, for each of the above-named periods.*

[PREPARED FOR THE SPECIAL COMMISSION OF THE REVENUE BY EDWARD YOUNG.]

Articles and occupations.	Receipts for fiscal year 1865	Per cent. of the whole receipts.	Receipts for fiscal year 1866	Per cent. of the whole receipts.	Receipts for fiscal year 1867.	Per cent. of the whole receipts.	Receipts for fiscal year 1868.	Per cent. of the whole receipts.
MANUFACTURES AND PRODUCTIONS.								
Boots and shoes	$3, 280, 627	1. 553	$6, 516, 814	2. 096	$2, 943, 420	1. 106	$1, 946, 963	1. 019
Brandy made from grapes	10, 546	. 005	44, 741	. 014	13, 070	. 005	158, 886	. 083
Bullion	379, 518	. 18	488, 337	. 157	441, 340	. 166	323, 002	. 169
Candles	326, 583	. 15	392, 822	. 126	290, 502	. 109	236, 650	. 124
Carriages, railroad cars, &c.	880, 021	. 416	1, 576, 662	. 507	1, 606, 762	. 604	559, 214	. 292
Chemical productions	317, 383	. 15	534, 780	. 172	279, 892	. 105	183, 640	. 100
Chocolate and cocoa	17, 980	. 008	36, 467	. 011	34, 453	. 013	24, 067	. 013
Cigars, cigarettes, and cheroots	3, 087, 421	1. 462	3, 476, 237	1. 118	3, 661, 984	1. 377	2, 951, 675	1. 544
Clocks, clock-movements, &c.	93, 838	. 044	153, 697	. 049	80, 963	. 030	71, 835	. 038
Cloth, other than cotton or wool.	376, 672	. 178	595, 728	. 191	1, 517, 683	. 571	123, 152	. 064
Cloth, painted, &c	150, 286	. 071	312, 924	. 100	289, 719	. 109	213, 722	. 112
Clothing	6, 820, 937	3. 230	12, 027, 697	3. 868	3, 195, 742	1. 202	204, 201	. 107
Coal	835, 994	. 395	1, 240, 106	. 398	....	.....	....	.....
Coffee, roasted and ground, and substitutes.	284, 070	. 134	221, 588	. 071	272, 665	. 100	251, 833	. 132
Confectionery	569, 474	. 269	995, 795	. 320	764, 825	. 287	592, 062	. 310
Cotton fabrics, yarns, thread, &c.	7, 331, 148	3. 47	12, 421, 934	4. 00	9, 229, 468	3. 471	6, 488, 855	3. 394
Cotton, raw	1, 772, 983	. 839	18, 409, 655	5. 921	23, 769, 079	8. 938	22, 500, 948	11. 767
Cutlery	84, 188	. 039	150, 762	. 048	158, 849	. 060	108, 336	. 057
Furniture and manufactures of wood.	2, 733, 248	1. 29	4, 540, 140	1. 46	2, 150, 480	. 809	1, 010, 469	. 529
Furs	222, 559	. 105	356, 503	. 115	415, 023	. 156	....	.....
Gas, illuminating	1, 348, 325	. 638	1, 842, 643	. 592	1, 834, 676	. 690	1, 902, 082	. 995
Glass, manufactures of	585, 430	. 277	922, 318	. 296	479, 102	. 180	242, 912	. 127
Gold manufactures, jewelry, diamonds, &c.	543, 430	. 26	640, 602	. 20	375, 652	. 141	393, 548	. 206
Glue	44, 517	. 021	78, 147	. 025	55, 419	. 021	....	.....
Gunpowder	248, 376	. 117	250, 669	. 080	180, 934	. 069	131, 418	. 069
India-rubber, manufactures of	635, 976	. 301	555, 842	. 178	391, 003	. 150	249, 772	. 131
Iron blooms, &c	52, 158	. 024	52, 258	. 016	....	.....	....	.....
Iron, advanced beyond blooms, &c.	457, 622	. 216	665, 102	. 213	526, 344	. 200	....	.....
Iron, band, hoop, and sheet	319, 142	. 151	566, 860	. 182	454, 344	. 171	....	.....
Iron, bar rod, &c	30, 475	. 014	55, 388	. 017	....	.....	....	.....
Iron, plate	150, 292	. 071	234, 916	. 075	150, 992	. 057	....	.....
Iron, railroad	284, 783	. 134	399, 669	. 128	....	.....	....	.....
Iron, railroad, rerolled	376, 265	. 178	668, 988	. 215	....	.....	....	.....
Iron, pig	1, 484, 383	. 703	2, 555, 893	. 725	....	.....	....	.....
Iron castings	798, 202	. 378	1, 367, 825	. 440	1, 061, 414	. 400	713, 851	. 373
Iron castings, (stoves and hollow ware.)	211, 849	. 101	297, 632	. 095	304, 475	. 114	213, 053	. 111
Iron, manufactures of	3, 944, 380	1. 869	5, 410, 181	1. 740	2, 584, 764	. 972	1, 069, 838	. 551
Iron, cut nails and spikes	382, 940	. 155	725, 146	. 233	741, 265	. 279	677, 623	. 354
Iron, rivets, nuts, &c	56, 498	. 026	101, 401	. 032	....	.....	....	.....
Lead, sheet, lead pipes, and shot.	125, 006	. 059	227, 610	. 073	165, 437	. 062	173, 824	. 09[illegible]
Lead, white	52, 067	. 024	102, 413	. 033	....	.....	....	.....
Leather of all descriptions	4, 337, 266	2. 05	5, 384, 813	1. 72	3, 445, 167	1. 300	1, 587, 746	. 831
Liquors, distilled	15, 995, 702	7. 58	29, 198, 578	9. 39	29, 151, 340	10. 962	14, 131, 845	7. 390
Liquors, fermented	3, 657, 181	1. 73	5, 115, 140	1. 64	5, 819, 345	2. 1[illegible]	5, 685, 664	2. 974
Machinery, steam engines, &c.	772, 360	. 366	1, 189, 485	. 383	2, 104, 655	. 791	1, 661, 606	. 869
Marble monuments, &c	170, 419	. 080	329, 217	. 105	121, 702	. 046	88, 568	. 046
Molasses	54, 972	. 026	90, 851	. 029	98, 750	. 037	....	.....
Musical instruments	259, 384	. 122	418, 144	. 134	425, 594	. 160	348, 900	. 182
Oil, coal, refin'd petroleum, &c.	3, 047, 213	1. 441	5, 317, 396	1. 71	4, 904, 762	1. 844	4, 281, 891	2. 240
Oil, lard, linseed, &c	414, 547	. 196	607, 225	. 195	....	.....	....	.....
Paper of all descriptions	1, 082, 476	. 512	1, 172, 115	. 376	743, 077	. 280	340, 398	. 178
Pickles, preserved fruits, &c.	172, 314	. 081	19[illegible], 860	. 062	....	.....	....	.....

A.—*Table showing the aggregate receipts of internal revenue, &c*—Continued.

Articles and occupations.	Receipts for fiscal year 1865.	Per cent. of the whole receipts.	Receipts for fiscal year 1866.	Per cent. of the whole receipts.	Receipts for fiscal year 1867.	Per cent. of the whole receipts.	Receipts for fiscal year 1868.	Per cent. of the whole receipts.
Pins	$24, 802	.011	$37, 993	.012	$31, 391	.012	$29, 827	.016
Pottery ware, &c	93, 221	.044	164, 857	.053	88, 307	.033	......	......
Salt	335, 349	.158	456, 101	.147	253, 306	.095	......	......
Screws, wood	122, 693	.058	226, 590	.072	172, 523	.065	73, 788	.039
Ships and other vessels	347, 218	.164	355, 478	.114	......	......	......	......
Silk, manufactures of	216, 189	.102	445, 766	.143	274, 890	.103	132, 912	.070
Silverware	59, 768	.028	128, 522	.041	88, 616	.033	58, 330	.031
Snuff	283, 352	.134	698, 174	.224	798, 365	.300	745, 308	.390
Soap	791, 416	.37	1, 326, 025	.426	727, 164	.273	411, 239	.215
Starch	61, 233	.06	112, 230	.036	......	......	......	......
Steel	174, 052	.07	212, 662	.068	17, 406	.006	......	......
Steel, manufactures of	549, 767	.26	714, 211	.229	......	......	......	......
Sugar, brown or raw	323, 790	.153	567, 531	.182	500, 296	.190	372. 930	.195
Sugar, refined	1, 720, 613	.82	2. 337, 405	.75	2, 065, 165	.776	1, 436, 394	.751
Tobacco, manufactured	8, 017, 020	3. 80	12, 339, 922	3. 97	15, 245, 478	5. 733	14, 947, 108	7. 818
Turpentine, spirits of	8, 462	......	248, 178	.079	423, 593	.160	417, 015	.218
Umbrellas and parasols	111, 147	.052	229, 491	.073	......	......	......	......
Varnish	149, 981	.071	251, 227	.080	151, 450	.057	......	......
Wine	43, 216	.020	66, 118	.021	2, 761	.001	4, 120	.002
Woollen manufactures	7, 947, 094	3. 764	8, 814, 101	2. 834	5, 405, 426	1. 933	3, 065, 786	1. 603
Miscellaneous articles	11, 381, 800	5. 395	17, 692, 357	5. 691	12, 741, 396	4. 792	6, 736, 093	3. 523
Total	104, 379, 609	49. 438	178, 356, 661	57, 366	146, 223, 674	54. 987	100, 274, 508	52. 451
GROSS RECEIPTS.								
Advertisements	227, 530	.107	290, 605	.093	288, 010	.108	......	......
Bridges and toll roads	75, 269	.035	108, 136	.035	115, 461	.043	53, 563	.028
Canals	92, 421	.043	99, 268	.032	45, 283	.017	9, 986	.005
Express companies	529, 276	.250	645, 769	.208	558, 359	.210	671, 950	.351
Ferries	126, 133	.060	48, 764	.015	137, 240	.052	132, 653	.068
Insurance companies	805, 992	.382	1, 169, 722	.37	1, 326, 014	.500	1, 288, 746	.674
Lotteries, and lottery-ticket dealers.	29, 249	.014	78, 072	.025	74, 484	.028	65, 127	.034
Railroads	5, 917, 293	2. 802	7, 614, 448	2. 449	4, 128, 255	1. 552	3, 134, 337	1. 640
Ships, barges, &c	431, 210	.204	39, 322	.013	4, 877	.002	44, 268	.023
Stage coaches	469, 188	.222	572, 519	.184	241, 297	.090	186, 586	.098
Steamboats	638, 812	.302	84, 846	.027	91, 805	.035	263, 450	.139
Telegraph companies	215, 050	.102	308, 438	.099	239, 595	.090	214, 699	.112
Theatres, operas, circuses, &c.	140, 442	.066	202, 521	.065	194, 039	.073	214, 704	.112
Total	9, 697, 866	4. 593	11, 262, 430	3. 622	7, 444, 719	2. 800	6, 280, 069	3. 284
SALES.								
Auction	410, 176	.19	503, 252	.162	240, 249	.089	186, 727	.098
Brokers, cattle	......	......	......	......	67, 674	.029	110, 859	.058
Brokers, gold, &c.	852, 801	.40	1, 046, 704	.336	......	......	......	......
Brokers, merchandise	596. 474	.28	870, 080	.280	415, 170	.156	286, 438	.150
Brokers, stock	2, 202, 793	1. 04	1, 582, 247	.509	......	......	......	......
Dealers, in excess of $50,000	......	......	......	......	2, 484, 383	.933	4, 244, 647	2. 220
Miscellaneous	......	......	......	......	906, 599	.340	9, 229	.005
Total	4, 062, 244	1. 924	4, 002, 283	1. 287	4, 114, 075	1. 547	4, 837, 900	2. 531
SPECIAL TAXES, (LICENSES.)								
Apothecaries	32, 872	.015	43, 713	.014	55, 447	.021	58, 377	.031
Architects and civil engineers.	10, 411	.005	12, 136	.004	15, 805	.006	15, 650	.008
Auctioneers	80, 545	.038	89, 724	.029	98, 085	.037	97, 448	.051
Bankers	846, 687	.40	1, 262, 849	.406	1, 433, 716	.539	1, 490, 384	.780
Billiard rooms	54, 025	.026	103, 929	.033	124, 711	.047	136, 993	.072
Bowling alleys	13, 490	.007	19, 749	.006	20, 353	.008	19, 603	.010
Brewers	77, 747	.037	105, 412	.033	238, 155	.090	270, 205	.141
Brokers	581, 450	.276	673, 260	.217	598, 855	.225	538, 417	.282
Builders	82, 273	.039	131, 178	.042	117, 531	.045	82, 234	.043
Butchers	152, 421	.07	224, 465	.070	217, 394	.081	225, 077	.118
Claim agents	56, 782	.027	70, 637	.023	84, 627	.032	63, 150	.033
Conveyancers and real estate agents.	33, 510	.016	84, 442	.027	99, 595	.037	97, 855	.051
Dealers, wholesale	3, 543, 105	1. 678	5, 428, 345	1. 745	3, 880, 281	1, 460	1, 854, 388	.970
Dealers, retail	1, 606, 778	.761	1, 949, 017	.626	2, 047, 861	.770	2, 163, 632	1. 132
Dealers, wholesale liquor	400, 693	.190	801, 531	.257	982, 135	.370	592, 046	.309
Dealers, retail liquor	2, 205, 866	1. 044	2, 807, 226	.903	2, 966, 684	1. 115	3, 242, 915	1, 696
Dentists	34, 475	.016	47, 149	.015	59, 461	.022	63, 663	.033
Distillers	59, 898	.029	101, 534	.038	253, 587	.095	115, 687	.113

A.—*Table showing the aggregate receipts of internal revenue, &c.*—Continued.

Articles and occupations.	Receipts for fiscal year 1865.	Per cent. of the whole receipts.	Receipts for fiscal year 1866.	Per cent. of the whole receipts.	Receipts for fiscal year 1867.	Per cent. of the whole receipts.	Receipts for fiscal year 1868.	Per cent. of the whole receipts.
Eating-houses	$36, 538	. 017	$50, 603	. 016	$53, 157	. 020	$54, 835	. 029
Hotels	415, 279	. 20	580, 022	. 186	763, 656	. 250	656, 795	. 344
Horse dealers	40, 160	. 019	27, 566	. 009	25, 635	. 009	23, 203	. 013
Insurance agents	21, 610	. 010	104, 867	. 033	148, 648	. 054	152, 143	. 078
Lawyers	190, 377	. 090	264, 837	. 085	357, 648	. 134	383, 031	. 200
Livery stable keepers	65, 211	. 031	90, 180	. 029	100, 856	. 040	101, 760	. 053
Lottery-ticket dealers	43, 480	. 020	54, 427	. 017	77, 686	. 030	70, 010	. 039
Manufactures	635, 115	. 300	1, 043, 031	. 335	1, 296, 487	. 487	1, 427, 669	. 746
Peddlers	459, 299	. 217	679, 014	. 218	708, 113	. 266	724, 210	. 379
Photographers	74, 608	. 035	93, 186	. 030	79, 170	. 030	53, 102	. 028
Physicians and surgeons	302, 847	. 143	425, 597	. 137	549, 369	. 207	280, 566	. 303
Rectifiers	48, 781	. 023	61, 301	. 020	80, 470	. 030	87, 770	. 045
Stallions and jacks	277, 166	. 131	306, 854	. 098	381, 032	. 143	395, 124	. 206
Theatres, museums, exhibitions, and circuses.	26, 143	. 012	1, 662	. 010	31, 893	. 012	48, 555	. 026
Tobacconists	13, 579	. 006	316, 675	. 005	59, 321	. 022	86, 004	. 045
Miscellaneous	90, 258	. 043	252, 180	. 081	279, 020	. 105	292, 046	. 152
Total	12, 613, 479	5. 974	18, 038, 098	5. 801	18, 186, 446	6. 840	16, 364, 547	8. 559
INCOME.								
From individuals	20, 570, 596	9. 742	60, 547, 882	19. 474	57, 040, 641	21. 450	32, 027, 611	16. 752
From other sources	169, 855	. 031	524, 050	. 169	....	.....	....	.....
From banks, railroad companies, &c.	....	.....	....	.....	7, 943, 796	2. 987	8, 384, 426	4. 385
Total	20, 740, 451	9. 823	61, 071, 932	19. 643	64, 984, 437	24. 437	40, 412, 037	21. 137
ARTICLES IN SCHEDULE A.								
Billiard tables	67, 754	. 032	17, 353	. 005	20, 761	. 008	23, 422	. 013
Carriages	322, 720	. 153	624, 458	. 200	183, 856	. 070	224, 605	. 118
Piano-fortes	7, 752	. 004	403, 572	. 130	....	.....	....	. 001
Plate, of gold	126	.....	84	.....	163	.....	218	.....
Plate, of silver	117, 987	. 056	216, 490	. 070	287, 679	. 108	252, 345	. 132
Watches	9, 139	. 005	426, 527	. 137	619, 063	. 232	605, 789	. 312
Other articles	254, 788	. 120	4, 609	. 002	1, 005, 152	. 378	27, 961	. 016
Total	780, 266	. 370	1, 693, 123	. 544	2, 116, 674	. 796	1, 134, 340	. 593
TOTAL RECEIPTS.								
From manufactures and productions.	104, 379, 609	49. 438	178, 356, 661	57. 366	146, 223, 674	54. 987	100, 274, 508	52. 451
Slaughtered animals	1, 261, 357	. 597	1, 291, 570	. 415	262, 211	. 099	6, 031	. 034
Gross receipts	9, 697, 866	4. 593	11, 262, 430	3. 622	7, 444, 719	2. 800	6, 280, 069	3. 285
Sales	4, 062, 244	1. 924	4, 002, 283	1. 287	4, 114, 075	1. 547	4, 837, 960	2. 531
Special taxes, (licenses)	12, 613, 479	5. 974	18, 038, 098	5. 801	18, 186, 447	6. 84	16, 364, 547	8. 559
Income	20, 740, 451	9. 823	61, 071, 932	19. 643	64, 984, 437	24. 437	40, 412, 037	21. 137
Salaries	2, 826, 333	1. 34	3, 717, 395	1. 195	1, 029, 992	. 387	1, 043, 561	. 546
Legacies and successions	546, 703	. 259	1, 170, 979	. 376	1, 865, 315	. 701	2, 823, 411	1. 477
Articles in schedule A	780, 266	. 370	1, 693, 123	. 544	2, 116, 674	. 796	1, 134, 340	. 593
Passports, &c.	29, 538	. 013	31, 759	. 010	28, 217	. 011	28, 280	. 015
Banks, railroad companies, &c.	13, 579, 594	6. 43	12, 109, 420	3. 90	2, 046, 562	. 770	1, 866, 746	. 976
Penalties, &c.	520, 385	. 25	932, 619	. 30	1, 459, 171	. 549	1, 256, 382	. 658
Sale of stamps	11, 162, 392	5. 287	15, 044, 373	4. 838	16, 094, 718	6. 052	14, 852, 252	7. 768
Special income tax	28, 929, 312	13. 702	....	.....	....	.....	....	.....
Collectors of customs, special treasury agents, &c.	....	.....	2, 184, 342	. 703	64, 262	. 024	....	.....
Aggregate	211, 129, 529	100.	310, 906, 984	100.	265, 920, 474	100.	191, 180, 564	100. 00

APPENDIX B.

LETTER

TO

HON. DAVID A. WELLS,

SPECIAL COMMISSIONER OF REVENUE,

ON THE

CURRENCIES OF GREAT BRITAIN, FRANCE, AND THE UNITED STATES.

BY

GEORGE WALKER,

LATE A BANK COMMISSIONER OF MASSACHUSETTS.

LETTER.

SPRINGFIELD, MASS., *November* 25, 1868.

HON. DAVID A. WELLS,
United States Special Commissioner of Revenue:

SIR: In compliance with your request, I have instituted an examination into the relative volume of the circulating medium of Great Britain, France, and the United States, to determine whether the complaint is well founded, which we have heard so frequently within the last few years, that the circulating medium of the United States, prior to the issue of the legal-tender currency was inadequate, to the business wants of the country, and relatively smaller than that of European nations. If such has been the fact, then the objection to a further contraction of the circulation of the United States is properly urged at the present time; for there will never be a better opportunity to settle the principles on which the currency should stand than now, when the public mind is alive to the question, and every intelligent proposition is likely to receive attention.

CONTRACTION AND EXPANSION.

There are two policies before the country in respect to the circulation: that of *contraction*, which has uniformly been advocated by the Secretary of the Treasury, and which two years ago had the consent of a great majority of Congress; and that of *expansion*, which has had its chief advocates in the western States and in Pennsylvania. Between these lies the expedient of inaction, which has so far prevailed upon Congress, as to put a stop to the contraction of the legal-tender notes, which had proceeded regularly under the direction of the Secretary of the Treasury for several months. Contraction rests upon the idea that the circulation of the country is excessive, and that specie payments can only be reached and maintained by contracting it, until by its scarcity it will exchange at par with gold. The views of the expansionists are well expressed in the following passage from the speech of an advocate of that policy in July last, in the House of Representatives:

> But we are met by the hue and cry of expansion. I am distinctly in favor of expansion. Our currency, as well as everything else, must keep pace with our growth as a nation. My plan is to increase our circulation until it will be commensurate with the increase of our country in every other particular. * * * Expansion is the natural law of currency, and a healthy growth as a nation. * * * *Five times as much postage is paid to-day as was paid ten years ago; consequently five times as much of a circulating medium to transact this little item of business as previously needed.* * * * Reduce the currency—*the means of the people*—and in my opinion you are fast finding the road to universal bankruptcy, from which may be seen leading repudiation. For my part I would issue as many greenbacks as the country can carry; how great that amount may be I will not pretend to say. * * * * *France has a circulation, per capita, of thirty dollars; England, twenty-five; and we, with our extent of territory and improvements, certainly require more than either.*

These passages, selected from different parts of the speech, embody the whole doctrine; they assert that expansion of the circulating medium means wealth—contraction, bankruptcy; that it should keep pace with the growth of business; that the circulation is "*the means of the people;*" and that England and France have more of it than we have, while we, on the contrary, require more than they do. I propose in this letter to consider the facts and the principles embodied in these assertions.

WHAT CIRCULATION INCLUDES—BANK DEPOSITS NOT CIRCULATION.

But before doing so it is necessary to settle what shall be included in the meaning of the word circulation. For the purposes of this inquiry, I consider circulation to mean only gold and silver coin, (or bullion, kept by banks as a part of their reserve,) and bank notes. There are no government notes circulating as money in either England or France, and in the United States there were none prior to the war. This definition of circulation is the popular one, and, I incline to believe, the only one which is strictly accurate. I am aware that it is quite common to treat as a part of the circulation both promissory notes and bills of exchange, and bank deposits. But none of these possess all the essential attributes of money, and they must all be regarded as only inferior instruments of credit. That notes and bills of exchange are not money, is evident from the fact that the delivery of them by the debtor to the creditor does not constitute the payment of a debt, but merely an acknowledgment of it and a promise to pay in future; while, on the contrary, nothing can answer to the word "money" which does not instantly pay the debt for which it is given. A bank note, though only a promise, is nevertheless money in a popular sense; because, if accepted, it discharges a debt precisely as coin would do. It differs from coin in this important particular, that it is not usually a legal tender, and may be refused. No other paper instrument has this capacity of instantaneous payment. A note, or bill of exchange, holds the parties to it till it is paid. A check is not payment until it is cashed by the bank on which it is drawn. Bank deposits, in like manner, lack these essential properties of money; they are not capable of manual delivery, nor of instantaneous liquidation between debtor and creditor. An act of a third party—the bank—is necessary to complete the transaction; and this completion may be delayed indefinitely by a failure of the holder to present the check, or a refusal of the bank to pay it. Deposits come much nearer to monetary circulation than any other instrument of exchange, but they do not perfectly fulfil all its conditions.

Lord Overstone, a very eminent and experienced banker, who is the real author of the existing banking system of Great Britain, (the act of 1844,) in his testimony before the parliamentary committee on banks of issue, in 1840, held that neither deposits nor bills of exchange could properly be included in the circulation. He says:

> Deposit business is a mode of economizing the use of the circulation; by means of resorting to that process, a greater amount of obligations or of transactions can be adjusted with a smaller amount of circulating medium, than could otherwise take place; but an economic use of the circulation is not itself circulation. * * * A less amount of the circulating medium of the country has been sufficient to perform certain functions, in consequence of that economic process of using the money, which arises out of banking deposits. The same thing exists to an enormous extent in the system of the clearing-house; but will any man in his common senses pretend to say, that the total amount of transactions adjusted in the clearing-house is part of the money or circulating medium of the country? The Bank of England, or any other banker, can clearly pay his deposits only to the extent of the banking reserve in his till. The banking reserve in his till is the money with which that business is worked, and constitutes the amount of circulation under his control. It is to mistake the amount of business done for the instrument with which it is done to call deposits circulation. Deposits are the business worked—the reserve in the banking till is the instrument with which they are worked, and the instrument by which your business is worked is the circutation or money of the country.

I think it proper to be thus distinct in excluding bank deposits from the circulation, because it has been very common, in the late discussions in this country, even for financial writers to speak of deposits as if they were a part of the circulation, instead of being, as Lord Overstone clearly shows, one of the economical substitutes for it. To make this a little clearer, let me define what a deposit really is. The first impression might be that it is, as the word literally implies, the money which I have taken to the bank, and left there as my property for safe-keeping. Such deposits there are, but they are known as *special deposits;* the bank makes no use of them, but takes them merely for safe-keeping until they are called for, when they are specifically surrendered to their owner. They cannot be drawn or transferred by check, but only in person or by special order. But general deposits are only entries in account on the bank books, expressing an indebtedness to me for so much money as I have deposited, to be paid on demand—that is, upon my check.* The money which I delivered is no longer my money, but became instantly the property of the bank. I parted with it in exchange for an entry to my credit of its amount, exactly as if I had loaned it on a mortgage. Payment by means of bank deposits is not therefore properly payment, by which a debt is wiped out of existence, but a liquidation, by the substitution of one debt for another. I owed my creditor; the bank owed me. By means of my check, I transfer to my creditor a claim of equal amount against the bank; he then ceases to be my creditor, but becomes the creditor of the bank, and the debt which he held, though I am discharged from it, is not paid, but shifted onto other shoulders, and it never will be paid till money is at last given for it. If deposits were really circulation, they would be capable of paying the whole debt of the bank to its depositors at any moment; but in fact they are not capable of paying any part of it. The special deposit pays itself; but the general deposit can only be paid out of such money as the banker has in his till. So long as all the depositors do not demand their money at once, it is very well; but if all should come to the counter together, the till would be emptied long before the deposits were paid.

Let it not be supposed that I overlook the important bearing which bank deposits have in determining the proper volume of the circulation. They affect the question very nearly, because they are among the simplest and most effective instruments of exchange; and the more they are used, the less need is there of using money. But the ingenious devices by which the use of money is economized are not money itself; they are rather what a French writer (J. E. Horn) denominates "procédés perfectionnés," perfected contrivances.

The eminent French economist, Michel Chevalier, speaks thus of these contrivances:

> Let me repeat, that all these instruments which, together with gold and silver, pass from hand to hand, to liquidate transactions; all those combinations which dispense with the use of any instruments of circulation whatever, among which the bank deposit is the most remarkable, are to be classed together under one precise and simple denomination, that of *credit.* All these contrivances and instruments of credit are *substitutes for money*, and not one of them is money itself; and any attempt to treat them absolutely as money would be attended with the most serious inconvenience. It would be as great a mistake as to confound the portrait with the original, the shadow with the substance.

THE BANK NOTE CIRCULATION OF GREAT BRITAIN, FRANCE, AND THE UNITED STATES.

Confining myself, therefore, to gold and silver coin and bank notes, which is all that is meant by circulation, when it is said that England and France have such and such sums per capita, let me first state the present amount of the *bank note* circulation of Great Britain and France,

* The French do not call them deposits, but "accounts current," which more nearly expresses their character, and does not convey the impression of substantial delivery which is involved in the word "deposit."

and compare it with that of the United States before the war, the period at which it is said we had too little circulation for the business of the country.

The bank note circulation of Great Britain consists of the notes of the Bank of England, and of such private and joint stock banks in the United Kingdom, out of London, as still retain the privilege of issue. No London bank has that privilege. For the four weeks ending August 15, 1868, (the latest return,) the note circulation of the United Kingdom amounted to $196,170,620, which, with a population of 30,000,000, gives $6 54 a head.

In France the only circulation of bank notes is that of the Bank of France, which has a monopoly of issue. On the first day of October, instant, (the latest date,) the circulation of the Bank of France was $251,782,750, or, with a population of 38,000,000, $6 63 a head.

The circulation of the banks of the United States on the first day of January, 1860, was $207,000,000, which, with a free population of 27,500,000, gave $7 52 a head. Thus it will be perceived, that in 1860 the *paper* money of the United States was 15 per centum, per capita, greater than that of England at the present time, and 13 per centum greater than that of France.

But it will be urged that the bank note currency of England and France forms much the smaller part of the whole circulation, and this is true. The smallest denomination of notes in England is of five pounds, or $25; in Scotland of one pound, or $5; and in France of fifty francs, or $10. The petty retail business of both countries must, therefore, be chiefly carried on by gold and silver coin. Very exaggerated notions, however, prevail in this country, and even in Europe, as to the amount of coin actually in circulation. It is necessarily a matter of estimate, as to which the judgments of competent persons will differ widely. All that I can do, therefore, is to present the estimates of those who seem to me to be the most trustworthy authorities.

TOTAL CIRCULATION OF GREAT BRITAIN.

Mr. Goschen, a banker of distinction, and a member of the last liberal ministry, in a recent article in the Edinburgh Review, (January, 1868, "Two per Cent,") states that the estimates of sovereigns circulating in Great Britain vary from 60,000,000 to 100,000,000 sterling ($300,000,000 to $500,000,000.) Dr. Lees, in his ingenious essay on the "Drain of Silver to the East, and the Currency of India," (London, 1863,) estimated the coin in circulation at £80,000,000 or $400,000,000; and he says "it has been estimated by various authorities at 70,000,000, 75,000,000, and even 90,000,000 sterling."

Michel Chevalier, who is hardly behind any Englishman in an accurate knowledge of English statistics, estimated it in 1853 at not more than 60,000,000 sterling, or $300,000,000, and that inclusive of the large mass of bullion then exceptionally held in the vaults of the Bank of England. (*Dictionnaire de l'Economie Politique*, article "*Monnaie.*")

Roswag, the latest and most learned writer on the precious metals, who gives much space to the consideration of the existing metallic circulation of Europe, ("*Les métaux précieux considérés au point de vue économique,*" Paris, 1865,) estimates the gold and silver coin of Great Britain in 1856 at 1,665,000,000 of francs, or $335,000,000.*

* In his speech in the House of Commons, February 11, 1826, the Chancellor of the Exchequer represented the total circulation of notes and coin at £46,000,000, and two years later, August 1828, the same officer represented it at £48,000,000.

As the average of these learned but conflicting authorities I think I am justified in assuming the estimate of Dr. Lees; and I shall accordingly put the metallic circulation of Great Britain at 80,000,000 sterling, or $400,000,000. The total circulation of the United Kingdom, coin and paper, will then stand as follows:

Gold and silver	$400,000,000	
Less in banks, August, 1868	131,000,000	
		$269,000,000
Bank notes, August, 1868		196,000,000
Total circulation		$465,000,000

This, with 30,000,000 of people, gives $15 50 a head. If I were to assume the highest estimate of the metallic circulation which I have seen anywhere given, namely, 100,000,000 sterling or $500,000,000, the amount per head would be $18 83. [See note at conclusion.]

TOTAL CIRCULATION OF FRANCE.

In France, as I have stated, the present bank note circulation is a little less than $252,000,000. This amount is large beyond any former precedent. During the whole of 1864 it averaged only $152,000,000, or $100,000,000 less than at the present time. Mr. Goschen has assigned the true reason for this increase. "Many symptoms," he says, "indicate that the greater part of the increase is due to the substitution of notes for gold." The gold has, in point of fact, been withdrawn from circulation with much greater rapidity than the note circulation has increased. In 1864 the average amount of cash and bullion in the Bank of France was only $50,000,000. It is now (October 1, 1868,) $254,764,350, or $3,000,000 greater than the whole amount of bank notes outstanding. These figures indicate a considerable decline of the circulation in the hands of the public since 1864; the coin withdrawn to the bank having exceeded $200,000,000, while the note circulation has increased only $100,000,000.*

With regard to the metallic circulation of France, the widest diversity of opinion exists among the authorities. The statistics of coinage are admitted, on all hands, to be no guide to a correct estimate, since it is impossible to tell how much has been recoined, carried to other countries, and used in the arts.

Roswag examines the subject with great detail and thoroughness, and arrives at the conclusion that the stock of coined money existing in France in 1865 did not exceed 3,000,000,000 francs, or $600,000,000. He quotes M. H. Bordet, ("*L'or et l'argent en* 1864,") and M. Villiaumé, ("*Nouveau Traité d'Economie Politique*, 3d edition,) as having each arrived at the same estimate in 1864. Michel Chevalier, in his article on money, in the "*Dictionaire de l'Economie Politique*," already quoted, estimated the metallic circulation of France at 2,500,000,000 francs or $500,000,000. This estimate was probably made in 1853, as the first edition of the book was published in that year, but the text stands unaltered in the edition of 1864.

M. Moreau de Jonnès, in a communication to the French academy in

* Such a decline is also rendered probable by the depressed condition of industry in France, which has driven the floating capital from all parts of the empire to Paris, and occasions the present seeming abundance of capital and low rate of interest. (See the first number of the new financial journal, "*Echo de la Bourse*," November 1, 1868.)

1855, (*Journal des Economistes*, November, 1855,) estimated it at 4,000,000,000 francs, *at the outside.*

M. Roswag estimates the amount in 1856 to have been from 4,000,000,000 to 5,000,000,000 francs; but he says there is no doubt that it considerably declined between 1856 and 1865, and he expresses a doubt whether in 1864 it really equalled 3,000,000,000 francs. The reasons which he gives for the decline are the large investments of French capital in foreign undertakings, such as public loans and railways; expenditures in Algeria and other colonies; the construction of the Suez canal; the purchase of foreign products, such as breadstuffs and cotton, and the cost of military expeditions, like those to Syria and Mexico.

M. Hippolyte Passy, formerly finance minister under Louis Phillipe, in his testimony before the banking commission in 1865, expressed the opinion that the ancient hoards of France were being constantly converted into productive property, and this would, of course, reduce the metallic circulation; "although," he says, "the practice of hoarding still prevails to too great an extent in France; the drain made at many points on the old savings has reduced the volume of available resources; and in view of the increasing number of new undertakings, it seems to me that the annual savings of the nation are not now sufficient to meet the wants which they have hitherto been able to satisfy."

I might easily multiply authorities, for the French are prolific writers on this class of subjects; but it seems to me that the conclusions of Roswag, whose work is not only very recent, having appeared in the autumn of 1865, but also far the most learned which has ever been given to the press on the subject of the precious metals, may fairly be accepted as true at the date at which they were made. Since 1864, however, (1865–'66–'67,) the imports of the precious metals into France have exceeded the exports by $266,000,000. How much of this gold and silver merchandise was in the form of coin, or has passed through the mint since its receipt, I have no means of judging. Roswag, however, cautions us against accepting the figures of the custom-house too implicitly, since they are known to give the imports more accurately than the exports, and in estimating the influence on the circulation of previous imports he makes very great abatement from the amount, which they seem to have added. I think the allowance will be sufficiently liberal if I add $100,000,000 to the $600,000,000 estimated by him as the stock of metallic money in France in 1864. The total circulation of France will then stand as follows:

Gold and silver	$700,000,000	
Less in bank October 1, 1868	255,000,000	
		$445,000,000
Bank notes October 1, 1868		252,000,000
Total circulation		$697,000,000

Which, with a population of 38,000,000, gives $18 34 a head.

CIRCULATION OF THE UNITED STATES IN 1860.

With regard to the amount of gold and silver coin in the United States before the war, the popular estimates are wider apart than even in Europe. They vary from $150,000,000 to $700,000,000.

Mr. Washburn, of Indiana, in the speech from which I have quoted, states the total coin in the country in 1861 at $385,000,000. Mr. Garfield, of Ohio, in his speech upon the currency, delivered at about the same time, puts the amount at $200,000,000. From the known habits of our people in the use of money, and their preference for bank notes over coin, I incline to the latter estimate, though it would be more easy to meet the arguments of expansionists as to the inadequacy of our former circulation, if I were to assume a high figure rather than a low one, as it would increase the per capita of the country. I shall, therefore, assume the metallic circulation of the United States in 1860 to have been $200,000,000. The total circulating medium of the United States will then have stood as follows:

Gold and silver	$200,000,000	
Less in banks and treasury	91,000,000	
		$109,000,000
Bank notes		207,000,000
Total circulation		$316,000,000

Which, to the free population of twenty-seven and one-half millions, gave $11 49 a head.

Thus it appears that the total circulating medium of Great Britain is now $15 50 a head, and that of France $18 34 a head; while that of the United States was in 1860, on a specie basis, $11 49 a head, being 74 per cent. of that of Great Britain and 63 per cent. of that of France. The popular estimate, therefore, which gives to Great Britain a circulation of $25 a head, and to France $30, is very wide of the truth.

POPULATION NOT THE MEASURE OF CIRCULATION.

It is, however, not more erroneous than the superstructure of argument which is built on this array of figures. The question is entirely misconceived when the wants of two countries, in respect of a circulating medium, are compared on the basis of population. These wants are not determined by population, for if they were, the savage tribes would come in for an important share of the circulation of the world. Population is an element to be considered, but the question mainly depends on the amount of a nation's wealth, the kind of property which composes it, and the magnitude of its trade. Roswag says:

> The circulation varies in different countries with the importance of their affairs and of their commerce, as well as with the activity of their dealings; the same pieces of money performing a given number of exchanges in a longer or shorter time, according as the nation is more or less active; in this respect England and the United States, for example, exhibit a rapidity of circulation altogether greater than that of France. It varies, also, according to the habits of saving and hoarding.

The people of the United States are essentially a saving people; witness the constant growth of property in the hands of the laboring classes, and especially the vast accumulations in the savings banks—but they are not a hoarding people, for reasons of which I shall speak hereafter. The people of France are, on the contrary, addicted to both saving and hoarding. Chevalier says "there is in France an inveterate love of metallic riches," and Villiaumé says "it is estimated that nearly a quarter part of the precious metals of France is concealed in the hoards of misers." With respect to such hoards Boisguilbert wisely wrote, two centuries ago, that "money at the bottom of a miser's chest is of no more utility than so much stone."

But the French people are beginning to learn the reproductive power of capital, and the importance of interest. Savings banks have had a continual though not very rapid growth among them. At the beginning of 1864, the 467 savings banks in France held deposits to an amount less than $90,000,000, against about $60,000,000 in Massachusetts and $100,000,000 in New York. The habit of hoarding in France, as well as the better knowledge of investment to which it is giving place, are well illustrated by the subscriptions to the public loans. The smallest sums are received, and the court-yards of the ministry of finance in Paris are thronged with applicants in every rank of life, from the richest to the poorest—the latter bearing with them their petty savings.

Last summer a loan of *rente* representing a capital of $90,000,000 was opened for subscriptions. The amount subscribed was for a capital of $3,000,000,000, or thirty-four times the sum desired. It is to this growth of intelligence in the matter of investing money, as well as to the operation of the special causes which I have already stated, that Roswag attributes the decline in the metallic circulation of France. The recent extraordinary exchange of notes for coin by the Bank of France, indicates that the tenacity with which the French people have heretofore held on to a metallic circulation, is fast giving way.

GREAT BRITAIN AND THE UNITED STATES COMPARED.

Let me now state some of the other elements which enter into a comparison of currencies. I will first compare the situation of the United States with that of Great Britain. The wealth of the United States, according to the census of 1860, amounted to $16,000,000,000; the wealth of Great Britain was estimated, in 1858, at $30,000,000,000, exclusive of property in the public funds. Allowing it to have increased since 1860 in the same ratio as before, it cannot now be less than $40,000,000,000, while the wealth of the United States, after five years of exhaustive war, which destroyed property of the value of not less than $5,000,000,000, deprived the country of the productive industry of 1,000,000 men, and manumitted slaves estimated in the last census at nearly $2,000,000,000, cannot now, by the most liberal estimate, be put at a higher figure than $20,000,000,000. If, therefore, the circulating medium were to be in proportion to wealth, Great Britain should have twice as much as the United States. But there is a wide difference, also, in the kinds of property which constitute the wealth of the two countries. Owing to its limited territory and the nature of its land tenure, the proportion of real to personal property in Great Britain is materially less than in this country. By the census of 1860 real stood to personal property, in the United States, in the relation of seven to five. Porter, in his "Progress of the Nation," estimated that in 1845 the property of Great Britain was about equally divided between real and personal. Since that date, the great commercial reforms have been adopted by which the country has not only been vastly enriched, but the preponderance of personal over real property in the national valuation has been fully established. Moreover, the real property of Great Britain is very different from that of the United States. While ours consists very largely of farming lands, of which five-eighths are returned as unimproved, theirs is, to a much greater extent, made up of manufactories, warehouses, docks and other productive property.

This difference in the nature of the property which constitutes the nation's wealth makes the greatest difference in the quantity of circulation necessary to do its business. It is not the ownership, but the exchanging of property which demands the use of money. A millionaire who is out of business, and has his property permanently invested, handles less currency than a thriving retail trader with a capital of

$10,000. Great Britain is eminently a trading country; she buys and sells not only for herself but for all the world. The United States, on the contrary, is not so much a trading as a producing and consuming country. Nearly the whole of our annual product is consumed at home, and a considerable part of it in the neighborhood where it is produced. England is the broker through whom other nations, to a very great extent, carry on their mutual dealings. Nearly all the foreign trade of the United States is done through London. We deal, in this way, with China, India and Australia, with Africa and South America, and to a considerable extent also with the continent of Europe. The United States government keeps but one bankers' account in Europe for its transatlantic disbursements; for its naval, diplomatic, consular and other expenditures; and that account is kept in London. The South American countries do the same. Wherever the traveller goes the trading world over, he finds that English merchants have gone before him, and English ministers or consuls are not slow to follow them. England is jealous of the trade which supports her national life, and she gives to the trading spirit of her sons the amplest national protection. The late exasperating and costly war with Abyssinia grew out of her insatiable desire to control the trade of all nations; even of the savage tribes which stand outside the pale of civilization. It results from this, that a bill on London is the highest type of mercantile exchange. It will pay debts everywhere, and in many countries it is the only instrument of exchange known to commerce.

Acting thus as the universal broker; taking commissions from all the world, London requires to make an infinity of exchanges, and these exchanges, in the last result, demand the use of money. Nowhere else, it is true, is so little money used to do so vast a business; but after all economical substitutes have been exhausted, money alone is the final liquidator.

The exports and imports of Great Britain indicate more strikingly even than her wealth the magnitude of transactions in that country, involving the use of a circulating medium. In 1867 the exports were £181,000,000 sterling, and the imports about £210,000,000; a total of £391,000,000, or $1,955,000,000 in gold. The director of the statistical bureau of the Treasury Department states the exports of the United States for the last fiscal year, on a specie valuation, at $353,000,000, including specie, and the imports at $350,000,000, making a total of $703,000,000, or only 36 per cent. of those of Great Britain.

It may, perhaps, be said that these figures are irrelevant; that foreign commerce does not involve the use of circulation; and that the question relates to domestic trade only. But this is not true. All trade, foreign and domestic, settles its balances in money, and foreign trade requires for that purpose the best sort of money, namely, gold and silver. In all trade the process of set-off is carried as far as it can be, from an instinct of economy, which is stronger than any economic law; but, in the last result, gold is the only thing which pays, for it lies behind even paper money, and gives it all the efficiency which it possesses as a circulating medium. Foreign trade is, moreover, a pretty sure index of domestic trade, of which no corresponding record is kept. It would be impossible to work up a great foreign commerce without an extent and variety of domestic exchanges proportionate to it. This is especially so when the exports consist of manufactured rather than raw products, as is the case in Great Britain.

The greatest absorbent of money is wages, because wages are paid in small sums, at short intervals, to many persons, and none of the instruments of credit are suitable for such payments. Now England, above all countries, certainly far more than ourselves, is a payer of wages. The nature of her industries, the tenure of land, and the social condition of the people, all conduce to this result. Levi, in his late essay on the "Wages and Earnings of the Working Classes," (London, 1867,) estimates the number of actual workers at 11,000,000 out of a population of 30,000,000, and if the families dependent on them are added, at not less than 22,000,000. He states also that, as a general rule, wages are paid weekly, and in cash.

Let me now sum up the facts which I have presented by way of comparing the condition and wants of Great Britain and the United States in respect of a circulating medium. The United States in 1860 (before specie payments were suspended) had a circulation of coin and paper of $11 49 a head; the wealth of the country was then estimated at $16,000,000,000, including slaves now emancipated, and it cannot now exceed $20,000,000,000; and the volume of foreign commerce amounts, at the present time, to $700,000,000 a year in gold. Great Britain has a present circulation of coin and paper of $15 50 a head; her wealth is not less than $40,000,000,000. and the volume of her foreign commerce is $1,950,000,000 a year. If her circulation were based upon wealth, in order to equal ours in 1860, it should amount to $23 50 a head; or, if based upon foreign trade, $32 50 a head. That that country was able to get along with so much less than ourselves in proportion to business, proves that it has learned to carry the process of set-off further than we have, her small territory enabling her to do so with greater ease; but, after making due allowance for the smallness of her territory, and the use of all economical substitutes, I think I shall be able to show, before I conclude, that prior to the war, the people of the United States had a larger circulating medium in proportion to their need of it, than the people of England, and that if we have stood at any disadvantage in our mutual dealings it has been from the over-abundance of our circulation and its poor quality, rather than from the inadequacy of it.

FRANCE.

It is not so easy to institute a comparison with France as with Great Britain. The two countries are very unlike, and there are considerations, political, social, and commercial, which conspire to influence the question of the monetary circulation on one side of the channel, which have little or no force on the other. I have shown that the circulation of France is probably about $18 34 a head, and the fact that it is so much greater than ours, is seized upon by the advocates of an increase of the circulation to prove that ours has hitherto been inadequate. But in presenting this argument, the bearing of national circumstances on the question has been wholly misconceived. It is popularly said, if a slow, sedentary people like the French require so large a circulation, how much more must be needed by a restless, energetic, moving population like our own. But this statement betrays ignorance of the laws which govern the circulation. The active, energetic nations need less, and the slow and sedentary nations more of a circulating medium to do the same business. It is precisely because the French people are so wanting in activity in social exchanges, that they absorb such an enormous and wasteful currency. They are behind the Anglo-Saxon races in commercial usages, and especially slow to adopt those substitutes for money by the use of which England and the United States have simplified and cheapened their business. This fact is both admitted and deplored by the best French writers. M. Horn, in his article on money in the "*Dictionnaire de Politique*," lays great stress upon the wastefulness of the French people in employing so large a mass of the precious metals to do a business which, in other countries, is as well done with a far less sum.

"All competent persons agree," he says, "in pronouncing the vast quantity of the precious metals absorbed by the circulation, as anything but an advantage to the country." This wasteful absorption exists in France "because the country has not yet learned to use that perfected mechanism of the exchanges, (checks, the clearing house, &c.,) which in England serves to keep the circulation down to a certain limit." I might quote Chevalier and many other eminent writers to the same point. All of them recognize the principle that the circulation is so much unproductive wealth, and that the amount of money which a nation employs, should be limited to what is absolutely necessary to make its exchanges without friction; and that to employ more than this is to keep idle a portion of the public wealth, which ought to be productive.

The political state of France has always led to hoarding. In a country where a revolution may at any time overturn the government, and put all visible property in jeopardy, there is a strong motive to put it out of sight and beyond the reach of contingencies.* The political disquietude of Europe has been one of the principal inducements to invest in United States bonds; there might be risk in it, but it was a different risk from that to which home property was exposed. This motive has operated largely in France to induce capitalists to invest their money in foreign enterprises and foreign loans, precisely as it has driven humbler people to hide away their savings in unproductive gold. How this national proclivity is giving way to more enlightened views in respect to the investment of capital, I have shown elsewhere; but it still operates to keep the circulating medium of the country immoderately large.

There is no such tendency as this in the United States. The people themselves govern the country, not by a figure of speech, but actually; their policy is peace, and they have shown in the most significant manner that a revolution is impossible, so that even rebellion is not likely to raise its defiant head again in the lifetime of this generation. The people of this country earn money and save it; and they know how to invest it so as not to lose interest. Real estate, the public funds, loans on mortgages, corporate shares, deposits in savings banks absorb the savings of the people, and prevent them from being locked up in money. They do not perhaps reason about it, but they instinctively know that money in the pocket-book is idle capital, and in a country where all must work for a living, we do not encourage idleness even in money.

The French are a sedentary people; living and dying where they were born; warmly attached to their country, incurious about strangers, rarely emigrating, seldom even travelling at home, and slow to adopt foreign fashions in business. There are very few banks in France. The Bank of France has a monopoly of issue, and this privilege gives it such an advantage, that there are few rivals to contest the field with either the parent institution or its branches. These are required to be established in every department of the empire, but though there are 89 departments, there are as yet but 56 branches; and yet the law has stood for twenty

* M. Rouher, the present prime minister of France, in the discussions of the imperial banking commission, of which he was the president, alluding to the national habit among business men of locking up money in their private tills, suggested whether it was not a habit "which grew out of political recollections, and of apprehensions not yet completely quieted; or to a state of manners which only time, and a long time, could cause to disappear." M. Hippolyte Passy, in the same investigation, attributes the slow growth of banks chiefly to political causes.

years upon the statute-book. Compare the operations of these 56 banks with those of the 1,673 now organized under the national banking law of the United States. Every one of these banks economizes the use of money in many ways. Practically speaking, every man of business in the United States, living in the neighborhood of a bank, keeps a bank account. He has his checks and his check-book for domestic payments, and if he wishes to make remittances to a distance, he gets drafts drawn by his bank on some convenient city correspondent—usually without any charge. He has no occasion, therefore, to use money except for the smallest payments. Large payments either in bank notes or coin have almost ceased in America. Now the case of the Frenchman is entirely different. He still keeps his strong box and his till; and when he makes a considerable payment, it is usually in packages of bank notes or in rouleaux of coin. He must therefore keep a good deal of money by him, and the aggregate of these individual reserves makes the heaviest item in the circulation. Even in great cities, the habit of depositing in bank is by no means general. The mass of Paris shopkeepers, tradesmen and small manufacturers know nothing of bank accounts or checks. One of the questions most earnestly debated in the late monetary discussions in France has been, whether checks and the clearing-house system should be introduced into Paris. I have before me an elaborate pamphlet, published in 1864, showing the nature and value of these institutions, ("*Les Chèques et le Clearing House, par M. P. J. Coullet.*" Paris, 1864.) Very little progress, however, has yet been made in transplanting these peculiarly Anglo-Saxon growths into the soil of France.

The Bank of France, on the first day of October, 1868, held private deposits to the amount of $76,000,000; but these deposits only represent the reserves of the great private bankers, precisely as the $95,000,000 held by the Bank of England, at the same date, represent the reserves of London bankers. None but the richest bankers and merchants keep accounts with either of these national institutions. In England the joint joint stock banks and the private banks and discount houses do the business of the trading community. The magnitude of the deposits belonging to this class in London, may be judged by the figures of the London and Westminster bank, which alone holds more than a hundred millions of dollars of private deposits, or more than half as much as all the corporate banks of the city of New York put together. There are important banks of discount and deposit in Paris, such as the Comptoir d'Escompte, the Crédit Industriel, the Crédit Agricole, the Crédit Foncier, and the Société Générale; but their operations are insignificant when compared with those of the banks of London. Several, perhaps all of them, are restrained by their charters from receiving deposits greater than once and a half their capital.* The London and Westminster holds twenty times its capital. Paris is, nevertheless, in the matter of banking economies, far in advance of the provinces. The 56 branches of the Bank of France held on the 1st of October only $10,000,000 of private deposits. Add to this the deposits of the parent bank, $65,000,000, and the total amount is $75,000,000. The banks of the United States, at the same date, held $602,000,000, of which $195,000,000 was in the city of New York. Thus it appears that France, with a population one-third greater than the United States, holds bank deposits, only one-eighth as large, and yet deposits are only one of several important auxiliaries to the circulation. Bills of exchange, promissory notes, and book accounts are other auxilia-

* M. Wolowski, in an article in the "Journal des Economistes" for October, 1868, says that the aggregate deposits in these institutions in Paris considerably exceed those of the Bank of France.

ries of the same character; whatever, in short, reduces the number and amount of payments, or effects them without the intervention of money, may be so reckoned. Now, of all these auxiliaries, France possesses less than we do. The obstacles thrown in the way of discounting mercantile paper may be cited to establish this position. Neither the Bank of France nor its branches can discount any paper unless it is guaranteed by at least three signatures, or by two signatures with collateral security of a defined and limited character. In the United States, on the contrary, more than two signatures are rarely required, and a great deal of paper is discounted upon a single name.

From all these circumstances it results, that the condition of the French people is so unlike our own, that their example cannot justly be invoked in favor of an expansion of the currency. Yet the circumstances indicated are wholly unlike those which in England justify the use of a larger circulation, per capita, than that of the United States. In England, it is the vast proportions and varied character of her trade, and the magnitude of her movable property, which gives employment to a large circulating medium, after all economical expedients have been exhausted. In France, it is the slow movement of all the exchanges, the indisposition of the people to adopt new methods of doing business, the restrictive character of banking legislation, and the insecurity to property resulting from political disquietude and changes of dynasty, which have conspired to put an undue portion of the national wealth into the unproductive form of money; which have, in short, converted it from a means into an end—from an instrument into an investment. There is no intelligent Frenchman who does not deplore this result, or who doubts that it has sensibly impeded the accumulation of wealth.

Although the excess of the French circulation over our own is mainly to be accounted for by the considerations which I have thus presented, it is no doubt partly due to the greater wealth and commerce of that country. I have not the means of showing, even conjecturally, the aggregate wealth of France, but the wonderful development of the empire, its great works of internal improvement, the varied and extensive operations of the Bourse, and the amount of French money which has gone into foreign investments, prove conclusively that the country is far richer in realized wealth than the United States. The magnitude even of its foreign trade proves the same thing, and yet we have not been accustomed to regard France as a commercial country. The exports and imports of 1867 amounted to $1,445,000,000, while ours were only $708,000,000. Thus the trade of that country would justify a circulation twice as large as ours, if it were as far advanced as we are in the use of substitutes for money, while the circulation is really only 50 per cent. greater without these substitutes.

OTHER EVIDENCE THAT THE CIRCULATION OF THE UNITED STATES HAS NOT BEEN INSUFFICIENT.

I have thus endeavored to show, by a comparison of currencies, and of national condition, that the complaint now so frequently made, that the circulating medium of the United States has in the past been insufficient to do the business of this country on equal terms with Great Britain and France, our most important rivals, is not well founded. But there is other and more conclusive evidence to be found at home. That evidence is, that under a system of bank-note issues, essentially free and unrestricted, the circulation of the country could not be carried above certain limits. The issue being unrestrained, except by the necessity of redeeming the bills in coin, the amount floated was governed by the laws of trade. The highest circulation which the banks ever attained while they continued specie payments, was $215,000,000, in 1857; but that figure was only arrived at by an excessive expansion of credits, which culminated in the crisis of that year. For several years prior to 1857, the banks had pushed their discounts to a dangerous point, for the sake of securing circulation. Loans were made in bank bills to distant customers, especially at the west; to railroad and other corporations, to contractors, and to banks, with a distinct agreement that the bills should be kept in circulation till the paper matured. The bills were marked, and as fast as they returned to the bank, they were sent back to the borrowers at their expense. In other cases the agreement was that the bills should be locked up in the safe of a borrowing bank, to constitute the reserve of eastern exchange, which was required to be kept by the laws of some of the western States. So extensive had these practices become, that Massachusetts passed a law to restrain them, and it now stands upon the statute-book in these words:

A bank which loans or issues any of its notes or bills, with an agreement or understanding that such notes or bills shall not be put into immediate unrestricted circulation, or that they shall not be returned to the bank within a limited time, shall forfeit a sum not exceeding one-half nor less than one-fourth part of the amount so loaned or issued. (General Laws of Massachusetts. Revision of 1859.)

Nobody now questions the irregularity and dangerous character of such loans. They were made for the sole purpose of stimulating the circulation, and in a spirit of resistance to those natural laws which govern its ebb and flow when left to itself. Although the crisis of 1857 cannot fairly be said to have been caused by this action of the banks, since, like all crises, it is referable to causes quite independent of any bank management, it was no doubt aggravated by it. A crisis is generally owing to the undue locking up of capital in enterprises which give no present return, thus gradually cutting off the supply necessary to regular business. Bank capital in this country is the principal aliment of trade, and if banks lend it in such a manner that it becomes locked up in fixed and unproductive property, they do much to promote commercial disturbances. After a while, these loans accumulate to such a degree as first to cramp, and finally to stop all legitimate business. The history of the last crisis in England is full of illustrations of this kind of banking; and so it was in America in 1857.

I claim, therefore, that the $215,000,000 of bank circulation in 1857 was in excess of the legitimate wants of the country at that time, *and yet it was far less than the banks had authority to issue.* In Massachusetts, which in this respect fairly represents the New England States, banks were allowed to circulate bills up to the amount of their capital, but the circulation never came near to that limit. In July, 1857, with a capital of $60,000,000, they maintained a circulation of only $24,000,000. In New York there was no restriction on the amount of circulation. Each bank could issue as many bills as it could secure at the banking department. Practically, therefore, it depended on the means of the banks to pledge securities and the demand of the public for bills. Yet in 1857, with a capital of $96,000,000, the circulation of the New York banks was only $34,000,000.

In the whole United States, the bank capital was $371,000,000, while the total circulation was $215,000,000. The circulation of the country was, in short, far within its statute limits, and this can only be attributed to the absence of a demand for more. The banks had the strongest motive to issue all that the public would take, and I have shown that this motive operated to lead them into a very hazardous business. The conditions on which they were allowed to issue it were always profitable, far more so than under the present national system. All they needed to have was the ability to put up the requisite securities, (when securities were required, and in many States they were not required,) to keep the necessary reserves of specie, (which were very small,) and to redeem the bills when presented. Is there any intelligent financier who would allow them to circulate more bills than they could thus secure, protect, and redeem? If there is, I cannot argue with him, for we should differ radically as to the principles on which a mixed currency rests.

WEALTH INCREASES FASTER THAN CIRCULATION.

It is popularly supposed that the circulation of a country keeps pace with the growth of its wealth. This is a mistake. There is, on the contrary, a steady retardation in the growth of the circulation, as compared with the increase of wealth and business. This is due to the increase of deposits, and other economising substitutes for money, and to the increased rapidity of movement which the circulation itself is constantly acquiring. Not merely by deposits, the clearing-house, and other banking agencies, but by the railroad, the express, the telegraph, and cheap postage, has the necessary amount of the circulation been reduced. Wherever society is most advanced in wealth and in the instrumentalities of exchange, this retardation shows itself most plainly. Thus circulation increases less rapidly in England than in the United States, and in the eastern States than in the west. The total bank-note circulation of the United Kingdom in November, 1844, was $198,352,985. In August, 1868, it was, as I have shown, only $196,000,000, a decline of $2,000,000 in 24 years. The highest point which it has touched in this period did not exceed $210,000,000. Yet in that period, the wealth of Great Britain has doubled, and the volume of domestic and foreign commerce has more than trebled. In the last debate in the House of Commons on the currency, (August, 1866,) it was asserted by the most experienced bankers, that notwithstanding the vast increase of trade, it took no more money (not capital) to operate it than in 1844.*

The same law governing the circulation is recognized in France. I have cited the opinion of Roswag, that the metallic circulation has probably declined since 1856. Chevalier says "although it is true that as society is developed the quantity of money which it uses increases for a certain time, it is not less true that there comes a time when the necessity for increasing the volume of money is no longer felt, and when, on the contrary, the industrial machinery becomes so perfected, as to perform the same quantity of transactions with a smaller quantity of money."

The same tendency which prevails in the world of mechanics, to get greater results out of inferior forces, extends to every other movement of society.

The slow growth of the circulation in some of the United States, is only less remarkable than its stationary position in England. In Massachusetts, from 1850 to 1860, the bank-note circulation increased only 22½ per cent., while bank capital increased 74 per cent. In the same period population increased 24 per cent., and property, by the census valuation, 42 per cent. In New York, during the same decade, the increase of circulation was only 15 per cent., against an increase in bank capital of 101 per cent., of population of 25 per cent., and of property of 71 per cent.

* In 1828, when the ministry represented the total circulation of notes and coin at £48,000,000 or $240,000,000, the exports and imports were only $440,000,000, or less than a quarter of their present amount.

The circulation of all the banks of the United States in 1837 was $149,000,000; in 1861 it was $202,000,000, an increase of 35½ per cent. Now compare this with the growth of wealth and population in the somewhat shorter period from 1840 to 1860. In 1840 the population of the United States was 17,000,000, in 1860 it was 31,000,000, an increase of 82 per cent. The census valuation of property in 1840 was $3,764,000,000; in 1860 it was $16,159,000,000, an increase of 329 per cent. When the more rapid growth of property in the United States is considered, together with its wide territory, and the imperfect machinery and slower movement of the exchanges, this inconsiderable growth of the circulation is even more remarkable, than that it should have remained stationary in Great Britain.

DISTINCTION BETWEEN MONEY AND CAPITAL.

It will probably be said, in reply to the foregoing suggestions, that it is for the new States, and not for the old ones that more currency is needed; that those sections of the country do not enjoy the same facilities for exchange as the eastern and middle States, and therefore require more circulation to do their business. But the great want of the west, as of all new countries, is not circulation, but capital; and it is a great mistake to suppose that without capital it can have money. And this leads me to consider the real nature and office of money, as distinguished from capital. It is from a misconception on this point, that most of the prevailing errors respecting the currency have arisen. *I define money to be a part of the wealth of the world, expressed in a coinage of the precious metals, which is withdrawn from reproductive uses for the purpose of measuring and exchanging the rest.**

If it were not for this necessity of constant measuring and exchanging, it would obviously be better if all the wealth of the world could be devoted to reproductive purposes. If money was not necessary for measuring and exchanging property, less labor would be spent in the mining of gold and silver, and more devoted to other services valuable to society. So in the social economy, a part of the men and women are employed in waiting on the rest and supplying their material wants, in order that they may not be diverted from more profitable occupation, by the necessity of each person waiting on himself. If there were no human necessities of the workers to be ministered to, the class of workers might be measurably increased.

It is just so with money in its relation to capital; it is its servant; it attends constantly upon it, fetches and carries for it, and sometimes, of necessity, stands idle, waiting for the bidding of its master. When the question of service is one of economy, and not of luxury, no more servants are employed than are necessary to save the more valuable time of the master. Now the use of money, as distinguished from other capital, is strictly a question of economy, and in a healthy state of society no more real money will ever be employed, than is necessary to give vitality and movement to the rest of its wealth. Money is a vehicle which performs a part of the social exchanges. It is of one family with the steamboat, the railroad, the express, the telegraph, the post-office. All of these are merely instruments of exchange, and not of production. If wealth could be increased by production only, without exchange, all these useful public servants would fall into the category of expensive

* M. Wolowski says of gold and silver, that they are "only vehicles for real productive capital, of which they immobilize the portion consecrated to the office of money, and destined to serve as a leaven to animate the rest of the mass." (See *Journal des Economistes*, October, 1863.)

luxuries. Every excess of them now is a burden to society. Two steamboats running where one can amply accommodate the travel, two railroads built side by side competing for the freight which one can carry, do not both increase the public wealth, for the support of one of them is a tax which the community must pay.

It is plainly a mistake, therefore, to suppose that a nation's wealth is to be measured by its money, that money alone or chiefly enriches it, or that it can ever have money at all except as an incident to capital. France is not richer, but poorer, for using so much more money than other nations to do the same business. If a manufacturer of clothing were to employ five women to do the work of one sewing machine, we should call him a bad economist; and precisely in this sense is France a bad economist, for refusing to avail herself of economies in exchange as manifest, as the superiority of the sewing machine is to the manual dexterity of the woman. In the order of civilization there must be first property, and then money, just as there must be passengers before coaches can be employed. It is equally a law of public economy that there should be no more money in existence, than is needed to exchange the property and services of a people with ample convenience, and yet with the smallest friction.

If the money of this country were wholly of gold and silver, I do not suppose any one would be found to controvert these propositions; but unfortunately the money of the United States is almost wholly paper money, and at all times it has consisted much more largely of paper than of coin. Because paper money can be increased at will, and almost without expense, it is supposed that it is not subject to the same laws as real money; but that certain valuable properties inhere in it, which are peculiar to itself. Now, paper money has two independent properties: it is an instrument of credit promising to pay money, just like any other promissory note, and in this aspect it is a useful agent, especially as it is transferable without endorsement; it is also a representative of real money lying behind it. Its only title to be called *money* is derived from the latter property. If money is wealth, then it is so because it is the product of labor, for no wealth can be produced without labor; and the value of a thing in exchange is measured by the labor that it has cost. It needs no argument to show that paper money, whether it be bank-notes issued by corporations or legal-tender notes issued by the government, will not stand the test of this definition, since it costs no more to print a note for a thousand dollars than for one dollar. We call it money, because it promises to pay money instantly on demand, and it assumes to be the representative of an exact sum which is waiting to be demanded, to fulfil the promise. But the assumption is groundless; there is no such sum of money waiting to redeem it; generally there is only a pitiful fraction of it. Paper money is not, therefore, wealth of itself, nor the representative of money, except so far as money lies behind it in the hands of the issuer of the bills, waiting to redeem them. Beyond this amount it is merely circulating credit. Most civilized nations have agreed in using this circulating credit in place of money, from the supposed economy of so doing. It is admitted not to possess all the properties of money, but its lack of them has been supposed to be less injurious to society than the idleness of an equal amount of capital locked up in coin. More and more doubt, however, is coming to be cast upon this theory, as is shown by the universal demand which is now made, that some proportion of coin shall be held by the issuers of bank-notes to protect their redemption. After the crisis of 1857, there was, in nearly all the States, a call for legislation in that direction. The treasury report upon the "Condition of the banks throughout the United States," at the beginning of 1858, is full of evidence that the bank currency of that period was vicious from the excess of its credit element; there was too little gold behind it, and it broke down the moment the strain upon it became serious. A circulation based upon a specie reserve is certainly stronger and better than one without such a basis; for the tendency to over issue is limited by the necessity of keeping the reserve; but there are occasions when such a currency is an engine of tremendous power for evil. Take the present national bank law, which requires a certain reserve of specie and legal-tender notes in proportion to deposits and circulation, and prohibits discounting whenever the reserve is not maintained. The locking up of a few millions of legal-tenders by speculators for a fall of stocks, acts with four-fold intensity upon the money market, where every dollar of the United States notes represents a credit currency of four dollars in deposits and notes of the national banks. One dollar drawn from the bank reserve practically withdraws four dollars from the loan fund of the locality. The banks cannot suddenly retire their notes, and they may not at once lose their deposits, so that the loss of their reserve compels them to stop discounting. This is what is actually taking place in New York as I am writing. It would be the same in principle, though a lock-up would be less manageable in practice, if we were on a specie basis, with a bank reserve of coin instead of United States notes. A sudden drain of gold for export, or a speculative locking-up of it, would act upon the loan market precisely as we are now witnessing. The reason is, that our laws permit a four-fold superstructure of pretended money to be raised upon a narrow basis of real money, and at the same time give to every man the right to take his pay out of the base, by making that alone the legal tender. If too many persons attack the base at once, it is not strange that the fabric of credit raised upon it topples to the ground.

But the locking up of gold could not be permanent. It would last only long enough to draw gold from other countries, or other sections of our own country; while on the other hand a strictly local currency of no intrinsic value, like United States notes, is a mere commodity like wheat or cotton, which may at any time be monopolized or locked up, and the lock-up will continue as long as the holders have the inclination and ability to do it. It differs, however, from all other commodities, in the fact that a speculation in it affects equally all other kinds of property, of which, in its character of money, it is the measuring and exchanging power. While the lock-up lasts it is a contraction of the currency, as absolute as if the bills were destroyed and never to be replaced. But it has the painfulness of contraction without its ultimate advantage. It causes a fall of prices which, as they are unnaturally high, is not a public evil, though it may occasion private losses. But as the contraction is only temporary, the fall of prices is temporary also. The bills locked up remain to menace the market, and to be let out as soon as the objects ot the speculation have been accomplished. Thus all values are unsettled, and no business can be undertaken safely.

On the 24th of October the banks of New York held $56,000,000 in legal-tender notes. On the 31st they held only $51,000,000, a loss of $5,000,000. On the 7th of November they held only $47,000,000, a loss of $9,000,000 in 14 days. The lock-up is said to have been really much greater than appears by the weekly statements, and to have equalled at one time $15,000,000. On the 5th of November United States bonds fell 3 to 4 per cent. below the quotations of the previous day, and within a week there was a decline in railway shares ranging from 5 to

35 per cent., the very soundest properties sharing the decline. I make no mention of the fluctuations in Erie railway stock, for which there were special disgraceful causes, desiring only to record the effects of currency speculations on the general market.

Witness now the other side of the picture. On the 14th of November the bank statement showed a return to the circulation of upward of $4,000,000, and on the 21st of $12,000,000 more, making a total increase of $16,000,000 in two weeks. Fluctuations like these, occurring at the time of a close money market, have brought fearful losses to innocent people, and they have given a rude shock to public confidence. People who have refused to see it before begin now to see that speculation thrives upon the debased quality of our artificial money, and that while we continue to use it no remedy for the abuse is possible, either by legislation or commercial restrictions. They cry loudly, therefore, for a return to specie payments, believing that any temporary suffering from a decline of prices is preferable to the continual danger and anxiety to which all business is now subject.

It may be thought that we should escape the difficulties incident to the maintenance of a reserve by letting the government issue all the notes, and taking away from the banks the privilege of circulation. But this would make no difference; practically the government issues all the notes now; the banks are only the agents for putting them into circulation, and the obligations imposed on them to redeem and protect them by proper reserves would revert to the government if they assumed to issue the notes without intervention. Could Mr. Spinner, at Washington, or Mr. Van Dyck, at New York, redeem the national bank issues, any better than the banks themselves, without keeping an adequate reserve to do it with? Certainly not. The danger of sudden contraction is incident to every credit circulation, redeemable in coin or its supposed equivalent, and so long as the redemption fund remains so small as compared with the amount having a right to be redeemed it will continue to be of a very serious character.

The cost of a metallic currency is easily calculated. It cannot exceed the average profit on so much capital productively invested. Suppose that this country could now maintain on a specie basis a note circulation —of the government or the banks, or both—of $300,000,000, (and I do not believe it possible to circulate more on such a basis,) what is the estimated saving to the country? In the first place, the coin reserve on this sum ought not to be less than one-third. There would remain, then, $200,000,000 at seven per cent. The saving realized by not putting so much capital into gold coin would be $14,000,000. Now the estimated wealth of this country is $20,000,000,000; the national revenue is $350,000,000, and the annual surplus out of which taxes are paid must considerably exceed the revenue. What, then, must be the volume of the exchanges incident to the creation of so much new wealth, and for the service of which the circulation is maintained? A loss of $14,000,000 to the production of the country would be many times repaid in the use of a currency by the slightest shade better than any other, so vast is the volume of transactions to be affected by it. On the other hand, who will attempt to measure the friction and loss entailed upon the country by the use of the best substitute for metallic money which we have hitherto been able to maintain? How much will the present lock-up of legal-tender notes in New York cost the country? Perhaps you will reply, Nothing; as somebody gains what others lose. But is it any satisfaction to the honest traveller, who has been robbed upon the highway, to be told that the country is no poorer for the robbery, since the thief has got his money? The highways of business should be safe against highwaymen, and it is the duty of government, as far as possible, to make them so. It is in times of commercial panic resulting from reckless speculation that the weakness of a paper currency becomes most apparent, but it is inherent in it always, and the friction with which it works is a heavy tax on business.

But if bank notes and United States notes are really money, as they are popularly claimed to be, then they must be subject to the laws of money. Their power is a delegated and representative power, and it cannot exceed that of their principal—coin. The same laws which regulate the supply and demand of real money must, therefore, govern paper money; and they will do so, unless artificially meddled with; and all such meddling serves only to destroy the monetary character of notes, and to render them unfit to perform their assumed office.

If the people of the west, therefore, would have more circulation they must begin by getting more wealth; and one evidence of that wealth will be the growth among them of moneyed institutions; for the trade in money comes last among the modes of employing capital, and can only spring up in communities which have an excess of capital waiting for profitable investment. In new countries there is no such excess. The first settlers of a country are always poor, for there is no motive to rich men to undergo the hardships of a pioneer life. In our western country the abundance and cheapness of land make the profits on capital very large—so much above the rate of interest, that there is no inducement to put capital into banking. Precisely for the reason that the old countries of Europe can afford to take our public debt at a lower rate of interest than we can, so the eastern States can afford to furnish loanable capital to the west cheaper than western capitalists can do. If the west is left free to furnish its own circulating medium, it will keep no more capital in this form, than is absolutely necessary to its business; and it is precisely the same while the currency is supplied by the government, or by eastern banks. In any case it is not furnished gratuitously; it has got to be paid for by the section which uses it out of its own earnings. It may, of course, be borrowed, like any other capital; but in that case other property has to be pledged for security, and the result is the same. As it is impossible to determine empirically when a country is rich enough in floating capital to furnish banks for itself, the system of banking should be eventually free; but this cannot take place so long as the bills to be issued are not redeemable in specie. With proper regulations as to the redemptions and the reserve, the obligation to redeem in coin will restrain the tendency to excessive issues within such limits of safety, as a mixed currency is capable of affording.

It is preposterous to talk about the currency being the "*means of the people*," if by that is meant, as I suppose, the wealth of the poor majority in contradistinction to the capital of the rich minority. Money has precisely the same properties in one man's hands as another's—gold money or paper money; and inasmuch as it is always unproductive capital, the last person who can afford to hold it is the poor man who has no margin. To the rich the loss of interest may not be important; but to the poor, all that is earned beyond necessary living should seek instant and safe investment; and this will always be done in the most civilized communities.

RESUMPTION OF SPECIE PAYMENTS.

I am not to be understood in what I have written as advocating any sudden change from the mixed currency of coin and paper which has hitherto formed our national circulation, to one of coin only. If I am right in believing that the truest economy would consist in using only the precious metals, (with some form of circulating paper, like gold notes, for convenience of handling and transmission,) the time for making so considerable a change in the habits of the country is not yet come. Any such change must be gradual, and it must be made with due regard to rooted opinions, as well as vested interests. We have a good way yet to travel before we get back to specie payments; and still another stage to arrive at the more solid ground occupied by European nations. When we have reached that point we can take counsel together, and see if the time has not come for trading at home as we always trade with other nations, on the basis of real money.

To get back to specie payments is the first object, and I know no other way of doing it than by the way once attempted and afterwards suspended, namely, by the painful process of contraction. It is useless to talk of growing up to the dimensions of the present circulation. Taking bank notes, legal-tenders and fractional currency together, the outstanding amount in the hands of the people is in the neighborhood of $585,000,000. In the face of all past experience of this and other countries, what possible justification can there be for such an increase of paper money over the figures of 1860? If left to the operation of natural laws, would the circulation have attained any such limits? Most certainly it would not; and the moment the touchstone of specie redemptions is applied to it, the volume of paper money will shrink to its natural proportions. To wait till we need so much circulating money would be to wait for years—an indefinite period; on the other hand, to force a resumption of specie payments with so much paper afloat, would cause such a sudden fall of prices as would inevitably lead to a crisis, and involve the ruin of many innocent persons. The only method left is to contract the circulation preparatory to redeeming it, to require beforehand a certain accumulation of specie in the banks, and I incline to believe also, to make the redemption partial to begin with. This might be done by redeeming at first only notes of certain dates or denominations, or by redeeming in gold, estimated at a higher price then par, as was done in England in 1820.

Contraction is not an agreeable process, for it involves a fall of prices; and as such a fall is never equal, some property and some people will suffer more than others. But so it was in the war, when the unavoidable losses and burdens to the nation were most unequally distributed among individuals. The restoration of a sound currency is one of the duties resulting from the war; it is a tax we have got to pay, and it cannot be adjusted with exact equality. The burden of contraction cannot, however, at its worst, fall as unequally upon the people as the burden of a depreciated currency. With a depreciated money and a fluctuating standard of value, the condition of industry can never be healthy. Values are all unsettled, and the fluctuations sudden and violent; both labor and capital have irregular employment, and there is a feverish habit imparted to all industries. So inseparable are these incidents from a depreciated currency, that if the national debt could be paid off to-morrow by an issue of legal-tender notes, and there were no considerations of good faith or national integrity involved in the question, it would be a most disastrous measure to the country, crippling its business to a degree far more burdensome, in the present and in the future, than honest payment, according to the intention of the contract. If there is to be any repudiation let it be by a square refusal to pay the bonds, principal and interest, as well as the notes, to be followed by a repeal of the legal-tender act. Large numbers of people would doubtless be ruined, and the national credit destroyed; but not more surely than by the greenback method of repudiation, which adds the vice of hypocrisy to the crime of dishonesty; while, on the other hand, the private business of the country, after the first violent shock, would be gradually resumed on a solid basis.

The heaviest burden of depreciated money falls upon the poor. As you have shown in your annual reports, and as all the evidence still goes to demonstrate, the laboring man is the heaviest tax-payer under our existing currency system. All the elements of his living have risen fully 20 per cent. above the rise in his wages. What capitalist has to suffer so severely as this? And it is not to be forgotten that the capitalist, because he is a capitalist, pays his taxes out of his abundance—the laborer out of his living. It is one of the worst features of a debased money that it widens the space between the rich and the poor; to those that have it gives more, and to those that have not it takes away even what they have.

I am, very respectfully, your obedient servant,

GEORGE WALKER.

NOTE.—Since the foregoing letter was issued from the press I have seen in the London Economist, of December 12, 1868, the statement of an estimate of the circulating medium of Great Britain recently made by Professor Stanley Jevons to the Statistical Society, which is considerably higher than my own. The method pursued by Professor Jevons in prosecuting his inquiry is a novel and ingenious one, and the high reputation of the author as a statistician entitles his conclusions to great respect. He estimates the gold currency alone at £80,000,000, the silver at £14,000,000, and the copper at £1,000,000, besides the bullion in bank, which he estimates at £15,000,000; making a total of £110,000,000, of which £89,000,000 are supposed to be in circulation and the rest in bank. The editor of the Economist considers the estimate of £80,000,000 for gold coin "a maximum figure," and probably beyond the truth. Professor Jevons puts the total circulation of coin and paper at £134,000,000; from which there should be deducted about £9,000,000 as the average amount of notes in the banking department of the Bank of England; leaving £125,000,000 sterling, or $625,000,000, in circulation. This would give $20 83 a head to a population of 30,000,000.

In assuming, on the authority stated, the sum of £80,000,000 as a probable figure of the metallic circulation, I supposed it to include the coin and bullion in bank, as has usually been done in estimating the amount of the precious metals in this country, and I was confirmed in that impression from the fact that Chevalier, in the passage quoted on page 6, makes his estimate of £60,000,000 to include "the enormous sum which lies to-day, exceptionally, in the vaults of the Bank of England."

Roswag, also, in his estimates of the French coinage, includes both that "*in circulation and in stock;*" and in arriving at the amount added by commerce, he includes in the importations bullion as well as coin. I can see no reason to doubt, therefore, that in his estimate of 3,000,000,000 francs ($600,000,000) for France, he includes all either "in circulation or in stock" which had been dedicated to the office of money; and this would include the coin and bullion in bank as well as in circulation.

In further examining Roswag's treatise I find an estimate of the metallic stock of England much lower than that given from his work on page 7. Comparing the increase derived from commerce—1858 to 1863—in the two countries, he finds that France gained three times as much as England; from which he reasons that the "monetary stock of France must be triple that of England," which would reduce the stock of Great Britain to 40,000,000 sterling, or $200,000,000.

It will be seen, therefore, that in striving to arrive at a just estimate on this difficult subject of the stock of the precious metals used as money in Great Britain, I have avoided both extremes of opinion; and that I seem to be considerably above the most learned and scientific of modern writers on the subject.

My only desire has been to arrive at the true fact, as nearly as it is possible to do so, and, from the facts established, to draw the proper deductions. In this spirit I have hastened to lay before the readers of my letter the later estimate of Professor Jevons, which lies midway between my own and the popular estimates already quoted. I find nothing in it to impugn the correctness of my general conclusion, that the circulation of the United States—coin and paper—was not inadequate to the wants of the country before the war, and that the amount now in use is, therefore, excessive.

APPENDIX C.

A statement of the indebtedness of the several States; before the war, (1861;) at its close, (1865;) and at the present time, (December, 1868.)

The following summary exhibits the financial condition of the several States immediately before and after the war, and at the close of the year 1868:

From official sources.

MAINE.

State debt December 31, 1860	$699,500 00
State debt December 31, 1865	5,164,500 00
State debt December 31, 1868	5,053,500 00
Showing a reduction in three years of 21.49 per cent., or	111,000 00
Amount of reduction in 1868 of 7.26 per cent., or	37,000 00

NEW HAMPSHIRE.

State debt June 1, 1861	$31,668 93
State debt June 1, 1866	4,002,070 13
State debt June 1, 1868	3,487,412 00
Showing a reduction in two years of 12.86 per cent., or	514,658 00
And a reduction in 1868 of 6.94 per cent., or	260,364 00

VERMONT.

State debt 1860–'61	None.
State debt 1865	$1,650,000 00
State debt November 1, 1868	1,168,000 00
Showing a reduction in three years of 29.21 per cent., or	482,000 00
And in 1868, 16.27 per cent. or	227,000 00

MASSACHUSETTS.

The debt of this State in 1861 consisted mainly of scrip issued to railroad corporations, and amply secured by bonds and mortgages paying interest. In addition, the State at that time possessed securities and property exceeding by more than one million of dollars in value all other obligations. Massachusetts, therefore, in 1861, had substantially no indebtedness.

The following table exhibits the apparent debt and resources of Massachusetts at the specified periods:

Date.	Aggregate debt.	Resources.	Debt unprovided for.
January 1, 1861	$7,132,627 56	$8,273,055 83	None.
January 1, 1866	23,047,873 36	14,793,008 65	$8,254,864 71
January 1, 1867	25,520,095 92	14,427,586 24	11,092,509 68
November 1, 1867	27,638,918 29	16,926,587 92	10,712,330 37
November 1, 1868	27,553,935 05	13,685,262 82	13,868,672 23

RHODE ISLAND.

State debt in 1860–'61	None.
State debt in 1865	$4,000,000 00
State debt in November, 1868	3,140,500 00
Showing a reduction in three years of 21.23 per cent., or	859,500 00
And a reduction for the year 1868 of 13.69 per cent., or	498,500 00

CONNECTICUT.

State debt in 1860–'61	None.
State debt in July, 1865	$10,400,000 00
State debt December 1, 1868	8,135,500 00
Showing a reduction in three years of 21.77 per cent., or	2,264,500 00
And in the year 1868, 3.46 per cent., or	286,900 00

NEW YORK.

The following table shows the amount and character of the debt of this State at the periods specified:

	Sept. 30, 1860.	Sept. 30, 1865.	Sept. 30, 1867.
Canal debt	$27,107,321 48	$19,424,585 49	$15,733,060 00
General fund debt	6,505,654 37	6,050,954 37	5,642,622 22
Contingent debt	570,000 00	224,000 00	130,000 00
Bounty debt	....	23,989,000 00	26,862,000 00
Total	34,182,975 85	49,688,539 86	48,367,682 22
Total debt September 30, 1868			44,968,786 40
Showing a reduction in the year of			3,398,895 82

Deducting the unapplied balances of the sinking funds in the treasury, the aggregate debt is reduced to $38,864,448 74.

NEW JERSEY.

State debt December 30, 1860	$104,000 00
State debt November 30, 1865	3,018,800 00
State debt November 30, 1868	2,219,697 30
Reduction in three years 26.47 per cent., or	799,102 70

PENNSYLVANIA.

The debt of this State on the 30th of November, 1860, was	$37,964,602 02
Which, during the first year of the war, increased to	40,575,420 60
This amount, gradually reduced, was—	
April, 1865	39,368,044 49
November 30, 1867	34,776,431 22
November 30, 1868	32,799,786 34
Showing a reduction in one year of 5.65 per cent., or	1,966,644 88

DELAWARE.

This State, which had no debt in 1860, reports an aggregate indebtedness in December, 1867, of	$1,242,000 00
State debt December, 1868, above investments	605,850 00

MARYLAND.

State debt September, 1867	$10,891,802 00
State debt September, 1868	(*)

Against this indebtedness, the State is reported to hold productive property to the extent of $8,059,487, and a sinking fund of $1,529,379—the two nearly covering the entire amount of the State debt.

OHIO.

State debt November 15, 1860	$14,250,173 00
State debt November 15, 1865	13,060,582 00
State debt November 15, 1868	10,529,675 43
Reduction in three years 19.37 per cent., or	2,530,906 57
Reduction in 1868, 4.55 per cent., or	502,271 57

INDIANA.

State debt October 31, 1861	$7,770,233 55
State debt October 31, 1864	8,687,960 55
State debt October 31, 1868	3,101,587 33
Reduction in four years 64.30 per cent., or	5,586,373 22
Reduction in 1868 22.92 per cent., or	922,234 00

MICHIGAN.

State debt January 1, 1861	$2,388,842 79
State debt November 30, 1866	3,979,921 25
State debt November 30, 1868	3,651,078 49
Reduction in two years 8.26 per cent., or	328,842 76
Reduction in 1868 6.45 per cent., or	250,164 21

ILLINOIS.

State debt November 30, 1860	$10,277,161 36
State debt December 16, 1864	11,178,564 45
State debt December 1, 1866	8,645,343 02
State debt October 15, 1868	5,988,453 53
Reduction in two years 30.73 per cent., or	2,656,889 49

* The amount of the debts of this State in 1868, although promised, has not yet been received, December 31, 1868.

WISCONSIN.

State debt January 1, 1861	$100,000
State debt December 31, 1865	2,692,467
State debt November, 1868	2,252,000
Reduction in three years 16.21 per cent., or	440,467

Of the remaining debt the greater portion is held by the school fund of the State.

MINNESOTA.

The debt of this State in 1860 was $250,000; and in 1866, $350,000; which last amount was increased in 1867 by the contraction of a loan of $100,000 for the purpose of erecting public buildings. This aggregate of $450,000 was reduced in 1867 to $325,000, through the redemption of $125,000 by the State sinking fund.

State debt November, 1868	$300,000

IOWA.

State debt in 1860	$200,000
State debt in 1865	500,000
State debt December 31, 1868	300,000
Reduction in three years 40 per cent., or	200,000

MISSOURI.

State debt in 1860	$24,734,000
State debt in January, 1865	37,000,000
State debt December 31, 1867	26,000,000
State debt October 1, 1868	20,557,000
Reduction in four years 44.44 per cent., or	16,443,000

Deducting bonds loaned to Hannibal & St. Joseph railroad, $3,000,000, the aggregate State debt is reduced to $17,557,000.

KENTUCKY.

State debt October 10, 1861	$4,729,234
State debt October 10, 1865	5,254,346
State debt October 10, 1868	3,619,191
Reduction in 1868 21.51 per cent., or	992,008

KANSAS.

This State had a debt in 1860 of $150,000; in 1865, of $452,975; and in 1867, of $819,975. In addition to this the legislature of 1867 made provisions for the payment of claims arising from the Price raid, and the Indian expedition of 1864, amounting to about $300,000. The State debt November, 1868, less treasury resources, was $974,882,42.

NEBRASKA.

This State had a debt of about $28,000 on October 31, 1868; but as the cash then in the treasury amounted to $67,810, a considerable surplus remained.

CALIFORNIA.

State debt in 1864, $5,290,640; expended since then for war and other extraordinary purposes, $2,807,363; total funded debt December 2, 1867, $5,126,500.

State debt December 1, 1868	$4, 695, 500
Reduction in one year 8.4 per cent., or	431, 000

GEORGIA.

State debt in 1860	*$2, 670, 750
State debt in 1867	6, 000, 000

The treasurer reports the assets of the State over all liabilities, $5,751,965.

LOUISIANA.

State debt in 1860	*$10, 023, 903
State debt in 1868	13, 566, 236

This amount includes $1,174,500 worth of State bonds held by the trust fund of the State, thus reducing the State indebtedness to $12,391,736.

MISSISSIPPI.

State debt in 1860	None.
State debt in 1868, about	$200, 000

ARKANSAS.

State debt in 1860	*$3, 092, 622
State debt in 1868, about	4, 577, 081

TENNESSEE.

State debt in 1860	*$16, 643, 666
State debt in 1868	36, 000, 000

From unofficial sources.

States.	Indebtedness in 1860.	Indebtedness 1866–'67.
Virginia	$33, 248, 141	$45, 119, 741
North Carolina	9, 129, 505	11, 433, 000
South Carolina	3, 691, 574	8, 378, 255
Florida	383, 000	638, 863
Alabama	5, 048, 000	6, 304, 972
Texas	....	2, 320, 360
Oregon†	55, 372	218, 574

* Obtained from unofficial sources.

† Funded debt of Oregon, September, 1868, reported by secretary of state, $176,156 50.

APPENDIX D.

TABLES

SHOWING

THE COMPARATIVE COST OF PROVISIONS, GROCERIES, DOMESTIC DRY GOODS, HOUSE RENT, ETC., IN THE MANUFACTURING TOWNS OF THE UNITED STATES IN THE RESPECTIVE YEARS 1860-'61 AND 1867-'68;

ALSO

THE AVERAGE WEEKLY WAGES AND EXPENDITURES OF THE FAMILIES OF WORKMEN IN THE YEAR 1867-'68, AS COMPARED WITH THOSE OF 1860-'61.

PREPARED, FOR THE

SPECIAL COMMISSIONER OF THE REVENUE,

BY EDWARD YOUNG.

NOTE.—In this Appendix, as well as in the report and other appendices, where British, French, or Belgian prices have been compared with those of the United States, the British shilling has been computed at twenty-five cents, and the French franc at twenty-cents. In reducing currency to gold the average rate of 140 per cent. has been adopted.

Table showing the average retail prices of provisions, groceries, and other leading articles of consumption; also prices of board and house rent in the manufacturing towns of the following States, and of the general average in the United States, in the years 1860–'61 and 1867–'68, with the percentage of increase of prices in the latter over the former year.

Articles.	Maine.		Percentage of increase.	New Hampshire and Vermont.		Percentage of increase.	Massachusetts.		Percentage of increase.	Rhode Island.		Percentage of increase.	Connecticut.		Percentage of increase.
	1860–'61.	1867–'68.		1860–'61.	1867–'68.		1860–'61.	1867–'68.		1860–'61.	1867–'68.		1860–'61.	1867–'68.	
PROVISIONS.															
Flour, wheat, (superfine)......per barrel.	$6 87	$14 17	106	$7 50	$15 00	100	$7 84	$15 48	97	$8 10	$16 15	99	$8 32	$15 83	90
Do........do..........per pound.	3.5	7.5	114	3.6	7.7	114	4.9	8.6	76	4.5	9	100	4.64	8.25	76
Flour, rye..................per barrel.	4 00	7 00	75	4 25	8 00	88	4 62	7 82	69	3 00	4 57	52	5 25	10 13	93
Corn meal.........................do....	3 00	4 75	58	3 76	5 47	45	3 52	5 63	60	2 38	4 25	78	2 95	5 53	87
Beef, fresh, roasting pieces....per pound.	9	19	111	10	19	90	11.6	24.1	108	13	25	92	12.81	24.38	90
soup pieces..........do....	5	9.5	90	4	8	100	4.3	7.8	63	6	10	67	5.67	10	76
rump steaks..........do....	11.5	28	143	12.5	23.5	88	13.4	27.3	104	14	28	100	12.06	24.50	103
corned......................do....	7	17	143	7	13.25	89	7.7	15.36	100	10	17.5	75	8.78	16.22	85
Veal, fore quarters..............do....	5.5	12	118	4.5	11.5	55	8.3	15.9	92	10.5	16	52	8.50	16.88	98
hind quarters..............do....	7	13.25	89	6.25	14.75	136	10.05	18.8	87	12.5	20	60	11	20.67	88
cutlets....................do....	9	15.5	72	11	18.25	66	11.9	23.11	93	16	23	44	13.43	26.57	98
Mutton, fore quarters............do....	5.5	12.5	127	5.75	12.25	113	8.33	16.11	93	10	16.5	65	9.81	18.22	86
legs......................do....	7	16	129	8.25	16.50	100	11.78	22.33	90	12	20	67	13.43	23.57	75
chops.....................do....	8	14	75	11	16.5	50	11.2	20.4	82	12.5	22	76	12.71	24.71	94
Pork, fresh.......................do....	8	14.5	81	7	12.5	78	9.8	18.6	90	13	19	46	10.28	18.22	77
corned or salted............do....	11	19	72	11	18	64	11.75	18.9	61	11.25	17	51	11.77	18.44	57
bacon.......................do....	12	19	58	8	14.25	78	10.25	19	85	10	16	60	11.50	19.67	71
hams, smoked................do....	12	21	75	10.5	17.5	60	12.15	22.3	83	13	22	69	13.83	23.89	73
shoulders...................do....	9	15	67	7.20	15.40	114	9.88	15.81	60	10	17	70	11.31	20	77
sausages....................do....	11	21	91	11	20	82	11.15	17.8	59	12	18	50	13	22.43	72
Lard..............................do....	12	17	42	12.5	17.5	40	12.23	18.64	52	12	16	33	13.33	18.78	42
Codfish, dry......................do....	4	7.5	87	5	10	100	4.55	8.33	84	4.5	8.5	89	4.78	8.56	79
Mackerel, pickled.................do....	7	13	86	7	13.30	90	8.86	14.41	62	7	14	100	9.06	13.88	53
Butter............................do....	16.67	33.33	100	17.5	29	66	21.27	35.73	81	20.5	38.5	88	19.89	40	101
Cheese............................do....	10.25	19.5	90	10	15.5	55	11.41	18.55	62	11.5	19	65	11.83	19.22	62
Potatoes.....................per bushel.	40	80	100	31.5	65	106	53.55	97.45	81	64	98	53	55	95	73
Rice.........................per pound.	6.25	14	124	5.75	13	126	6.33	13.33	114	6.5	13	100	6.44	14.22	121
Beans........................per quart.	6	14.5	142	7	14	100	7.67	13.89	81	8	14	75	7.14	12.79	79
Milk..............................do....	4.25	7	65	4	6.5	62	4.77	7.27	52	5	6	20	4.75	7.67	62
GROCERIES, ETC.															
Tea, Oolong or other good black.per pound	75	1 20	60	50	1 25	150	56.45	1 33.17	136	62	1 18	90	70	1 35.78	94
Coffee, Rio, green................do....	14.5	32.5	159	14.5	30.5	110	14	34.10	143	17	37.5	120	16.75	39.38	135
roasted.............do....	16	33.5	109	17.5	35	100	18.38	41.67	127	20	45	125	20.75	42.5	105
Sugar, good brown.................do....	8.5	14.5	72	8.25	14.5	76	8.82	14.73	67	9	14	55	8.56	14.56	70

yellow C.....do....	9	16	78	8.75	15.25	94	8.70	15.29	75	9.5	15	58	9.75	16.56	70
Molasses, New Orleans.....per gallon.	42	1 00	138	50	85	70	50.20	99.50	98	47	1 09	132	51.50	92.50	80
Porto Rico.....do....	35	68	94	43.5	83.5	92	42.36	88.13	108	41	90	119	52.50	83.50	59
Sirup.....do....	55	87.5	59	62.5	1 22	95	76.36	1 36.82	79	83	1 50	81	1 01.25	1 65	63
Soap, common.....per pound.	8.5	14.25	68	8.5	12.75	50	7.86	13.05	66	8	11	62	8.78	13.61	55
Starch.....do....	10	16.25	60	9	14.31	59	10.36	14.80	43	9	14	56	11.31	16.13	42
Fuel, coal.....per ton.	8 33	9 50	11	5 00	11 00	122	6 63	9 16	37	5 50	7 50	36	6 61	9 05	37
wood, hard.....per cord.	4 31	6 25	45	3 20	5 60	75	5 89	8 50	44	5 50	9 20	67	3 64	5 56	53
pine.....do....	2 37½	4 00	68	1 75	3 33	90	3 89	6 00	54	3 50	6 00	71	3 17	4 75	50
Oil, coal.....per gallon.	83	72.5	(*)	90	72	(*)	77.63	62.56	(*)	95	65	(*)	78.33	67	(*)
DOMESTIC DRY GOODS, ETC.															
Shirtings, brown, 4-4 stand'd qual. p. yard.	8.5	18	112	9	19	111	9.80	18.70	91	10	19	90	9.15	20.56	125
bleach, 4-4 stand'd qual...do....	10	20.5	105	12	23	92	12.46	23	78	11.25	23.5	109	11.92	22.83	92
Sheetings, brown, 9-8 stand'd qual..do....	10	21	110	10	19.25	92	11.55	20.20	75	10.5	22	109	11.57	23	99
bleached, 9-8 stand'd qual.do....	12	26	117	13	23.25	79	14.75	26.10	77	13	27	108	13.30	28.8	116
Cotton flannel, "Hamilton," (or similar quality).....do....	14	31.5	125	13	25	92	13.27	27.36	106	13	25	92	13.21	27.14	105
Tickings, good quality.....do....	20.5	36.5	78	16	36.5	128	18.05	40.60	125	17	40	135	17.59	35.62	102
Prints, Merrimac.....do....	12	18	50	10.5	18.25	74	11.73	17.17	46	11	16.25	48	12.28	21.89	78
Mouseline de Laines, (domestic).....do....	16	25	56	18.20	26.50	46	19.82	24.45	23	16	24	50	19.69	25.75	31
Crash, (domestic).....do....	9	18	100	10.75	18.75	74	10.50	15.92	52	8.25	15	82	9.81	17.67	80
Satinets, medium quality.....do....	50	67.5	35	55	78.75	43	56.32	78.14	39	50	70	40	68.33	97.92	43
Boots, men's heavy.....per pair.	3 42	5 00	46	2 85	4 75	67	3 20	5 02	57	2 90	5 31	83	3 53	5 50	56
HOUSE RENT.															
Four-roomed tenements.....per month.	3 25	5 67	74	2 42	3 68	52	5 86	10 28	75	5 93	9 63	62	4 04	5 77	43
Six-roomed tenements.....do....	4 67	8 17	75	3 17	5 75	81	6 54	10 14	55	9 11	11 69	28	4 56	6 81	49
BOARD.															
For men.....per week.	2 50	4 33	73	2 00	3 28	64	2 59	4 25	64	2 70	4 90	81	2 78	4 42	59
For women.....do....	1 67	3 16	89	1 40	2 69	92	1 67	2 96	77	1 94	3 37.5	74	2 04	3 46	69

* Decrease.

Table showing the average retail prices of provisions, groceries, and other leading articles of consumption, &c.—Continued.

Articles.	New York. 1860–'61.	New York. 1867–'68.	Percentage of increase.	Pennsylvania. 1860–'61.	Pennsylvania. 1867–'68.	Percentage of increase.	New Jersey. 1860–'61.	New Jersey. 1867–'68.	Percentage of increase.	Delaware. 1860–'61.	Delaware. 1867–'68.	Percentage of increase.	General average. 1860–'61.	General average. 1867–'68.	Percentage of increase.	Prices in 1867 reduced to gold value.†
PROVISIONS.																
Flour, wheat, (superfine) ......per barrel	$7 02	$13 32	90	$7 00	$13 30	90	$7 83	$15 00	91	$6 83	$12 67	85	$7 48	$14 55	94.53	$10 39
Do........do ....per pound	3.86	7.03	82	3.5	7	100	4.17	8.33	169	3.25	6	85	3.99	7.71	93.21	5.51
Flour, rye ....per barrel	4 86	9 00	85	4 15	9 00	117	6 25	9 50	52	4 50	8 00	78	4 44	8 11	78.62	5.79
Corn meal.......................do....	2 94	5 47	86	3 19	5 50	72	2 50	5 14	106	3 94	6 25	59	3 13	5 33	70.3	3 81
Beef, fresh, roasting pieces......per pound	10.25	20.5	100	12	22	83	12	25	108	12.5	25	100	11.46	22.66	97.73	16.19
soup pieces ....do....	5.25	10.33	98	7.3	13.9	90	7	15	114	7.5	15	100	5.78	11.06	91.33	7.9
rump steaks ....do....	10.33	20.10	94	12	21.5	79	12	25	108	12.5	22	76	12.25	24.4	99.38	17.5
corned ....do....	7.67	14.22	85	8	16	100	10	19	90	10	15	50	8.46	15.95	109.6	11.4
Veal, fore quarters ....do....	7.25	14.11	95	8	15	87	9	14	55	11	15.5	41	8.06	14.54	80.41	10.4
hind quarters.................do....	9.14	17.38	90	9.5	18.5	95	12	24	100	15	19	27	10.27	18.48	89.95	13.2
cutlets......................do....	11.43	22	92	12.5	20	75	13	26	100	18	25	39	12.92	22.16	71.54	15.83
Mutton, fore quarters.................do....	8.8	11.75	34	7	13.5	93	8	15	87	9	15.5	72	8.02	14.59	81.92	10.42
legs.........................do....	9.63	16.67	73	9	18	100	11	19	72	10.5	19	81	10.29	19.01	84.75	13.58
chops ....do....	10.14	18	77	10	19.5	95	12	22	83	15	21	40	11.39	19.79	73.69	14.14
Pork, fresh...........................do....	9.75	15.11	55	9	18	100	9	17	89	10	18.25	82	9.54	16.79	76.10	12
corned or salted..............do....	10.25	16	56	8.5	17	100	9	16	78	9	18	100	10.39	17.59	69.31	12.56
bacon ....do....	10.75	17.5	64	10.5	18	71	11	18.75	70	8.5	16.5	94	10.28	17.63	71.53	12.6
hams, smoked.................do....	11.25	20.17	79	12.5	25	100	12.5	25	100	13.5	23	63	12.36	22.21	79.69	15.86
shoulders ....do....	9	16.5	87	8.75	17.5	100	10	18	80	10	18.5	85	9.46	17.08	80.54	12.20
sausages ....do....	11	18.33	66	11.25	22	95	11.5	18	56	12.5	19	50	11.6	19.67	69.6	14.05
Lard ....do....	12	18.36	52	12	17	42	10	18	80	13.5	19	70	12.17	17.88	46.84	12.72
Codfish, dry.........................do....	5	9	80	4.5	8.1	80	5.75	10.5	83	5.75	8	39	4.87	8.73	79.31	6.24
Mackerel, pickled....................do....	9.18	13.45	47	9	12.5	39	7	15.75	125	8	12	50	8.01	13.59	69.51	9.71
Butter ....do....	18	35	94	22	41	86	18	42	133	23.5	45	91	19.7	37.73	91.48	26.95
Cheese ....do....	10.7	17.7	65	12	21	75	10	23	130	14.75	23	56	11.38	19.61	72.27	14
Potatoes.........................per bushel	46	90	96	65	1 19	83	60	1 34	123	83	1 12	35	55.34	98.94	78.79	70.67
Rice..............................per pound	6	13.27	110	6.25	12.5	100	5	14	180	6.25	12.5	100	6.09	13.31	118.73	9.51
Beans............................per quart	6.36	11.18	76	6.5	13	100	6	15	150	8	12	50	6.96	13.37	92.05	9.55
Milk ....do....	4.25	7.50	76	5	8	60	4.5	9.5	111	5.25	8	52	4.64	7.49	61.45	5.35
GROCERIES, ETC.																
Tea, Oolong or other good black.per pound	63	1 44	128	75	1 50	100	75	1 50	100	83	1 38	66	67.72	1 34.88	99.19	96.34
Coffee, Rio, green ....do....	15.4	32.7	112	15	30	100	15.5	31	121	13.5	31	130	14.96	33.19	121.82	23.71
roasted..................do....	20	40.44	102	18.75	37.5	100	17.5	40.5	131	15.5	32	106	18.26	38.67	111.74	27.62
Sugar, good brown ....do....	8.20	14.10	72	8.5	15	88	7.5	15.5	107	7.75	15	94	8.34	14.65	75.67	10.46
yellow C.................do....	9.50	16.20	70	9.5	16	68	8	16	100	8.5	16	88	9.02	15.80	75.13	11.29
Molasses, New Orleans ....per gallon	48	1 00	108	57	1 16	103	54	1 25	131	48	93	94	49.74	1 02.22	105.49	73.02
Porto Rico.................do....	45.54	93.63	105	45	91	102	42	92	119	50	90	80	44.1	88.87	115.14	63.48

Sirup ....do....	63	1 22.4	91	64	1 22	91	61	1 29	111	62	1 07	72	9.79	1 15.75	65.85	82.68
Soap, common ....per pound.	8.63	12.36	43	6	12	100	6.5	12.5	92	8	13	62	7.86	12.72	61.82	9.09
Starch ....do....	10.73	14.63	39	10	14	40	9.5	15	58	9.25	15	62	9.91	14.9	50.39	10.64
Fuel, coal ....per ton..	5 62	7 48.33	34	2 80	5 05	80	4 19	6 62	58	5 50	7 67	39	5 58	8 11	45.53	5 80
wood, hard ....per cord.	4 50	6 94	54	4 00	6 00	50	4 25	8 50	100	4 83	7 67	59	4 44	7 14	60.87	5 10
pine ....do....	3 41	5 25	55	3 62	5 43	50	3 50	6 00	71	3 83	7 00	83	3 23	5 31	64.44	3 78
Oil, coal ....per gallon.	87.5	62.5	(*)	90	65	(*)	90	60	(*)	92	52	(*)	87.05	64.28	* 35	45.92
DOMESTIC DRY GOODS, ETC.																
Shirtings, brown, 4-4 standard qual..p. yard.	9.63	20	107	11	20.25	84	9.5	20	110	10	19	90	9.62	19.39	101.56	13.85
bleached, 4-4 standard qual.do....	13	25	94	12	24	100	10	22	120	13.5	26	92	11.79	23.31	97.71	16.65
Sheetings, brown, 9-8 standard qual..do....	10.25	22	115	12.5	25	100	11	29	164	13	27	108	11.15	23.16	107.68	16.54
bleached, 9-8 stand'd qual..do....	12	24	100	13.5	27	100	13.5	30	122	17	29	70	13.56	26.79	97.59	19.14
Cotton flannel, "Hamilton," (or similar quality) ....do....	13.33	31.8	138	13	26	100	13	29	123	12.5	30	140	13.14	28.09	113.68	20.06
Tickings, good quality............do....	19.50	37	90	25	45	80	17	39	129	16.5	43.75	159	18.57	39.33	111.78	28.1
Prints, Merrimac ....do....	11.3	18	60	12	18	50	11.5	18.75	63	12	19	58	11.59	18.37	58.48	13.12
Mouseline de Laines, (domestic) ......do....	18.5	25.3	36	18	25	39	19	25	32	17	27	59	18.02	25.33	40.56	18.10
Crash, (domestic)............do....	11.33	18.75	67	10	17	70	12.5	21	68	10	18	80	10.24	17.79	73.75	12.71
Satinet, medium quality ....do....	61.20	98	60	57	95	67	55	88	60	55	90	64	56.43	84.81	50.30	60.58
Boots, men's heavy ....per pair.	3 47	5 05	46	3 35	5 13	53	3 25	5 75	77	3 75	6 25	67	3 30	5 31	60.61	3 79
HOUSE RENT.																
Four-roomed tenements ....per month.	4 20	6 85	51	5 60	9 60	71	4 67	10 00	114	4 00	5 00	25	4 44	7 39	66.31	5 28
Six-roomed tenements ....do....	5 78	9 37	62	8 00	15 20	90	7 17	15 00	109	5 17	6 33	22	6 02	9 83	63.32	7 02
BOARD.																
For men............per week.	3 15	4 75	51	3 00	5 25	75	3 25	6 50	100	2 75	4 50	64	2 75	4 69	70.63	3 85
For women ....do....	2 53	4 00	58	2 00	4 00	100	1 75	3 75	114	1 75	3 00	71	1 86	3 38	81.47	2 41

* Decrease.

† Calculated at $1 40.

Table showing the comparative average weekly expenditures of families in the manufacturing towns of the United States in the respective years 1860–'61 *and* 1867–'68.

Articles.	Average expenditures of families, consisting of—																General average.		Percentage of increase.
	Parents and 1 child.		Three adults.		Parents and 2 children.		Parents and 3 children.		Parents and 4 children.		Parents and 5 children.		Parents and 6 children.		Parents and 7 children.				
	1867.	1860.	1867.	1860.	1867.	1860.	1867.	1860.	1867.	1860.	1867.	1860.	1867.	1860.	1867.	1860.	1867.	1860.	
Flour and bread	$1 09	$0 56	$0 78	$0 41	$1 43	$0 73	$1 32	$0 70	$2 79	$1 46	$2 25	$1 18	$2 00	$1 00	$4 27	$2 25	$1 99	$1 03½	92.
Meat of all kinds	1 50	81	1 02	52	1 94	1 60	2 83	1 60	2 56	1 35	3 17	1 66	2 90	1 53	3 79	2 00	2 46	1 31	88.
Butter	66	34	46	25	82	45	1 10	57	1 38	75	1 31	70	87	53	2 35	1 32	1 12	61	82.
Cheese	16	09	12	07	19	11	34	20	33	19	33	19	......	......	55	33	26	15	75.
Sugar and molasses	73	41	47	27	87	50	1 09	62	1 08	61	1 18	65	70	40	1 99	1 08	1 01	57	79.
Tea	26	13	22	11	26	12	41	21	51	25	63	32	70	35	67	34	46	23	100.
Coffee	20	10	09	04	21	10	39	19	34	17	35	17	15	07	39	15	25	12	105.
Soap and starch	21	13	11	06	20	12	40	26	32	18	28	15	30	18	46	27	29	17	79.
Lard	26	18	17	11	27	17	33	23	26	18	23	16	48	35	64	40	33	22	50.
Milk	40	25	34	22	54	35	47	28	41	25	44	28	42	26	67	42	46	29	59.
Eggs	20	12	11	06	27	16	40	24	31	19	32	19	......	......	85	48	31	18	71.
Salt and spices	09	05	08	05	10	06	17	09	18	10	14	08	15	09	37	20	16	09	77.
Potatoes and other vegetables	57	32	32	19	65	36	97	50	90	49	96	54	90	45	1 40	80	83	45	83.
Fruits, fresh and dried	06	04	34	19	40	23	48	30	63	40	38	24	......	......	58	37	36	22	62.
Fuel—coal, wood, &c	77	50	1 09	75	1 01	70	94	63	1 13	71	79	47	40	23	1 13	70	91	59	54.
Oil or other light	30	41	15	18	18	24	20	27	30	40	14	18	20	25	30	40	22	29	*24.
Other articles of consumption	35	19	48	26	99	52	80	42	1 22	64	52	28	......	......	1 50	79	73	39	89.
House rent	2 43	1 47	2 00	1 33	1 93	1 16	2 38	1 46	3 14	1 75	1 81	95	1 50	1 00	1 96	1 09	2 14	1 27½	68.
Total for groceries, provisions, &c	10 24	6 10	8 35	5 07	12 26	7 08	15 02	8 77	17 79	10 07	15 23	8 39	11 67	6 69	23 78	13 39	14 29	8 19	74.40
Balance for clothing, housekeeping goods, &c	6 76	3 86	9 17	5 24	6 49	3 71	4 48	2 56	5 54	3 11	1 88	1 07	1 83	98	1 22	70	4 67	2 66	76.02
Weekly wages	17 00	12 17	17 52	12 00	18 75	11 50	19 50	12 41	23 33	14 15	17 11	10 37	13 50	9 50	25 00	15 17	18 96	12 16	55.92
Surplus in 1861	......	2 21	......	1 69	......	71	......	1 08	......	97	......	91	......	1 83	......	1 08	......	1 31	......

* Decrease.

Table showing the average weekly expenditures of families in the manufacturing towns of the United States in the year 1867-'68.

Articles.	Average expenditures of families consisting of—								
	Parents and one child.	Three adults.	Parents and two children.	Parents and three children.	Parents and four children.	Parents and five children.	Parents and six children.	Parents and seven children.	General average.
Bread and flour	$1 00	$0 78	$1 43	$1 32	$2 79	$2 25	$2 00	$4 27	$1 99
Meat, fresh and salted	1 50	1 02	1 94	2 83	2 56	3 17	2 90	3 79	2 46
Butter	66	46	82	1 10	1 38	1 31	87	2 35	1 12
Cheese	16	12	19	34	33	33		55	26
Sugar and molasses	73	47	87	1 09	1 08	1 18	70	1 99	1 01
Tea	26	22	26	41	51	63	70	67	46
Coffee	20	09	21	39	34	35	15	30	25
Soap and starch	21	11	20	40	32	28	30	46	29
Lard	26	17	27	33	26	23	48	64	33
Milk	40	34	54	47	41	44	42	67	46
Eggs	20	11	27	40	31	32		85	31
Salt and spices	09	08	10	17	18	14	15	37	16
Potatoes and other vegetables	57	32	65	97	90	96	90	1 40	83
Fruits, fresh and dried	06	34	40	48	63	38		58	36
Fuel—coal, wood, &c	77	1 09	1 01	94	1 13	79	40	1 13	91
Oil or other light	30	15	18	20	30	14	20	30	22
Other articles	35	48	99	80	1 22	52		1 50	73
House rent	2 43	2 00	1 93	2 38	3 14	1 81	1 50	1 96	2 14
Total for provisions, &c	10 24	8 35	12 26	15 02	17 79	15 23	11 67	23 78	14 29
Weekly wages	17 00	17 52	18 75	19 50	23 33	17 11	13 50	25 00	18 96
Surplus for clothing, housekeeping articles, &c	6 76	9 17	6 49	4 48	5 54	1 88	1 83	1 22	4 67

A comparative table, showing the weekly expenses of families of workmen in the United States in 1867, and in Belgium in 1853.

Articles.	Families consisting of— Two adults and 3 children. Unit'd States.	Two adults and 3 children. Belgium*.	Two adults and 4 children. Unit'd States.	Two adults and 4 children. Belgium*.
Bread and flour	$1 32	$1 13	$2 79	$1 27
Meat, fresh and salted	2 83	....	2 56	....
Butter and lard	1 43	27	1 64	64¼
Cheese	34	....	33	....
Sugar, molasses, spices, vinegar, &c.	1 26	16	1 26	8½
Tea	41	....	51	....
Coffee and chicory	39	17½	34	15
Soap and starch	40	5½	32	9
Milk	47	8	41	10
Eggs	40	....	31	....
Potatoes and other vegetables	97	67½	90	63
Fruits, fresh and dried	48	....	63	....
Fuel	94	27	1 13	27
Oil or other light	20	....	30	....
Other articles	80	57	1 22	28
House rent	2 38	40½	3 14	34¼
Total, except clothing	15 02	†3 79	17 79	†3 86
Add 20 per cent. for advance in prices since 1853	....	76	....	77
	....	4 55	....	4 63
Increased cost in United States	....	10 47	....	13 16
	15 02	15 02	17 79	17 79

* In United States currency, the franc computed at 27 cents.

† These were the expenses in 1853. Since that period provisions have advanced in price from 10 to 20 per cent.

APPENDIX E.

TABLES

SHOWING

THE AVERAGE WEEKLY WAGES OR EARNINGS OF WORKMEN EMPLOYED IN THE MANUFACTURING ESTABLISHMENTS OF THE UNITED STATES IN THE RESPECTIVE YEARS 1860-'61 AND 1867-'68, WITH THE PERCENTAGE OF ADVANCE IN THE LATTER YEAR;

ALSO

THE AVERAGE WAGES PAID TO WORKMEN IN SIMILAR ESTABLISHMENTS IN GREAT BRITAIN, WITH THE PERCENTAGE OF EXCESS IN THE RATES PAID IN THE UNITED STATES OVER THOSE IN EUROPE.

PREPARED, FOR THE

SPECIAL COMMISSIONER OF THE REVENUE,

BY EDWARD YOUNG.

COTTON MILLS.

Table showing the average rates of wages paid to persons employed in the cotton mills of the United States in the respective years 1860–'61, *and* 1867; *also the percentage of increase in the latter year.*

Occupation.	AVERAGE RATES OF WAGES OR EARNINGS PER WEEK.								Percentage of increase.
	In Massachusetts		In New England.		In Middle States.		Average in the United States.		
	In 1860–'61.	In 1867.	In 1860–'61.	In 1867.	In 1860–'61.	In 1867.	In 1860–'61.	In 1867.	
CARDING.									
Overseer	$17 18	$20 00	$12 90	$17 61	$9 58	$16 30	$12 66	$17 60	39
Second hand	9 18	13 33	7 36	11 25	6 26	10 55	7 23	11 14	54
Picker tenders	5 00	7 42	4 77	8 22	4 78	8 84	5 13	8 18	59
Railway tenders	2 83	4 70	2 80	4 51	3 67	5 75	2 83	4 61	63
Drawing-frame tenders	2 87	5 02	3 00	5 00	2 81	4 16	2 93	4 82	64
Speeder tenders	3 61	6 26	3 54	5 96	3 07	5 16	3 54	5 81	64
Picker boy	....	....	....	....	2 92	4 50	2 92	4 50	54
Grinders	5 78	9 80	5 85	9 37	....	....	5 85	9 37	00
Strippers	5 17	7 18	4 54	7 86	5 12	7 50	4 74	7 41	56
SPINNING.									
Overseer	16 65	20 60	11 88	16 98	9 80	16 72	11 71	16 90	44
Second hand	8 85	13 21	6 93	10 90	5 55	10 04	6 46	10 27	59
Mule spinners	5 93	11 16	6 10	10 18	6 25	11 18	5 80	10 14	74
Mule backside piecers	1 64	3 17	1 83	3 14	1 72	3 46	1 69	3 09	81
Frame spinners	3 33	6 05	2 83	5 18	2 13	4 50	2 64	4 76	80
DRESSING.									
Overseer	15 15	21 44	12 19	18 09	8 75	16 50	12 02	17 70	48
Second hand	8 30	13 45	7 70	12 42	5 76	13 00	7 44	12 53	68
Third hand	6 50	10 75	5 57	9 18	....	13 50	5 71	10 11	77
Spoolers	3 40	6 49	3 12	4 71	2 48	3 99	2 85	5 03	76
Warpers	3 96	6 81	3 59	6 09	4 13	5 87	3 62	6 00	64
Drawers and twisters	3 72	6 75	3 75	6 41	4 15	6 66	4 10	6 77	65
Dressers	5 10	9 89	7 03	11 40	7 22	13 17	7 64	11 66	52
WEAVING.									
Overseer	15 94	21 11	12 73	17 84	10 31	16 08	12 18	17 36	42
Second hand	8 83	14 23	7 08	11 42	6 66	11 17	6 95	11 50	65
Third hand	7 12	11 83	5 89	9 10	6 25	9 59	5 60	9 40	67
Weavers	4 50	9 06	4 63	7 80	4 75	6 85	5 24	8 48	62
Drawing-in hands	3 45	6 02	4 07	6 65	4 50	8 00	4 10	7 21	76
REPAIR SHOP, ENGINE ROOM, ETC.									
Foreman or overseer	14 89	19 20	12 65	18 11	11 65	17 25	12 60	17 77	41
Iron workers	8 82	13 75	8 71	13 65	7 92	13 20	8 60	13 95	62
Wood workers	9 09	13 83	8 70	13 66	9 39	14 13	8 78	13 76	57
Engineer	....	14 00	6 42	10 78	11 50	18 00	7 24	11 61	6[illegible]
Laborers	6 15	9 17	5 98	9 09	6 00	9 38	5 96	9 14	53
CLOTH ROOM, ETC.									
Overseer	13 31	17 03	11 31	14 41	7 32	11 19	9 75	13 22	35
Second hand	7 46	10 54	6 77	9 77	4 83	9 00	5 93	9 25	56
Other hands—males	5 85	8 92	5 95	8 97	....	....	5 90	8 96	52
Females	3 57	5 50	3 21	5 14	2 44	4 23	2 82	4 68	66

Hours of labor per week 66
Apparent average increase of wages in 1867 over those in 1860–'61, per cent 56
True average, per cent 63

COTTON MILLS.

Table showing the comparative rates of wages paid to persons employed in the cotton mills of the United States and Great Britain in the year 1867.

Occupation.	AVERAGE WEEKLY WAGES OR EARNINGS.				
	In the United States.		In Great Britain.		Percentage of excess in United States over Great Britain.
	Currency.	Gold, (at 140.)	60 hours per week.	Add 10 per cent. to make it equal to 66 hours.	
CARDING.					
Overseer	$17 60	$12 57	$7 25	$7 97	57.71
Picker tenders	8 18	5 84	2 14	2 35	148.51
Railway tenders	4 61	3 29	1 75	1 92	61.10
Drawing-frame tenders	4 82	3 44	2 50	2 75	25.09
Speeder tenders	5 81	4 15	2 50	2 75	50.91
Picker boy	4 50	3 21	2 14	2 35	36.59
Grinders	9 37	6 70	4 88	5 37	24.76
Strippers	7 41	5 30	3 87	4 26	24.41
SPINNING.					
Overseer	16 90	12 07	6 75	7 42	62.56
Mule spinners	10 14	7 24	4 87	5 36	35.08
Mule backside piecers	3 09	2 21	1 50	1 65	33.94
Frame spinners	4 76	3 40	2 37	2 61	30.27
DRESSING.					
Spoolers	5 03	3 59	2 25	2 47	45.34
Warpers	6 00	4 29	3 50	3 85	11.43
Drawers and twisters	6 77	4 84	3 00	3 30	46.67
Dressers	11 66	8 33	....	....	....
WEAVING.					
Overseer	17 36	12 40	10 00	11 00	12.73
Weavers	8 48	6 06	4 12	4 54	33.48
Drawing-in hands	7 21	5 15	2 38	2 61	97.32
REPAIR SHOP, ENGINE ROOM, ETC.					
Iron workers	13 95	9 96	6 75	7 42	34.14
Wood workers	13 76	9 83	6 75	7 42	32.39
Engineer	11 61	8 29	6 00	6 60	25.61
Laborers	9 14	6 53	4 50	4 95	31.92
CLOTH ROOM, ETC.					
Overseer	13 22	9 44	} 5 00	5 50	45 82
Second hand	9 25	6 61			

NOTE.—Hours of labor per week in the United States, 66; in England, 60. Apparent average excess of wages paid in the United States in 1867 (in gold) over the rates in Great Britain, 47 per cent. True average excess United States over Great Britain in 1867, 35½ per cent. Wages in the cotton mills of the United States having been reduced in 1868, the average excess in the rates paid in that year over those in England in 1867 is 28.72 per cent.

Omitting overseers, the average weekly earnings of operatives in the cotton mills of the United States in 1867 was 21*s.*, or $5 25, (gold,) and in Great Britain 15*s.* 6*d.*, or $3 87.

WOOLLEN MILLS.

Table showing the average rates of wages paid to persons employed in the woollen mills of the United States in the respective years 1860–'61 and 1867–'68, with the percentage of increase in the latter year; also the rates paid in England, with the percentage of excess in the rates paid in the United States over that country.

Occupation.	AVERAGE WEEKLY WAGES OR EARNINGS.											
	In New England.		In New York State.		Gen'al average in New England and New York.		Percentage of increase.	Rate of 1867–'68 in gold, (at 140.)	In England.		Percentage of advance in United States over England.
	In 1860–'61.	In 1867–'68.	In 1860–'61.	In 1867–'68.	In 1860–'61.	In 1867–'68.			Sixty hours per week.	Adding 10 per cent. to equal 66 hours.	
PREPARING.												
Wool sortors	$8 05	$12 35	$7 53	$11 00	$7 84	$11 86	51.28	$8 47	$6 00	$6 60	28.33
Wool washers	5 65	9 46	5 13	8 31	5 42	9 00	66.05	6 43	4 85	5 34	20.41
Dyers	6 13	10 13	4 80	8 22	5 46	9 17	68.32	6 56	5 00	5 50	19.27
Overseers	12 00	19 13	12 38	22 00	12 19	20 56	68.66	14 69	10 00	11 00	33.55
Assistants	8 50	11 50	7 75	11 00	8 13	11 25	38.38	8 04	......	......	......
CARDING AND SPINNING												
Pickers	5 25	8 03	4 90	8 63	5 11	8 25	61.45	5 89	4 60	5 06	16.40
Carders	4 15	5 96	4 00	6 35	4 08	6 12	50.00	4 37	3 50	3 85	13.50
Spinners	6 74	11 34	7 00	11 25	6 84	11 30	65.20	8 07	5 50	6 05	33.38
Warpers and beamers	5 48	9 04	5 00	11 00	5 27	9 88	87.48	7 06	5 12	5 63	25.40
Reelers	2 90	4 62	2 50	3 67	2 73	4 21	54.21	3 01	2 50	2 75	9.46
Overseers	11 50	18 43	12 38	23 25	11 85	20 27	71.06	14 48	10 00	11 00	31.64
Assistants	7 50	11 10	7 88	13 13	7 69	12 00	56.04	8 57	......	......	......
WEAVING.												
Weavers	4 44	7 73	4 88	8 38	4 66	8 02	72.10	5 73	4 25	4 67	22.70
Burlers	3 14	5 34	2 69	4 50	2 92	4 95	69.52	3 04	2 25	2 48	22.58
Overseers	11 70	17 75	13 13	24 75	12 33	20 55	66.67	14 68	10 00	11 00	33.45
DRESSING AND FINISHING.												
Fullers	6 00	8 88	5 88	10 69	5 93	9 78	64.92	6 99	5 25	5 77	21.14
Dressers or giggers	5 00	8 81	4 50	7 88	4 77	8 34	74.84	5 96	5 00	5 50	8.36
Finishers	6 50	9 00	4 13	8 50	5 55	8 80	59.45	6 29	5 50	6 05	4.00
Press tenders	6 50	9 00	5 38	8 75	6 05	8 90	47.10	6 36	5 25	5 78	10.04
Drawers	4 50	9 00	3 75	7 50	4 12½	8 25	100.00	5 89	3 75	4 13	42.15
Brushers	2 25	3 50	6 00	9 00	3 50	5 33	52.28	3 81	2 50	2 75	38.55
Packers	5 00	7 50	4 50	8 25	4 75	7 75	63.15	5 54	5 00	5 50	00.73
Overseers	7 88	14 25	11 75	17 25	11 12	18 62	68.34	13 30	10 00	11 00	21.00
Assistants	7 50	12 00	8 63	12 00	8 06	12 00	48.88	8 57	......	......	......
ENGINE ROOM, YARD, ETC.												
Engineers	9 62	14 00	10 50	20 75	9 97	16 70	67.50	11 93	7 50	8 25	44.61
Mechanics	9 31	15 98	8 84	16 00	10 54	15 98	51.61	11 41	7 50	8 25	38.30
Laborers, watchmen, and yard hands	6 13	10 50	5 83	7 50	6 00	9 64	60 66	6 84	4 50	4 95	38.18
Foremen	13 50	18 00	......	......	13 50	18 00	33 33	12 86	7 50	8 25	55.88

NOTE.—General average hours of labor per week in New England and New York, for 1860–'61, 71, and for 1867–'68, 66; in England, 60; adding 10 per cent., 66. Average increase in rates of wages in 1867–'68 over those of 1860–'61, 60.65 per cent. Average advance in rates of wages paid in the United States over those of England, (both in gold,) 24.63 per cent.

WORSTED MILLS.

Table showing the comparative rates of weekly wages paid in the worsted mills of Massachusetts in the respective years 1860–'61 *and* 1867, *also in England in* 1866.

Occupations.	Average weekly wages in three worsted mills in Massachusetts.		Increase of 1867 over 1860.	Rates of 1867 in gold, (at 140.)	Average weekly wages in Bradford, England, in 1866.		Excess in U. S. over England.
	1860–'61.	1867.	Per c't.	1867.	For 60 hours.	Equal at 66 hours to—	Per c't.
WORSTED YARNS AND FABRICS.							
Wool sorters	$7 20	$12 07	68	$8 62	$7 00	$7 70	12
Wool washers	6 00	9 80	63	7 00	4 12	4 53	54
Combers	5 73	9 00	36	6 43	3 50	3 85	67
Gill box and drawing hands. females	4 20	7 17	70	5 12	2 37½	2 51	95
Spinners do	3 48	5 75	65	4 11	2 50	2 75	49
Twisters do	3 30	5 40	64	3 86	....	....	....
Reelers do	3 30	6 30	90	4 50	3 25	3 58	26
Overseers males	15 00	24 00	60	17 14	8 75	9 63	78
Assistant overseers	7 50	13 03	73	9 31	5 50	6 05	54
Dyers	6 00	10 17	67	7 26	4 50	4 95	47
Weavers	5 94	11 40	92	8 14	4 50	4 95	64
Weavers females	4 50	7 62	70	5 44	3 25	3 38	61
Finishers males	4 02	9 80	144	7 00	6 00	6 60	6
ENGINE ROOM, YARD, &C.							
Engineers	11 19	17 75	58	12 68	8 00	8 80	15
Mechanics	8 51	15 16	78	10 83	7 25	7 98	35
Laborers, watchmen, and yard hands	5 80	10 68	84	7 63	4 50	4 95	54

Hours of labor per week: in Massachusetts, 66; in Bradford, England, 60; adding 10 per cent., 66.
Average increase of the rates of 1867 over those of 1860–'61, 79 per cent.
Average excess of the rates paid in the United States in 1867 (in gold) over those in England in 1866, 58 per cent.

SUGAR REFINERIES.

Table showing the average weekly earnings of persons employed in the sugar refineries of the United States in the years 1860–'61 *and* 1867, *and in those of Great Britain in* 1866.

Occupation.	Average weekly earnings.		Percentage of increase in 1867 over 1860–'61.	Earnings in 1867 in gold.	Wages in England in 1866.	Percentage of advance in U. S. over Eng'd.
	1860–'61.	1867.				
Boilers	$13 00	$21 50	65. 38	$15 36	$8 25	86. 18
Panmen	7 67	12 00	56. 45	8 57	7 50	14. 26
Filtermen	6 50	11 00	69. 10	7 85	4 37½	79. 04
Warehousemen	5 80	9 50	63. 80	6 78	4 50	50. 66
Upstairsmen	6 00	10 00	66. 67	7 14	4 37½	63. 20
Engineers	14 00	21 50	53. 58	15 36	7 00	119. 43
Stokers	7 75	11 00	41. 93	7 85	5 75	36. 52

Average increase of earnings in 1867 over 1860–'61, 59 per cent.
Average advance in the United States over England, (both in gold,) 65 per cent.

IRON ROLLING MILLS.

Table showing the average weekly earnings of workmen in the iron rolling mills of the United States in the respective years 1860–'61 and 1867–'68, with the percentage of increase in the latter year; also the earnings in England in 1867, with a comparison of the earnings in the two countries.

Occupation.	Average weekly earnings. In 1860–'61.	Average weekly earnings. In Sept., 1867.	Percentage of increase in 1867 over 1860.	Earnings in 1867 in gold.	Earnings in England in 1867.	Percentage of excess in United States over England.
Puddlers	$13 37	$23 17	73. 30	$16 54	$8 75	89. 03
Puddlers' helpers	7 27	13 46	85. 14	9 61	4 50	113. 55
Shinglers	12 06	22 27	84. 66	15 90	11 25	41. 33
Shinglers' helpers	5 33	9 50	78. 24	6 79	6 75	....
Puddle-mill rollers	9 77	19 02	94. 68	13 58	11 25	20. 71
Top and bottom rollers	10 75	25 06	133. 12	17 90	15 00	19. 33
Forge rollers	10 25	21 25	107. 32	15 18	11 25	34. 93
Merchant-mill finishers	18 50	35 00	99. 31	18 50	13 75	35. 54
Rail-mill rollers	27 00	37 69	39. 60	26 92	12 00	124. 33
Sheet and plate rollers	12 00	20 67	72. 25	14 76	20 00	dec. 26. 20
Second rollers	8 97	16 41	82. 94	11 72	6 00	inc. 95. 33
Third rollers	8 75	13 87	58. 51	9 90	4 50	120. 00
Furnace-men or heaters' helpers	7 39	11 91	61. 16	8 51	6 00	41. 00
Shearmen	9 04	14 98	65. 71	10 70	6 00	78. 33
Catchers	6 71	14 80	120. 57	10 57	6 00	76. 16
Roughers	8 67	20 24	133. 45	14 46	8 00	80. 75
Heaters	14 83	25 36	71. 00	18 11	12 50	44. 88
Foremen or superintendents	14 87	24 90	67. 45	17 78	12 00	48. 17
Machinists	12 08	18 11	49. 92	13 64	7 50	81. 86
Engineers	9 64	14 28	48. 13	10 20	7 50	36. 00
Carpenters	8 44	15 42	82. 70	11 01	7 00	57. 28
Blacksmiths	8 07	14 66	81. 66	10 47	7 50	39. 60
Laborers and unskilled workmen	5 34	9 10	70. 41	6 50	4 00	62. 50
Teamsters	6 00	10 25	70. 83	7 32	4 00	83 00
Apprentices and boys	2 80	4 34	55. 00	3 10	2 50	24 00

Average increase of wages in 1867 over the rates in 1860–'61, 76 per cent.

Average price of puddling in the New England and Middle States in 1867, $6 63 per ton; in 1868, $6 per ton.

The prices for puddling, rolling, &c., having declined in 1868, the average increase of 1868 over 1860 is thereby reduced to about 67 per cent. But although the cost of labor has advanced but 67 per cent., the real advance over 1860 in the cost of making iron, is believed to be about 75 per cent.

The average advance in the earnings of the workmen employed in the rolling mills of the United States over those of Great Britain (both in gold) is 48.34 per cent.

[For prices of puddling in Europe as compared with the United States, and for other information in regard to the manufacture of iron, reference is made to page 69 of the report.]

STEEL WORKS.

Table showing the average weekly earnings of workmen employed in the steel works of Pittsburg, United States, in 1867–'68, as compared with those in Sheffield, England, in 1866–'67.

Occupation.	Average weekly earnings in— Pittsburg, 1867–'68. Currency.	Pittsburg, 1867–'68. Gold.	Sheffield in 1866–'67.	Percentage of excess in Pittsburg in 1867–'68.
Converter	$19 50	$13 93	$10 00	3. 93
Converter's laborer	12 00	8 57	5 25	3. 32
Common laborers	9 00	6 43	4 50	1. 93
Melter	32 50	23 21	11 25	11. 96
Puller-out	16 25	11 61	8 00	3. 61
Moulders	12 00	8 57	5 00	3. 57
Cokers	12 00	8 57	5 00	3. 57
Forgeman and tilter	30 00	21 43	12 50	8. 93
Forgeman's heater	12 00	8 57	6 00	2. 57
Roller	38 00	27 14	18 00	9. 14
Roller furnace-man	18 00	12 85	7 50	5. 35

Average advance of wages in the steel works of Pittsburg over those of Sheffield, 62.23 per cent.

IRON FOUNDRIES AND MACHINE SHOPS.

Table showing the average weekly wages paid to persons employed in the iron foundries and machine shops of the United States in the respective years 1860–'61 nad 1867, with the percentage of increase in the latter year; also the wages paid in England in 1866, and the percentage of advance in the rates paid in the United States over those of England.

Occupations.	AVERAGE WEEKLY WAGES OR EARNINGS.											PERCENTAGE.
	In New England.			In Middle States.			General average in United States.				In England.	
	1860–'61.	1867.	Percentage of increase 1867 over 1860.	1860–'61.	1867.	Percentage of increase 1867 over 1860.	1869–'61.	1867.	Percentage of increase.	1867 in gold.	1866.	Excess of wages in U. S. over England.
Moulders	$10 00	$15 68	56. 80	$10 19	$16 51	62. 02	$10 08	$16 13	60. 02	$11 52	*$8 00	44. 00
Machinists, best	11 29	17 60	55. 89	11 58	18 80	62. 35	11 54	18 19	57. 62	12 99	8 50	52. 82
second	10 67	16 29	52. 67	9 39	16 00	70. 40	10 21	16 15	58. 17	11 54	7 00	64. 86
ordinary	8 73	13 10	50. 06	8 88	14 82	66. 90	8 76	13 82	57. 88	9 87	6 50	51. 85
inferior	6 89	10 50	52. 40	7 00	12 19	74. 14	6 92	11 13	60. 84	7 95	5 00	59. 00
helpers	5 85	9 19	57. 10	5 99	9 86	64. 61	5 92	9 54	61. 15	6 81	4 50	51. 33
Blacksmiths	10 92	19 08	74. 72	10 03	15 41	53. 64	10 47	17 25	64. 76	12 32	*7 12	73. 03
helpers	7 00	10 67	52. 43	5 94	10 04	69. 02	6 57	10 35	57. 53	7 39	4 50	64. 22
Riveters	10 00	15 48	54. 80	10 25	16 61	62. 05	10 15	16 14	59. 01	11 53	7 50	53. 73
Holders-on	6 50	10 10	55. 38	6 68	10 85	62. 42	6 60	10 50	59. 09	7 50	5 00	50. 00
Boiler-makers	10 96	17 80	62. 50	10 71	17 55	63. 87	10 70	17 70	65. 42	12 64	*7 50	68. 53
helpers	6 20	10 52	69. 68	6 52	10 69	63. 96	6 39	10 62	66. 20	7 59	4 50	68. 67
Flangers	12 95	21 60	66. 80	13 00	20 71	59. 31	12 80	21 20	65. 63	15 14	7 50	101. 87
helpers	6 35	10 62	67. 24	6 81	11 35	66. 67	6 60	11 02	66 97	7 87	4 50	74. 89
Engineers	9 19	15 90	73. 01	9 84	15 87	61. 28	9 50	15 96	68. 00	11 40	6 25	82. 40
Pattern-makers and carpenters	9 00	18 52	105. 78	10 38	17 37	67. 34	9 81	18 00	83. 48	12 86	*8 50	51. 29
assistants	9 00	13 58	50. 89	6 38	10 95	71. 63	8 05	12 77	58. 63	9 12	7 50	21. 60
Laborers, carters, &c	6 07	9 90	63. 10	5 98	9 68	61. 87	6 02	9 84	63. 45	7 03	*4 50	56. 22
Apprentices	3 81	5 58	46. 46	3 03	5 21	71. 95	3 50	5 46	56. 00	3 90	*2 50	64. 00
Brass founders	11 00	19 00	72. 73	11 00	17 75	61. 36	11 00	18 28	66. 17	13 06	7 50	74. 13
fitters and turners	10 33	16 50	59. 74	10 20	15 57	52. 64	10 26	15 97	55. 65	11 41	6 50	75. 54
Millwrights	12 75	19 50	52. 94	10 25	16 70	62. 93	11 50	18 10	57. 39	12 93	7 50	72. 40
assistants	9 00	15 00	66. 67	....	....	....	9 00	15 00	66. 67	10 71	6 50	64. 77
Painters, 1st class	9 17	13 83	50. 82	....	....	....	9 17	13 83	50. 82	9 88	7 00	41. 14
2d class	8 00	13 50	68. 75	....	....	....	8 00	13 50	68. 75	9 64	6 00	60. 67

Hours of labor per week .... 60.
Average increase of wages paid in 1867 over 1860 .... 60. 45 per cent.
Average increase of wages paid in 1867 over 1860, both in gold .... 14. 61 per cent.
Average advance of wages in the United States in 1867 over England in 1866 .... 57. 72 per cent.

* The rates of wages given in this column were those paid in Sheffield, Hull, and other manufacturing towns of England. In Glasgow the rates were lower, being as follows: Moulders, $7 25; blacksmiths, $6; boiler-makers and machinists, $6 25; engineers, $4 50; pattern-makers, $5 75; carters, $4 75; and common laborers, $3 75.

HARDWARE MANUFACTORIES.

Table showing the average weekly wages of persons employed in the hardware manufactories of the United States in 1860–'61 and 1867, with the percentage of increase in the latter year; also the rates in similar establishments in Great Britain in 1866, compared with those of the United States in 1867.

Occupation.	AVERAGE WEEKLY WAGES OR EARNINGS.					
	In 1860–'61.	In 1867.	Percentage of increase 1867 over 1860.	Rates of 1867 in gold.	Wages in England in 1866.	Percentage of excess in United States over England.
Moulders	$7 95	$13 18	65.79	$9 41	$7 50	25.46
Cupola tenders	7 15	10 65	48.95	7 61	....	....
Annealing-furnace tenders	7 06	11 02	56.09	7 87	....	....
Filers	7 57	11 21	48.09	8 02	6 25	28.32
Japanners	7 33	11 58	57.98	8 27	....	....
Forgers	11 03	17 25	56.39	12 32	8 50	45.00
Helpers	6 61	10 18	54.01	7 27	5 00	45.40
Grinders	8 87	12 16	37.09	8 69	6 50	33.69
Polishers	8 11	11 58	42.79	8 27	6 75	22.51
Turners	7 92	11 50	45.20	8 21	7 50	9.46
Lockmakers	12 00	15 00	25.00	10 71	7 50	42.80
Machinists	11 48	18 18	58.36	12 99	7 50	73.20
Engineers	10 70	16 50	54.21	11 79	7 50	57.27
Laborers	6 00	9 60	60.00	6 86	5 25	30.60
Packers	7 29	12 00	64.61	8 57	....	....
Do..females	3 88	5 85	50.77	4 18	2 50	67.20
Diemakers	13 00	20 40	56.92	14 57	10 00	45.70
Press-workmen	8 34	11 79	41.37	8 42	....	....
Do....females	3 75	6 00	60.00	4 29	....	....
Rollers	10 50	15 00	42.86	10 71	....	....
Welders	10 50	15 00	42.86	10 71	....	....
Jointers	9 00	14 25	58.33	10 18	....	....
Stampers	12 00	15 00	25.00	10 71	....	....
Graduators	12 00	13 50	12.50	9 64	....	....
Finishers	9 19	13 94	51.69	9 96	6 75	47.85
Patternmakers	11 50	17 86	55.30	12 76	8 50	50.00
Carpenters	9 64	16 52	71.37	11 80	7 00	68.57
Trip-hammer men	11 10	16 20	45.95	11 57	10 00	15.70
Crimpers	10 50	16 50	57.14	11 79	....	....
Twisters	10 50	18 00	71.43	12 86	....	....
Fitters up	7 75	10 50	35.48	7 50	....	....
Screw cutters	6 26	10 10	61.34	7 21	....	....
Blacksmiths	9 22	14 53	57.59	10 38	7 50	38.40
Helpers	6 48	9 50	46.60	6 79	5 00	35.80
Foremen	13 06	19 87	52.14	14 19	10 00	41.90
Apprentices or boys	3 59	5 64	57.10	4 03	3 12	22.75

Hours of labor per week 60
Average increase in rates of wages in 1867 over 1860–'61 .... per cent.. 50
Excess of rates of wages in United States in 1867 over those of England in 1866....do..... 40

MANUFACTORIES OF EDGE TOOLS.

Table showing the average weekly earnings of persons employed in manufactories of edge tools in the United States in 1860–'61 and in 1867, with the percentages of increase in the latter year; also the comparative rates in similar establishments in Sheffield, England, in 1866–'67.

Occupations.	AVERAGE WEEKLY EARNINGS.					
	In the United States, 1860–'61.	In the United States, 1867.	Percentage increase of 1867 over 1860.	Earnings in 1867 in gold.	In Sheffield, England, 1866–'67.	Percentage of excess in U. S. over England.
Forgers	$13 50	$17 50	29. 63	$12 50	$8 50	47.
Helpers	10 50	13 50	28. 57	9 64	5 00	92.
Temperers	10 50	15 00	42. 86	10 71	6 50	65.
Grinders	12 00	18 00	50. 00	12 86	9 25	39.
Polishers	10 50	14 50	38. 10	10 36	6 75	53.
Laborers	6 00	10 25	70. 83	7 32	5 50	33.
Carpenters	10 50	16 50	57. 14	11 79	7 50	57.
Foremen	11 00	17 25	56. 82	12 32	10 00	23.
Apprentices or boys	6 00	8 00	33. 33	5 71	3 75	52.
Machinists	12 00	18 00	50. 00	12 86	7 50	71.
Trip-hammer men	15 00	21 00	40. 00	15 00	10 00	50.

Hours of labor per week 60
Average increase of earnings in 1867 over 1860–'61 .... per cent.. 44
Average excess of earnings in the United States over England .... do..... 50

MANUFACTORIES OF AGRICULTURAL IMPLEMENTS.

Table showing the average rate of wages paid to persons employed in manufactories of agricultural implements in the United States in the respective years 1860–'61 and 1867–'68, with the percentages of increase in the latter year.

Occupation.	Aver'ge weekly earnings.		Percentage of increase.
	In 1860–'61.	In 1867–'68.	
Moulders	$10 97	$17 29	57. 61
Machinists	8 68	15 69	80. 76
Blacksmiths	8 50	15 57	80. 32
Blacksmiths' helpers	5 75	8 90	54. 78
Woodworkers	8 75	14 61	66. 90
Painters	7 77	12 23	57. 40
Ploughmakers	9 00	15 00	66. 67
Teamsters	6 82	10 52	54. 25
Grinders	7 87	12 05	53. 11
Patternmakers	9 08	17 25	89. 97
Watchmen	8 97	12 69	41. 47
Clerks	18 22	31 96	75. 96
Engineers	9 00	15 00	66. 67
Laborers and unskilled workmen	5 33	9 92	86. 12
Apprentices or boys	2 62	4 53	72. 90
Foremen or overseers	13 12	23 54	79. 42

Hours of labor per week 60
Average increase of wages in 1867 over 1860–'61 .... per cent.. 68

FIRE-ARMS MANUFACTORIES.

Table showing the average weekly wages or earnings of persons employed in fire-arms manufactories in the years 1860-'61 and 1867, with the percentages of increase in the latter year; also a comparison with the rates paid in England in 1866.

Occupations.	Average weekly earnings in the United States.*		Percentages of increase 1867 over 1860-'61.	Rates reduced to gold, at 40 per cent. premium—1867.	Wages in England, 1866.	Percentages of advance in United States over England.
	1860-'61.	1867.				
Gun-barrel browners	$12 62	$17 19	36	$12 27	$10 00	22.7
filers	12 00	16 81	40	12 01	10 00	20
grinders	13 37	19 12	43	13 65	7 50	82
riflers	12 00	16 87	41	12 06	10 00	20
welders	15 50	22 00	42	15 72	10 00	57.2
drillers	9 75	15 00	54	10 71	....	....
breech forgers	12 38	18 00	45	12 86	7 50	71.4
case makers	10 83	15 50	43	11 07	7 50	47.6
finishers	12 00	17 00	42	12 14	7 50	61.8
nipple makers	11 19	16 87	51	12 06	6 25	93
polishers	12 87	18 00	40	12 86	8 75	47
stockers	12 19	16 81	38	12 01	7 50	60
tool makers	13 56	20 37	50	14 54	8 75	66.2
work forgers	13 50	20 25	50	14 46	8 75	65.2
lock filers	12 12	16 87	39	12 06	7 50	60.8
lock forgers	14 00	20 00	43	14 29	7 50	90.5
Machinists	12 31	17 62	43	12 58	8 25	52.4
Engineers	12 50	20 00	60	14 29	....	....
Laborers, or unskilled men	6 31	9 37	48	6 69	4 50	48.9
Apprentices or boys	4 67	6 17	32	4 40	2 50	76
Foremen or overseers	20 00	30 00	50	21 43	....	....

* Chiefly in the States of Connecticut and New York, embracing Colt's and Sharp's manufactories in Hartford, Connecticut, and that of Remington & Sons, at Ilion, New York.

REMARKS.—It appears from the table that the wages paid in 1867, when reduced to a gold standard, differed but little from those of 1860, and, with gold at 140, exhibited an *average* increase of only 3½ per centum. In France the wages of operatives in this branch are lower than in England. In 1860, 564 hands employed in Paris received the following wages: 62 received 3 fr. 50c., or less; 62, 4 francs; 11, 4 fr. 25c.; 58, 4 fr. 50c.; 234, 5 fr.; 24, 5 fr. 50c.; 70, 6 fr.; 5, 6 fr. 50c.; 23, 7 fr.; 10, 8 fr.; and 15, 10 fr. each per day—the average being 5 fr. 20c., equivalent to 99 cents in gold. The average weekly earnings (in gold) in the three countries named were as follows: In France $5 94, in England $7 79, and in the United States $12 22. In the United States, therefore, the workmen in this branch earn 56 per cent. more than those of England, and 105 per cent. more than those of France. The hours of labor are 60 per week in each of the countries named.

SAW MANUFACTORIES.

A comparative table showing the average weekly earniags of persons employed in saw maufactories in the United States in 1860-'61 and in 1867-'68; also in Sheffield, England, in 1866-'67.

Occupations.	Average weekly earnings in—					Percentage of excess in U. S. over England.
	United States.		Percentage of increase in 1867-'68.	Wages in 1867-'68 in gold.	Sheffield.	
	1860-'61.	1867-'68.			1866-'67.	
Saw-makers	$12 50	$25 00	100	$17 85	$11 25	58
Grinders	11 67	20 39	74	14 56	12 50	16
Polishers	11 00	16 50	50	11 79	7 00	68
Turners	14 09	24 00	71	17 15	8 50	100
Filers	7 50	10 00	33	7 15	6 25	14
Laborers	6 00	9 42	57	6 73	4 50	50
Helpers	7 70	11 52	50	8 21	5 00	64
Boys	3 75	5 50	46	3 92	2 50	57

Average increase of earnings in 1867 over 1860-'61, 65 per cent.
Average excess of rates in United States in 1867-'68 over England in 1866-'67, 52 per cent.

GAS WORKS.

Table showing the average weekly wages paid to persons employed in the gas works of the United States in the respective years 1860–'61 and 1867–'68, with the percentages of increase in the latter year; also the rates paid in Great Britain in 1866, as compared with those in the United States in 1867.

Occupation.	Average weekly earnings in— United States.* 1860–'61.	1867–'68.	Percentage of increase in 1867.	Wages in 1867 in gold.	Great Britain in 1866.†	Percentage of advance in U. S. over G. Britain.
Firemen	$9 13	$17 25	89	$12 32	$6 75	81
Second-men	8 10	15 11	86	10 79	....	....
Yardmen	6 75	9 60	42	7 86	....	....
Purifiers	7 00	11 90	70	8 50	....	....
Engineers	11 25	18 06	60	12 90	10 00	29
Carpenters	10 50	18 60	77	13 28	7 25	83
Masons	12 02	22 36	86	15 97	8 25	94
Blacksmiths	9 67	16 75	73	11 96	7 50	60
Pipe layers	7 31	13 13	80	9 37	7 50	25
Gas fitters	7 80	13 20	70	9 42	6 25	50
Lamp-lighters	7 10	9 70	37	6 93	4 00	73
Laborers	6 00	10 05	67	7 18	4 50	60
Foremen	11 62	19 51	68	13 93	8 13	71

Average increase of wages in 1867 over 1860, 70 per cent.
Average advance of wages in the United States in 1867 over the rates in Great Britain in 1866, 62 per cent.

* Chiefly in the cities of Boston, New York, Philadelphia, Baltimore, Washington, and Chicago.
† Chiefly in Edinburgh and Leicester.

LEATHER MANUFACTORIES.

Table showing the average weekly wages paid to persons employed in manufactories of leather in the United States in 1860–'61 and in 1867; also the rates paid in Scotland in 1866, as compared with those in the United States in 1867.

Occupation.	Average weekly earnings in— United States. 1860–'61.	1867–'68.	Percentage of increase in 1867.	Wages in 1867 in gold.	Edinburgh, Scotland in 1866.	Percentage of excess in U. S. over Scotland.
Tanners	$7 00	$15 00	114	$10 71	$6 25	4.46
Curriers	9 00	15 00	67	10 71	8 50	2.21
Dressers	9 00	15 00	67	10 71	8 50	2.21
Beam-men	10 00	18 00	80	12 86	6 25	6.61
Shed-men	7 00	10 00	43	7 14	6 25	0.89
Tanners' laborers	6 00	9 00	50	6 43	3 75	2.68

Average increase of wages in 1867 over 1860–'61, 71 per cent.
Average advance of rates in the United States in 1867 over those of Scotland in 1866, 48 per cent.

GLASS WORKS.

Table showing the average earnings of persons employed in glass works of the United States in the years 1860–'61 and 1867–'68, with the percentages of increase in the latter year; also the earnings in glass works of England in 1866, compared with those in the United States in 1867.

Occupation.	Average weekly earnings in the United States.		Percentage of increase.	Earnings of 1867 in gold.	Earnings in England in 1866.	Percentage of excess in United States over England.
	1860–'61.	1867–'68.				
Glass blowers	$14 00	$22 73	62. 36	$16 23	$12 00	35
Vial blowers	12 00	18 00	50. 00	12 86	10 50	22
Assistants	6 00	10 00	65. 67	7 14	5 41	32
Batch mixers	8 50	14 25	67. 65	10 18	6 25	63
Master teasers	12 00	18 00	50. 00	12 86	....	....
Assistant teasers	6 50	13 00	100. 00	9 28	6 25	48
Potmakers	11 50	19 00	65. 22	13 57	....	....
Assistant potmakers	7 00	12 00	71. 43	8 57	....	....
Packers	7 50	14 50	93. 33	10 35	6 25	65
Blacksmiths	13 00	17 50	42. 31	12 50	7 50	53
Carpenters	8 50	14 25	67. 65	10 18	7 00	45
Demijohn coverers	8 00	14 00	75. 00	10 00	....	....
Skilled boys	3 25	6 00	84. 61	4 28	....	....
Engineers	10 25	15 00	46. 34	10 71	....	....
Laborers or unskilled workmen	5 50	9 32	69. 45	6 66	....	....
Apprentices or boys	2 50	4 25	70. 00	3 03	....	....
Foremen or overseers	13 50	19 50	44. 44	13 93	....	....

Average increase of earnings in 1867 over 1860–'61, 63 per cent. Average excess in United States over England, 45 per cent.

FLINT GLASS WORKS.

Table showing the average weekly earnings of persons employed in the flint glass works of the United States in the respective years of 1860–'61 and 1867–'68, with the percentages of increase in the latter year.

Occupation.	Average weekly wages or earnings.		Percentage of increase.
	1860–'61.	1867–'68.	
Workmen	$15 66	$27 87	78. 00
First servitor	12 00	19 31	61. 00
Second servitor	8 83	14 51	64. 33
Footmakers	7 82	12 74	62. 66
Finishers	10 25	20 08	95. 90
Leechers	7 00	14 00	100. 00
Mixers	7 00	14 00	100 00
Liersmen	7 00	14 00	100. 00
Tiseurs	8 00	17 00	112. 50
Pressmen	13 12	23 37	78. 12
Gatherers	5 50	10 62	93. 10
First-class gaffer	28 00	45 00	60. 72
Second-class gaffer	25 00	40 00	60. 00
Potmakers	10 50	13 50	28. 57
Potmaker's assistant	12 00	18 00	50. 00
Mould makers	14 37	26 00	80. 93
Blowers	13 00	19 50	50. 00
Glass cutters	10 97	16 82	53. 33
Engravers	13 50	25 00	85. 26
Packers	7 00	14 50	107. 14
Engineers	9 20	16 80	82. 61
Laborers	6 07	10 61	74. 80
Foremen	13 67	21 33	56. 04
Boys	2 72	4 90	80. 15
Superintendents	20 00	30 00	50. 00
Apprentices	5 00	9 50	90. 00
Watchmen	7 00	13 50	92. 86
Carpenters	8 00	17 00	112. 50
Blacksmiths	9 50	17 00	78 95

Average increase of earnings in 1867–'68 over those of 1860–'61, 71 per cent.

FELT-HAT MANUFACTORIES.

Table showing the average weekly earnings of persons employed in the felt-hat manufactories of the United States in the years 1860–'61 and 1867–'68.

Occupation.	Average weekly earnings.		Percentage of increase.	Rates of 1867 in gold.
	1860-'61.	1867-'68.		
Body-makers	$7 00	$12 00	71.43	$8 57
Finishers	14 00	21 00	50.00	15 00
Blockers	14 00	21 00	50.00	15 00
Stiffeners	14 00	19 25	37.50	13 75
Trimmers	5 37	7 50	39.57	5 36
Engineers	12 00	20 25	68.75	14 47
Laborers or unskilled workmen	6 50	10 87	67.30	7 76
Apprentices or boys	2 00	3 00	50.00	2 14
Foremen or overseers	17 50	27 00	54.29	19 29

Average increase of earnings in 1867–'68 over 1860–'61, 50 per cent.

SILK-HAT MANUFACTORIES.

Table showing the average weekly earnings of persons employed in silk-hat manufactories of Philadelphia in 1867, and of Glasgow in 1866.

Occupation.	Average weekly earnings in—			Percentage of excess in U. States over Scotland.
	Philadelphia.		Glasgow.	
	1867.	1867.	1866.	
	Currency.	*Gold.*		
Body-makers	$23 50	$16 78	$8 50	97
Silk finishers	20 52	14 65	9 00	63
Tippers-off	....	....	10 00	....
Curlers	30 97	22 12	....	....
Crown sewers, (females)	6 55	4 68	2 50	87
Trimmers, (females)	11 55	8 25	3 00	....

Apparent average excess of earnings in Philadelphia over Glasgow, 80 per cent.

PAPER MILLS.

Table showing the average weekly wages paid to persons employed in paper mills in the United States in the respective years 1860–'61, and 1867–'68, with the percentage of increase in the latter year; also the rates paid in Scotland in 1866, with the percentage of advance in the United States.

Occupation.	Average weekly earnings in—					
	United States.		Percentage of increase in 1867-'68.	United States in 1867, (gold.)	Edinburgh & vicinity in 1866.	Percentage of advance in U. S. over Scotland.
	1860–'61.	1867–'68.				
Machine tenders	$9 67	$15 67	62	$11 19	$5 50	103
Assistant tenders	4 50	9 00	100	6 43	....	....
Rag cutters—males	7 17	12 17	70	8 69	4 00	117
Rag cutters—females	3 67	6 00	60	4 29	....	....
Loft-men or dryers	6 17	10 83	75	7 74	4 00	93
Callender men	8 75	14 25	63	10 18	....	....
Finishers	7 50	12 67	69	9 05	4 50	101
Engine men	7 50	12 00	60	8 57	5 00	71
Helpers on engines	4 75	8 50	79	6 07	....	....
Bleachers	7 00	11 00	57	7 86	4 50	75
Sizers	4 50	10 25	127	7 32	4 44	65
Millwrights	10 50	19 00	81	13 57	7 00	94
Masons	10 00	20 00	100	14 29	6 25	128
Carpenters	9 50	16 50	73	11 78	6 25	88
Blacksmiths	9 00	14 00	55	10 00	5 75	74
Laborers, carters, watchmen, &c	5 92	8 92	50	6 37	3 75	69
Apprentices or boys	4 00	6 00	50	4 29	....	....
Firemen	9 00	14 00	55	10 00	4 50	122

Average increase of wages in 1867–'68 over 1860–'61, 84 per cent.
Average advance in rates paid in the United States in 1867 over Scotland in 1866, 93 per cent.

SHIP-BUILDING.

Table showing the average weekly wages paid to persons engaged in ship-building in the United States in 1860–'61 and 1867–'68, with the percentage of increase in the latter year; also the rates paid in Great Britain in 1866 as compared with those in the United States in 1867.

Occupation.	Average weekly wages in— United States. 1860–'61.	1867–'68.	Percentage of increase in 1867.	Wages in 1867 in gold.	Great Britain in 1866.	Percentage of advance in U. S. over G. Britain.
WOODEN SHIPS.						
Shipwrights	$12 00	$18 00	50	$12 85	$7 50	71
Ship-smiths	12 00	18 37	53	13 11	7 50	74
Sawyers	11 00	16 50	50	11 78	6 75	74
Joiners	9 00	16 50	83	11 78	7 00	68
Strikers	7 50	10 50	40	7 50	4 50	67
Caulkers	13 50	24 00	78	17 14	....	....
Laborers	6 75	10 50	55	7 50	4 50	67
Foremen	12 00	21 00	75	15 00	10 50	43
IRON SHIPS.						
Moulders	9 00	15 50	72	11 07	9 00	23
Machinists	9 00	16 00	78	11 43	7 50	50
Riveters and platers	9 00	12 00	33	8 57	7 50	14
Boiler-makers	9 00	15 00	67	10 71	7 50	43
Helpers and strikers	7 00	10 50	50	7 50	4 50	67
Blacksmiths	10 00	15 50	55	11 07	7 50	47
Chippers	9 00	12 00	33	8 57	6 00	43
Carpenters	12 00	18 00	50	12 85	7 50	71
Painters	9 00	15 00	67	10 71	6 00	78
Laborers or unskilled workmen	6 00	10 00	67	7 14	4 50	57

Average increase of wages in ship-yards in 1867 over 1860–'61, 61.63 per cent.
Average advance in rates paid in the United States in 1867 over those of Great Britain in 1866, 62.17 per cent.
Average increase of wages on iron ships in 1867 over 1860–'61, 56.74 per cent.
Average advance of rates in the United States in 1867 over those of Great Britain in 1866, 47.58 per cent.

In other branches the average increase of wages in 1867 over those in 1860 were as follows: in manufactories of chemicals, (in Philadelphia,) 66 per cent.; of clocks, (Connecticut,) 78 per cent.; of leather belting, 77 per cent.; of machine card clothing, (Massachusetts,) 75 per cent.; of silk trimmings, sewing silk, &c., (Paterson, New Jersey,) 94 per cent.; of cotton hosiery, (New Hampshire,) 50 per cent., and of railroad cars, 52 per cent.

In the town of Zanesville, Ohio, skilled mechanical labor has advanced since 1860 on an average from $9 to $15 per week, or 66⅔ per cent.; while in unskilled labor the increase has been from $6 to $9 per week, or 50 per cent., and the earnings of miners from $11 25 to $15 75, or nearly 40 per cent.

The average advance in the rates of agricultural labor, in the same period, in the States of Massachusetts, New York, and Ohio, was 50 per cent.; and this was about the average in the New England, the Middle, and the older Western States.

In the building trades, such as carpenters, bricklayers, plasterers, painters, &c., where the men work by the day and are not constantly employed, the rates of wages are not given, as they differ so widely in different localities, owing to the varying demand for and supply of such labor, and to strikes and local causes, that no fair average rates can be given. Indeed, it is impossible to give the weekly or monthly *earnings* of men who are not *constantly* employed. For instance, a house-joiner may obtain, during part of the year, $4 or $4 50 per day, and another carpenter, employed in a manufactory, get but $3. The latter, however, receives his $18 every week for about 50 weeks in a year, earning, therefore, $900 per annum; while the former, owing to unfavorable weather, may not earn over $600 or $700.

The aim has been in the foregoing tables to state the *average earnings of workmen constantly employed* in some branch of industry during the periods and in the countries therein mentioned.

APPENDIX F.

THE TARIFFS OF THE UNITED STATES.

Statement showing the revenue collected each year from 1789 *to* 1868, *the amount of dutiable imports and free goods imported annually, and the average rate of duty on imports, annually.*

	Tariffs.	Customs.	IMPORTS.			Per cent. on dutiable.	Per cent. on aggregate.
			Free.	Dutiable.	Total.		
From Mar. 4, 1789, to Dec. 31							
1790—Aug. 10..	General						
1791—Mar. 3..	Spirits	$4, 399, 473 09			$52, 200, 000		8½
1792—May 2..	General	3, 443, 070 85			31, 500, 000		11
1793		4, 255, 306 56			31, 100, 000		13½
1794—June 7..	General	4, 801, 065 28			34, 600, 000		14
1795—Jan. 29..	Supplementary	5, 588, 461 26			69, 756, 268		9
1796		6, 567, 987 94			81, 436, 164		8⅓
1797—Mar. 3..	General	7, 549, 649 65			75, 379, 406		10
1798		7, 106, 061 93			6[illegible], 551, 700		10⅓
1799		6, 610, 449 31			79, 069, 148		8½
1800—Mar. 13..	Sugar and wines	9, 080, 932 73			91, 252, 768		9¼
1801		10, 750, 778 93			111, 363, 511		9
1802		12, 458, 235 74			76, 333, 333		16
1803		10, 479, 417 61			64, 666, 666		16
1804—Mar. 26..	Mediterranean fund	11, 098. 565 33			85, 000, 000		14
1805—Mar. 27..	Light money	12, 936, 487 04			120, 600, 000		10½
1806		14, 667, 698 17			129, 410, 000		11½
1807		15, 845, 521 61			138, 500, 000		11½
1808		16, 363, 550 58			56, 990, 000		30
1809		7, 296, 020 58			59, 400, 000		12
1810		8, 583, 309 31			85, 400, 000		10
1811		13, 313, 222 73			53, 40[illegible], 000		25
1812—July 1..	War: double duties	8, 958, 777 53			77, 030, 000		11⅓
1813—July 13..	Salt	13, 224, 623 25			22, 005, 000		60
1814		5, 998, 772 08			12, 965, 000		47
1815		7, 282, 942 22			13, 041, 274		55
1816—April 27..	Min. for protection	36, 306, 874 88			147, 103, 000		25
1817		26, 283, 348 49			99, 250, 000		27
1818—April 20..	Iron and alum	17, 176, 385 00			121, 750, 000		14
1819—Mar. 3..	Wines	20, 283, 608 76			87, 125, 000		23
1820		15, 005, 612 15			74, 450, 000		20⅓
1821		18, 475, 703 57	$10, 082, 313	$52, 503, 411	62, 585, 724	35. 6	29. 5
1822		24, 066, 066 43	7, 298, 708	75, 942, 833	83, 241, 541	31. 7	28. 9
1823		22, 402, 024 29	9, 048, 288	68, 530, 979	77, 579, 267	32. 7	28. 8
1824—May 22..	General rise	25, 486, 817 86	12, 563, 773	67, 985, 234	80, 549, 007	37. 5	31. 6
1825		31, 653, 871 50	10, 947, 510	85, 392, 565	96, 340, 075	37. 1	32. 8
1826		26, 083, 861 97	12, 567, 769	72, 406, 708	84, 974, 477	34. 6	30. 7
1827		27, 948, 956 57	11, 855, 104	67, 628, 964	79, 484, 068	41. 3	35. 1
1828—May 19..	Min. extended	29, 951, 251 90	12, 379, 176	76, 130, 648	88, 509, 824	39. 3	33. 8
1829		27, 688, 701 11	11, 805. 501	62, 687, 026	74, 492, 527	44. 3	37, 1
1830—May 20..	Coffee, tea, molasses	28, 389, 505 05	12, 746, 245	58, 130, 675	70, 876, 920	48. 8	40
1831		36, 596, 118 19	13, 456, 625	89, 734, 499	103, 191, 124	40. 8	35. 4
1832—July 14..	Modifications	29, 341, 175 65	14, 249, 453	86, 779, 813	101, 029, 266	33. 8	29
1833—Mar. 2..	Compromise	24, 177, 578 52	32, 447, 950	75, 670, 361	108, 118, 311	31. 9	22. 4
1834		18, 960, 705 96	68, 393, 180	58, 128, 152	126, 521, 332	32. 6	15
1835		25, 890, 726 66	77, 940, 493	71, 955, 249	149, 895, 742	36. 0	17. 2
1836		30, 818, 327 67	92, 056, 481	97, 923, 554	189, 980, 035	31. 6	16. 2
1837		18, 134, 131 01	69, 250, 031	71, 739, 186	140, 989, 217	25. 3	12. 4
1838		19, 702, 825 45	60, 860, 005	52, 857, 399	113, 717, 404	37. 8	17. 3
1839		25, 554, 533 96	76, 401, 792	85, 690, 340	162, 092, 132	29. 9	15. 8
1840		15, 104, 790 63	57, 196, 204	49, 945, 315	107, 141, 519	30. 4	14. 1
1841—Sept. 11..	Free list taxed	19, 919, 492 17	66, 019, 731	61, 926, 446	127, 946, 177	32. 2	15. 6
1842—Aug. 30..	General rise	16, 662, 746 84	30, 627, 486	69, 534, 601	100, 162, 087	23. 1	16. 6

The tariffs of the United States, &c.—Continued.

	Tariffs.	Customs.	IMPORTS.			Per cent. on dutiable.	Per cent. on aggregate.
			Free.	Dutiable.	Total.		
1843		$10, 208, 000 43	$35, 574, 584	$29, 179, 215	$64, 753, 799	35.7	15.7
1844		29, 236, 357 38	24, 766, 881	83, 668, 154	108, 435, 035	35.1	26.9
1845		30, 952, 416 21	22, 147, 840	95, 106, 724	117, 254, 564	32.5	26.4
1846—Aug. 6	Revenue tariff	26, 712, 668 00	24, 767, 739	96, 924, 058	121, 691, 797	26½	21.9
1847		23, 747, 865 00	41, 772, 636	104, 773, 002	146, 545, 638	22½	16.2
1848		31, 757, 071 00	22, 716, 603	132, 282, 325	154, 998, 928	24	20.4
1849		28, 346, 739 00	22, 377, 665	125, 479, 774	147, 857, 439	23	19.2
1850		39, 668, 686 00	22, 710, 382	155, 427, 936	178, 138, 318	25.2	22.3
1851		49, 017, 568 00	25, 106, 587	191, 118, 345	216, 224, 932	26	22.6
1852		47, 339, 326 00	29, 692, 934	183, 252, 508	212, 945, 442	26	22.2
1853		58, 931, 865 00	31, 383, 534	236, 595, 113	267, 978, 647	25	22
1854		64, 224, 190 00	33, 285, 821	271, 276, 560	304, 562, 381	23.5	21.1
1855		53, 025, 794 00	40, 090, 336	221, 378, 184	261, 468, 520	23	20.3
1856		64, 022, 863 00	56, 955, 706	257, 684, 236	314, 639, 942	25	20.3
1857—Mar. 3	General	63, 875, 905 00	66, 729, 306	294, 160, 835	360, 890, 141	21.5	17.7
1858		41, 789, 621 00	80, 319, 275	202, 293, 875	282, 613, 150	20	14.8
1859		49, 565, 824 00	79, 721, 116	259, 047, 014	338, 768, 130	19	14.6
1860		53, 187, 511 00	90, 841, 749	279, 872, 327	362, 166, 254	19	14.7
1861 { Mar. 2, Aug. 5, Dec. 24 }		39, 582, 186 00	*134,559,196	218, 180, 191	352, 739, 387	18.1	11.2
1862—July 14	General	49, 056, 398 00	*91, 603, 481	183, 843, 458	275, 446, 939	26.7	17.7
1863—Mar. 3		69, 059, 64[illegible] 00	44, 826, 029	208, 093, 891	252, 919, 920	33.2	23.7
1864—June 30	General	102, 316, 153 00	*54, 244, 183	275, 320, 951	329, 565, 134	37.2	31
1865—Mar. 3		84, 928, 260 00	54, 329, 588	194, 226, 064	248, 555, 652	43.7	34.2
1866 { Mar. 14, May 16, July 28 }		179, 046 630 00	69, 728, 618	375, 783, 540	445, 512, 158	47.06	40.2
1867—Mar. 2	Wool and woollens	176, 417, 811 00	39, 105, 708	372, 627, 601	411, 733, 309	47.34	42.8
1868		164, 464, 599 56	29, 804, 147	343, 605, 301	373, 409, 448	47.86	44

* In these amounts are included imports into the southern ports during the war, from which no revenue was derived, viz: In 1861, $17,089,234; in 1862, $90,789; and in 1864, $2,220.

www.ingramcontent.com/pod-product-compliance
Lightning Source LLC
LaVergne TN
LVHW021409110826
845150LV00007B/1853

* 9 7 8 1 4 2 5 5 1 1 5 1 7 *